The A–Z of Us

JIM KEEBLE

PENGUIN BOOKS

PENGUIN BOOKS

Published by the Penguin Group
Penguin Books Ltd, 80 Strand, London WC2R ORL, England
Penguin Group (USA) Inc., 375 Hudson Street, New York, New York 10014, USA
Penguin Group (Canada), 10 Alcorn Avenue, Toronto, Ontario, Canada M4V 3B2
(a division of Pearson Penguin Canada Inc.)
Penguin Ireland, 25 St Stephen's Green, Dublin 2, Ireland
(a division of Penguin Books Ltd)
Penguin Group (Australia), 250 Camberwell Road, Camberwell, Victoria 3124, Australia
(a division of Pearson Australia Group Pty Ltd)
Penguin Books India Pvt Ltd, 11 Community Centre, Panchsheel Park, New Delhi – 110 017, India
Penguin Group (NZ), cnr Airborne and Rosedale Roads, Albany, Auckland 1310, New Zealand
(a division of Pearson New Zealand Ltd)
Penguin Books (South Africa) (Pty) Ltd, 24 Sturdee Avenue, Rosebank 2196, South Africa

Penguin Books Ltd, Registered Offices: 80 Strand, London WC2R ORL, England

www.penguin.com

Published in Penguin Books 2005
1

Set in 12.5/14.75 pt PostScript Monotype Garamond
Typeset by Rowland Phototypesetting Ltd, Bury St Edmunds, Suffolk
Printed in England by Clays Ltd, St Ives plc

Acknowledgements

With special thanks to my agent Stephanie Cabot for her belief, to Louise Moore and Mari Evans for their vision, and my parents David and Valerie for years of everything.

To Jessica, for your wisdom and laughter

Ian Thompson and Gemma Cook meet on their third day at university in September 1993. He is twenty and she is eighteen. They become best friends. They say they are not attracted to each other.

No one believes them.

THE BEGINNING

Gemma had never really travelled. Spain, Greece, Dublin once for a hen weekend – the usual holiday destinations that seemed so dull now that you could fly anywhere on earth for the price of a coffee table. The other junior architects laughed at her because she hadn't even been to New York.

'You haven't lived,' they declared, chuckling.

She countered by boasting that her best friend Ian was a travel writer, he'd been everywhere, including places even these geeky architects with their Hoxton fins and latest Levi's had never heard of, like Kyrgyzstan, Kiribati and the Aleutian Islands. But he was no happier for it.

'Your best friend's a bloke?' The architects smirked. 'Is he gay?'

'I don't think so,' she replied, testily. 'He's been going out with my sister for the last eight months!'

'Kinky,' they said.

'Piss off, idiots,' she retorted, and hurried to the toilets to worry, as usual, about her inability to come up with instant, impressive put-downs.

Gemma was afraid of travel. The word itself sounded like 'travail' – 'a painful or laborious effort'. She'd looked it up once in a dictionary. It came from the Latin 'tripalium', a Roman instrument of torture. Which raised the question: 'why would you willingly partake in an activity that derives its name from a three-pronged spear used to eviscerate Roman prisoners?'

She admitted she was nervous of things she didn't understand. She thought it was a natural human tendency – the fear of the unknown. Gemma was constantly surprised that so many people paid good money to go abroad, throwing themselves into situations that made them feel disorientated and scared.

Gemma wasn't proud of her fears. She wanted to be braver. She wanted to challenge herself. Now, more than ever.

'Don't worry about it,' said Ian. 'There's nowhere left worth visiting anyway. Everywhere's accessible, everywhere's touched by tourism, there's no dusty corner of the world that a Canon Ixus hasn't snapped to show the folks back home. There's nothing left to explore.'

Of course she nodded agreement, her instinctive reaction when faced with something she felt ignorant about. But secretly she wondered. Maybe there was somewhere left to explore. Maybe each of us explores new territory, new lands, every day.

'How's that?' she imagined Ian questioning her, with his lopsided grin.

'Love, emotions, relationships . . .' she imagined herself replying, faltering as she tried to formulate confused thoughts into words. 'There are no maps, no charts any more. We're like those people who went out to Australia in the 1800s; they had nothing to tell them what was there, they had to draw their own maps, build new roads, new towns, new railways . . . we're the same . . . with relationships. Everything's new, the old maps don't work any more. Don't you think?'

ATTRACTION

It was my dream house. I felt dizzy when Raj stopped the Audi and asked softly:

'Do you like it?'

Number 26 Raleigh Street was part of a four-storey terrace on Victoria Park in one of the more fashionable streets of London's East End borough of Hackney. The property had just come on the market following the demise of its ninety-three-year-old owner, and was being sold at auction. It was run-down, 'in need of considerable refurbishment', but in every other way it was as perfect as the house I'd imagined as a little girl, when I used to walk the long way home from school in Richmond in order to see the vast mansions on Palmerston Road with their long curtains and warm, inviting living rooms. I'd stand across the street, holding my satchel, and stare into them, imagining my future life with a tall, dashing husband and four picture book-pretty children in every window.

I could have *carte blanche*, Raj said, it would be a good investment for him, for us, in an area that was up-and-coming, just ten minutes drive from the City. He loved my style, my understated elegant taste. I knew that few of my clients would ever live in such a house, let alone a junior second-in-command architect like me.

I stood, looking up, hardly daring to believe. It was a clear winter's day. The sun glinted off the windows like diamonds. I felt like that little girl once more, brimming with excitement and hope. Only now I knew how to build, how to design, how to plan. I knew how to make the dream come true. It would be my masterpiece. I would make Raj proud of me.

My attraction to Raj had been immediate – partly because he was undeniably handsome – and partly because there was something about him that reminded me of my father, even though Raj was dark-skinned, and hadn't been dead for ten years.

Like my father, Raj wasn't tall (in contrast to almost all my previous boyfriends), and his slender body lacked the bulk I'm instinctively drawn to. Yet for some reason, I wanted to put my arms around him and hold him tight, as the ten-year-old daughter used to do to her father when he returned from work, exhausted by numbers and deadlines.

Raj approached me at a bar in Hoxton Square. I looked round and there he was: alongside, but not too close to be threatening. He inquired whether it would be too old-fashioned to ask if he could buy me a drink. His tone was quiet, but within it I thought I detected a concealed strength. I imagined him standing in a formal garden, his slender form complementing the small slim trees and shrubs.

I asked for a vodka and soda, which was strange since I hadn't touched vodka since the Corfu debacle, seven years previously. He ordered a pint of bitter, which was something nobody under the age of forty drank. My father had always preferred bitter to lager.

'An English tipple,' he used to say. 'A man's beer.'

At the bar another man tried to push in, and Raj turned to him and said:

'Excuse me, I'm just getting my order,' in the same measured, direct tone. The man apologized, Raj made a joke and he laughed.

Later, Raj told me that he'd been drawn to my beautiful face, my lush blonde hair, and my vulnerable smile. With his small grin and careful, measured ways, he made me feel wholly and warmly significant. He was immensely polite, constantly aware of his surroundings and the reactions of others.

'The curse of the immigrant offspring,' he would smile.

He was bright, I knew, a first in law at Oxford, a clerkship at a top London firm, with a wonderfully polished accent that sounded more English than Prince Charles's. And he worked so hard, he was so dedicated. If he showed half such devotion to me, I thought, I'd be the happiest woman in London.

He was dedicated from the outset. There was champagne, dinners and presents of gold jewellery, which I shuddered at instinctively, but grew to enjoy more and more, especially after his mother, the formidable Geeta Singh, informed me that 'Gold is the metal of trust.'

He needed me, I quickly realized. And I needed to prove to myself that my talent for love had not waned.

We had two weddings, on consecutive days. 'Two for the price of three!' Raj quipped, several times. On Saturday we were married in the eyes of the Greater London Authority at the registry office on the Marylebone Road, followed by dinner for twenty at an expensive restaurant in Notting Hill. On Sunday it was the turn of Ganesh,

Vishnu and Maha Lakshmi to bless us, in a wholly more gaudy, raucous affair at the Holiday Inn, Hounslow with five hundred guests, few of whom I knew. I was so laden with bullion that I almost passed out. But Raj took my hand gently, as if holding glass, and asked me so sweetly if I could manage to carry on that I threw my jangling braceleted arms around him and burst into joyful tears.

Raj left on a Saturday in August. It began, like most break-ups, out of nothing. We were disagreeing about the colour for the bedroom, in our gentle stilted way. This led to a disagreement about when to throw the party to celebrate the house's prospective completion in mid-September, which Raj wanted to coincide with his review at work, which in turn led to me mentioning that I felt Raj didn't consider my job to be as important as his own. He laughed sarcastically, and said that since he earned five times what I did as an architect, on the basis of pure mathematical equation his job was indeed more important than mine. The next thing I knew, I'd swigged a large glass of wine and told him that I didn't love him.

'I don't love you any more.'

Six words. Barely a second of speech, a second of breath. How many breaths do we take in a lifetime? How can one of them, so short, change your life?

I hadn't been planning to say it. But alcohol and truth have a strange sibling relationship. Sometimes it's hate, but sometimes it's love. There are times when all it takes is half a bottle of Sainsbury's Rioja to loosen the binds on thoughts that have been pirouetting around your head for weeks, if not months.

'I don't love you.'

I even repeated the words, for effect. I couldn't help myself. It was as if they had become malicious little children, chasing each other around my head, hell-bent on disruption.

'I don't love you, Raj,' I chimed once more like a playground bully.

I didn't expect his reaction. To be honest, I'd not thought further than the moment of releasing the words from my head. It was very unlike me.

Raj said nothing. His beautiful mahogany eyes narrowed, he breathed out quickly, and he started to pack a bag. I was impressed with his energy – he flew around our bedroom like a Punjabi Russell Crowe – before storming down the stairs, slamming the front door and speeding away in the Audi with a cinematic screech of the tyres.

The silence after he left was deafening.

I spent a careful hour checking the bedroom, methodically. He'd packed well, as I knew he would. He was organized, I had to give him that. He'd taken his three favourite ties, his new Calvin Klein briefs, and the god-awful book on cricket he was reading. He'd taken all his toiletries, even the Boots pre-shave lotion I'd bought him the previous month after he'd seen it on television.

Following my search of the bedroom, I did something strange, that I didn't know I was going to do. I checked in the medicine cabinet to see if he'd taken the condoms. It was silly, I knew, but I felt relieved that the packet of eighteen 'Elite Pleasure Ribbed' remained on the top shelf, unopened.

I lay on the bed until the late summer night cast shadows

up the walls. My hand touched his side of the duvet and it was cold. There was no sense of his presence. On Friday evening he'd fallen asleep next to me and I'd listened to his breathing, unable to sleep. Twenty-four hours later I was lying on top of the blanket, fully clothed and alone.

The bastard! The childish, self-important, immature bastard! It was so fucking typical, he always did this, he always overreacted rather than be calm and listen and talk and work it through! This was exactly the problem! For someone who earned his impressive living from a measured, patient analyzing of the facts, he was like a stroppy little boy when it came to working out his own emotions.

Almost immediately, my anger turned, a coin tossed; to guilt. He'd left because of me, because of what I'd said. Oh God, why had I said those things? I was so stupid. I'd tried to excuse it as he rushed around the bedroom – throwing clothes into his Burberry bag like a thief – it was my period, I was under stress at work, I hated the thought of turning thirty, I was drunk (none of these close to the real reason, but who could face that?).

But it was no good apologizing. I'd said it. It was out. Like seeing someone naked, like losing my virginity, like cutting off my ear, I could never turn back.

If only he'd call, maybe I could placate him. I was good at calming him after a stressful day at work, after he'd had another run-in with the senior partner.

But this time it was different. I was the perpetrator. I was the one who'd upset him.

'I don't love you.'

How had this happened? It wasn't like we were a couple

who argued. We got pissed off with each other, of course, who doesn't? But big blow-up arguments? It wasn't our style. We prided ourselves on being skilfully restrained. Whenever we were at dinner parties and a couple would row, we'd glance at each other with imperceptible nods, confident in our self-control, in our maturity.

How had we been transformed from the most peaceful couple in London, a poster-couple for clever, successful, loving bi-racial relationships, into World Champions of marital abuse, hurling spite into each other's faces like acid?

Oh fuck! I felt tears coming, but I fought them back, gulping in air, my hands in tight fists. This wasn't what I did. I was measured, in control, with a strategy for every occasion. I was not a woman who gave up, who changed her mind, her direction.

I needed a plan. I needed to take control.

I looked around the bedroom. The walls had been stripped, but not yet rendered. Exposed bricks mocked me, the uneven floorboards jeered me, the gaping wounded holes in the walls scorned me. I thought about the plans that I'd drawn, such loving and detailed drawings with their own essential order and beauty. They bore no relation to the chaotic mess I was now lying in the middle of.

'Bollocks,' I said, loudly. My voice echoed in the empty space. '. . . ocks . . . ocks . . .'

There was only one thing for it. Downstairs, I opened another bottle of wine. Painfully aware that I was fulfilling the stereotype of the recently-abandoned-woman-approaching-thirty, I turned on the portable television and proceeded to drain the bottle while waiting for the phone to ring.

Every so often I pressed the mute button on the remote control and listened, but the phone remained silent.

Fuck, fuck, fuck, fuck, fuck. FUCK!

If you said it loudly enough, it made you feel a little better.

It didn't help that my parents, Susan and Bill Cook, were happily and resolutely married for twenty years until my father's sudden death from a brain aneurysm at the age of fifty-six. I'd been his favourite daughter, mainly because I loved to run and climb trees and hit golf balls and watch James Bond films, unlike Molly who preferred the more feminine pursuits that our mother encouraged, such as buying dresses, trying on make-up and watching *The Sound of Music*.

'My little urchin,' my father used to call me, tousling my short cropped hair. Later, when I entered puberty and fought constantly with my mother, I always sought out 'daddy' in his study, where occasionally he allowed me a puff on his cigarette, a Dunhill that made me splutter and choke from laughter. He was an accountant for a City firm, a safe, dull job that concealed what I saw as his inherent strength and energy, which he expressed most visibly in his garden – an *avant-garde* creation heavily influenced by Japanese design and philosophy, which he studied intermittently.

He went to work one Thursday with a smile and a wave; he dropped dead in his office near Waterloo Bridge. The postmortem indicated that the wall of one of his cerebral arteries had thinned, like a worn car tyre, and popped suddenly, causing a massive rupture into the brain.

'It was instant,' our mother told us, her shoulders wracked with sobs.

I didn't cry at his funeral. I told Mum that I didn't want to talk about Daddy. Three weeks later, I attacked a girl at school who'd made a comment about my new Converse high-tops, leaving her with a bloody nose.

The headmaster informed my mother that I would be suspended for two weeks, a lenient punishment, granted solely with regard to the family's recent bereavement. Outside in the car park, my mother's face hardened, her knuckles white on the steering wheel, as she turned to me and asked:

'Why don't you ever tell me anything?'

I could not answer. Since I was little, I'd always chosen my father rather than my mother to confide in. When he died, I was unable to transfer the allegiance, preferring instead to speak to my father in my head, a habit I continued for a year or more, until one day I woke and told myself that he was dead and gone and I would have to cope on my own.

I wish things were different. I wish I could call Mum and tell her about Raj. I wish I could just pick up the phone and spill out everything that's happened in the past couple of weeks, like those daughters whose smugly glowing accounts of their 'wonderfully honest' daughter–mother relationships adorn the various women's magazines I pretend not to read.

But I'm not ready for another lecture. I have no desire

to hear my mother blame me, telling me that I've always been an introverted and self-centred girl, unlike my older sister who sometimes blunders into caring for others more than is good for her. (As was evidenced by how badly Molly was treated by the evil and heartless Will.)

It's so unfair. Molly got divorced two years ago, and yet our mother laid all the responsibility for the break-up at the size twelve feet of Molly's ex-husband Will, whom she categorized as a weak, infantile philanderer. Yet I know my mother will view her younger daughter's situation differently, as she always does. She will side automatically with Raj, whom she loves for his posh voice, good manners and expansive bank account. In Susan Cook's mind, her two daughters' personalities have been clear since childhood – Molly, good, Gemma, not so good.

I can almost hear her wail:

'How could you, Gemma? What will I do for grand-children?!'

I wonder if I can tell Molly? I want to. She also lives in London in a chic Clerkenwell apartment that estate agents label 'urban loft', but I think is sterile and unimaginative. But again something stops me. Because Molly is The Victim. Will Masterson screwed an easyJet stewardess from Glasgow – 'she lived up to the company name' is Molly's tragi-comic refrain. In contrast, I am The Perpetrator, The Guilty Bitch.

Like my mother, Molly will judge me. Even though my elder sister is far from the saint our mother classifies her as – to her credit, Molly readily and frequently points this out to both mum and I – she does possess our mother's tendency towards moralizing, towards seeing the world in cheerfully black-and-white terms. She'll ask me for reasons, seeking explanation, looking for swift and absolute clarity.

I have no answers.

Why did I do it? I don't know.

Do I really not love my husband? Maybe, maybe not.

What's going to happen now? I've no idea.

I spent the next few days waiting for Raj's return. I was constipated (my stomach resisted my rebellion and was as tight as a walnut each morning). My head felt like someone had dropped a heavy iron on it. And I looked like shit.

On Monday morning, I stood and surveyed myself in the bedroom mirror for the first time in two weeks, as if challenging my reflection to explain what had happened, and where I was going to go next. I touched my left breast, tentatively, a child prodding meat. God I hated my body.

I've always hated my thighs. My face is still pretty, even with the bloodshot eyes and bags under them, but those fucking thighs. I've often fantasized about taking a kitchen knife and cutting down the length of them, like severing cheese. But hating my breasts is something new.

I went to work because I couldn't decide not to. I followed habit, sat down at my desk, drew plans, did meetings, met contractors, ignored my boss's flirtatious asides, and drank numerous cups of coffee, as if nothing had happened.

Then my boss, Duncan Archer, came up to my desk, sat on the corner and told me 'in strictest confidence' that he was getting a divorce and he'd very much like to take me out for dinner one of these nights, 'just for a wee chat'.

When he'd departed, disappearing around the model of the new tower KPSG were designing in Southampton, I stood calmly and walked to the ladies' toilets.

I sat for half an hour in a cubicle. I would not cry. I could not cry. I was blowing my nose with toilet paper when Sophie Watson knocked on the toilet door.

'Are you pregnant, Gemma?' she whispered, in a voice that could not disguise the hope.

'Piss off, Sophie!'

'We're worried about you, that's all.'

'You can't have my bloody job! I'm not fucking pregnant! Just piss off and leave me alone!'

So much for the fucking sisterhood! So much for fucking mutual support amongst women, helping each other on the jagged way up the corporate ladder! Sophie couldn't wait to get me fired. I wondered, just for a moment, if the evil bitch hung around the ladies' toilets taking urine samples.

I'm not pregnant. That's one thing I'm sure of. More sure than I've ever been. You can't get pregnant if you don't have sex. Raj hasn't been inside me in two months. He was too tired, I was too tired, we were both too fraught. I'm glad in some ways. I can't be pregnant. Not now. I can't look after myself, let alone a human being the size of a telephone directory.

And anyway, Raj doesn't want kids yet. He's afraid that any hint of impending children might harm his chances of a partnership.

'If they think something might detract from your concentration on the job, forget about it. Thank God Jerome's getting married next year, there's no chance they'll choose

15

him,' he informed me, happily. I smiled and nodded, feeling a mixture of pride and concern that Raj's senior partners weren't worried that he had anything in his life to distract him from his work.

'The house will be our baby,' he added, with a big smile.

At the time, I was inspired by this remark. The house could be our baby, I agreed, it could bring us closer together. We could create our own nest, our own perfect Gemmarajworld, Rajgemmaworld.

In the end, the house was exactly like a baby – it gave us sleepless nights, caused us to row and drink more, and took nine months to get to a state where we could see its true, solid form.

And now I hate it, our child. It's nothing like my dream. It's dark, dank and unruly, and will never be finished. It's in an area far from my friends, an area full of young mothers and laughing, shrieking children. I don't want to think about it any more. I don't want to think about anything any more.

Raj did not return. On the third evening I drank more wine, trying to muster the strength not to call him. I missed talking to him. I missed preparing stories in my head, waiting for the sound of his key in the door, lying in bed recounting my day until he fell asleep. After half a bottle of Australian Merlot I dialled his mobile number.

The conversation lasted approximately four minutes. He told me that I was selfish, which I acknowledged, and that we had nothing to talk about, which I did not acknowledge. He informed me that he was in the middle of a very complex merger deal and needed to concentrate on more important things than a woman who didn't love him.

I called him again the next day, forcing myself to be calm and strong, to mimic the detached tone of my husband. Before I could ask him when he was intending to come back home and talk about things like a normal, mature-minded adult, he explained in careful language worthy of a high-flying lawyer that he felt his eyes had been opened and he was doubtful whether he wanted to be married to me any more. I tried pleading with him, asking if we could just meet somewhere to talk things through, but he put down the phone.

This left me in a state of small shock. I'd been so obsessively preoccupied by the thought that I didn't love Raj, and by how I could possibly express this to him, that I hadn't stopped to ask myself whether Raj loved me. I'd simply assumed it – he'd always seemed so grateful to be married to me, his 'cultured, stylish, beautiful woman' (his words). I couldn't believe that this had been a pretence, that he didn't seem to love me either.

I took the pictures in the silver and gold wedding present frames and placed them in a box, face down.

On the second Sunday morning after he left, I woke feeling so alone. I was the smallest, most inconsequential thing on the planet. I was unloved, and unable to love. It was as if I was already dead and forgotten and the world was hurtling towards a future that I would be no part of.

And what was worse was that I knew Raj was feeling just as alone, and there was nothing I could do to make him feel better. It was all my fault.

I went downstairs, made some coffee and took out the plans I'd drawn for the house. I stared at them. The straight lines, the solid marks on white paper. The numbers, words and angles. The drawings reassured me. I breathed; out, in, out. As long as I concentrated on the A3 paper and the mapped-out integral worlds delineated there, I felt okay.

But you can't look at plans for ever, Gemma. You have to look up and see the reality around you.

The reality was that the house was in disarray, the builders wouldn't return until after the bank holiday, and the project's principle financial backer, my husband, was now living in a hotel, refusing to speak to me.

It was a mess. A big fucking mess of a mess.

I ripped the plans from the makeshift kitchen table, mashing them together like a schoolgirl crumpling paintings.

Maybe my mother was right. Maybe I am bad to the bone. Maybe I deserved all this.

I called Ian out of panic. I needed to hear his voice. I needed something familiar, a kind word. But most of all, I needed that particular form of male ambivalence I knew Ian would be able to offer. He would not judge me. He would simply try to help. I needed his energy, his overwhelming enthusiasm for giving assistance.

The surprising thing was that the moment he answered the phone I wanted to smash the receiver down, run upstairs to the unmade bed and crawl under the covers, for ever. Suddenly, the last thing on earth I wanted to do was to tell Ian about Raj. To admit that I had failed.

So I tried with all my might to be normal, to chat with

him as old friends do, and then he asked me if I was okay, in that soft reassuring voice that almost requested me not to be okay, so that he could take care of me, so that he could be my best friend once more and come to the rescue as he had done all those times in the past. I'd almost cried, but managed to contain myself at the last moment.

'Fuck it,' I said to the empty house, as if these were the only two words I had left, the only words I'd ever be able to use again.

And now I lie in the bath twisting my wedding ring round and round my finger. I'm terrified, I know that. I have always feared the unknown, a trepidation that worsened after my father's death. As a little girl I always thanked my parents (silently) for producing me second.

I used to ask Molly incessant nervous questions about what my future had in store. How high was the diving board you had to leap from to pass the swimming exam? Which teachers accepted late homework? How did a tampon work? What was it like to kiss? Was beer disgusting? Was a man's penis really like an uncooked Sainsbury's pork and onion sausage?

To escape my fear, I plunged into romantic fiction – Catherine Cookson, Maeve Binchy, even Jane Austen, intoxicated by the adventurous heroines who laboured and loved, who acted as my surrogates, doing deeds of derring-do and high romance that I knew I'd never be capable of. The funny thing is, now I'm in my own story, I just wish I could turn to the end. To see what happens.

The doorbell rings. For an instant I wonder if it's Raj, returning to talk things through, a bunch of flowers in hand. My heart races. But Raj has keys, and he never buys flowers. That's my job. I'm the 'artistic' one. Then I remember calling Ian, and I feel sick once more. I put my head under the water, but the bell keeps ringing.

I open the front door in pyjamas and Raj's big blue towelling bathrobe. Ian stands there, crutches and an *A to Z* map in one hand, a bunch of cheap chrysanthemums in the other, as if on his way to the funeral of someone he doesn't know very well. He looks good, as always – tall, dark-haired, blue-eyed, square-jawed with a faint suntan, like a young Pierce Brosnan – despite the fact he's wearing a pair of Adidas waterproof jogging trousers over a thick white plaster cast.

'What the hell happened to you?'

'I broke my ankle in Venezuela. It's a long story.'

Ian puts out his arms, a gesture that's been his way of greeting me since university. I hesitate on the doorstep, terrified that any human contact will somehow soften the taut, agonizing control I've managed to exert over my muscles, mind and heart.

But I know I need this.

Ian steps forward into me, closing his arms around my narrow back, the plastic wrapping of the funeral flowers rustling crisply as he does so. He hugs me gently. I know this feeling, these arms, this scent of faint sweat and Right Guard.

I close my eyes tightly, and let the tears come, finally, like soothing summer rain.

THE BEGINNING: 2

Ian Thompson met Gemma Cook on his third day at Sheffield University. He wandered into the Freshers' Fair looking for something to join (one of the many things he'd learned on his two-year 'Gap' travels through south-east Asia, Australia and the States, he believed, was that you couldn't just sit back and wait for things to happen, you had to be proactive). Yet his fellow students, with their Kurt Cobain and Che Guevara T-shirts, their un-kempt hair and slouching, affected poses seemed so naive, so full of themselves, that he couldn't bear to sign up for anything – especially not the 'Traveller's Club' with its long-haired private school boys and mis-spelled 'Zimbwawbe'. Rather than helping him feel more connec-ted to the other students, the Freshers' Fair left him feeling even more alienated, more different, and, Ian admitted secretly to himself, even more superior.

He entered the pizza-eating competition because he felt he had to sign up for something, and it would only last one evening. He was fairly confident of winning. Few people would be able to devour as much pizza as Ian Thompson, following his three-month stint at Zeppy's in Hermosa Beach, California, during which he'd consumed an extra large Spicy American every night, without taking breath.

Sitting down at the trestle table in the student union

on that first Friday night, Ian felt supremely confident, and vaguely hopeful (like most other male students in the bar, he had visions of finding an instant freshers' week girlfriend). He was happy to see that five of the twenty contestants were female, including one slender brunette who glanced at him with a swift smile, sending flashes of tequila-charged excitement spinning around his belly.

Yet the competition wasn't quite what he'd expected. It was to be speed, not quantity. He almost gave up before the first round − he'd not planned to make a fool of himself. But the brunette glanced at him again, and the bell rang, and he discovered that the months at Zeppy's had not been in vain. The pizzas were only small, after all. Ian crammed and gobbled and came second in the first round.

The brunette came last, barely finishing a third of her nine-inch Margarita. Ian tried smiling sympathetically, but she pushed back her chair and hurried away from the table. He never saw her again.

By the fourth round, there were only five contestants left, one of whom was female. She was blonde, with a pretty, gentle face, but a little on the heavy side. Ian preferred slim, small-titted women, preferably with some exotic blood in them. This woman looked consummately English, with her pale skin flushed with drunken embarrassment. She was gulping beer, trying to ignore the jokes and supportive cries of the small group of boys standing behind her. She seemed awkward, as if she had embarked on something she was regretting. Ian wondered if she was an only child, like him. As he stared at her, she glanced up, and he smiled at her. She looked away and then the bell rang once more.

Ian folded and gulped and won the heat. The blonde came third, scraping into the semi-final. Behind her, the boys whooped and cheered, and she tried to smile more confidently, a forced smile that only served to emphasize her timidity. Ian wanted to speak up, to tell her that it was all right, that it was a stupid competition and everyone would have forgotten about it in the morning. He wanted to tell her to lose, deliberately, if she was feeling uncomfortable. Then the bell pealed. The next pizza, a Neptune with anchovies, proved more difficult to swallow. Ian glanced up as he ripped into the final piece to see the blonde gulp down her last crust. He was third, and out.

He thought about leaving, but he wanted to see what the shy girl with the large appetite would do. He bought a pint and stood opposite her, then the bell rang and he watched carefully as she ignored all the male voices, nimbly folding the nine-inch Spicy American, complete with chilli sauce, cramming it into her mouth. It was a big mouth, Ian noted. He wondered for a moment what it would be like to have his cock in that mouth, but then she gagged on the chilli, turned, and threw up.

The four lanky boys behind her leapt away, shouting and gesticulating as vomit spattered their shoes. Everyone cheered. The blonde girl grabbed a napkin and threw up again, pizza splattering the table. Instinctively, Ian stepped to her side, grasped a pile of napkins, handed them to her and pulled her arm.

'Come on! The toilet!'

The blonde looked up at him, morsels of vomited pepperoni clinging to her chin and cheeks, and said quietly: 'I'm Gemma. Very pleased to meet you.'

BELIEF

I was looking for a map. My father, the Reverend John Thompson, loved old maps, in particular anything purporting to be of the Holy Land, pre-1948. I loved them too. They made cheap presents, and they made dad happy. Which was something I didn't seem to achieve very often.

The antiques market took place at strange times, never on the same day. Occasionally I would be in the area and make a quick detour to the Old Seamen's Hall on Gutter Lane, but it would be closed. The randomness of the market's openings intrigued me. There was no number to call, you just had to turn up and hope. It was a canny marketing move. It meant that if you were lucky enough to find the hall open, you were so overjoyed and grateful that you ended up spending far too much money on secondhand junk.

Not that I was lavish. I couldn't exactly afford to be. As a freelance travel writer, I sometimes got to stay in five-star hotels in exotic locations, but I rarely made more than £2,000 a month from my articles, before tax.

And now, even this meagre income was in doubt, following my early morning meeting at the newspaper.

I limped carefully past the antiques market's trestle tables adorned with the immaculately arranged detritus of other people's lives, neatly delineated like museum exhibits – umbrellas, old brass lamps, an animal skull, a strange blunt tool that might once have been used for amateur dentistry or bludgeoning hedgehogs. The secondhand map stall was hidden at the back of the hall as usual, beneath a low coving.

The bald old man sat behind his table wearing his customary baggy cardigan that looked like his mother might have knitted it sometime during the First World War, and a cloth cap that appeared to have been molested by a small rodent. He nodded at me, then glanced down at my left leg and the heavy white plaster cast that began just below my knee, before returning to his newspaper crossword.

I leaned my crutch gently against one of the cardboard boxes, unbuttoned my linen shirt sleeves and began my search.

The five cardboard boxes were precisely labelled – Americas, Africa, Australasia, Europe, Asia – but I knew from experience that the maps never lurked in the right sections. Here, the world was shifted into chaos – Burgundy could be found in the Middle East, whilst Lebanon sometimes turned up in the Western Isles of Scotland. It was a fluid atlas, full of bizarre geographical partnerships.

I started methodically with the Americas, in the hope that a map of Judea might be loitering in New Mexico, Montana or even Tierra del Fuego. I flicked quickly but meticulously through the maps, each one neatly encased in secondhand cellophane, each with a handwritten affirmation of its antiquity. I didn't really care whether these scrawled attestations were true or fabricated. If the map looked attractive, with intricate line drawing and subtle shading, and it seemed to resemble somewhere that could be passed off as the Holy Land, I would buy it. My father always seemed grateful.

At the next box, a middle-aged couple was methodically plucking through the maps. They were dressed in matching tracksuits, as if they'd taken time off from intensive training for some domestic sport that had been newly included in the Olympics – synchronized ironing or pairs dusting.

Nonchalantly, I listened to their matrimonial murmurings, a travel writing habit perfected after almost ten years of eavesdropping around the world.

'I want something pretty,' the woman was saying.

'Of course, Lovekins. We both do. How about this one? Antarctica. Look, there are drawings of penguins . . .'

'I don't know, it's not got any cities or nothing . . . you know I like ones that have those little houses . . . there's nothing there, just ice . . .'

'It's amazing,' I interjected, quickly. I couldn't help myself. Antarctica is one of my favourite destinations; I've been fortunate enough to go there twice, on small adventure cruises.

'Sorry?' chirped the man, looking up with alarm.

'Antarctica.'

'You've been there?'

'I'm a travel writer.'

'We're looking for something nice for the living room,' interjected the woman, with a welcoming smile. 'We're having it done.'

'Fall off a horse?' said the man, gesturing to my plaster and crutches.

'Wrestling a crocodile,' I replied, with a grin.

'Really?' exhaled the woman, her voice high and squeaky. 'How brave!'

'No, Mary, he's joking.'

'Oh.'

'I fell off a bus.'

'Tough luck.'

I nodded, they smiled, I smiled, and we returned to our neighbouring boxes.

To my relief, I found a little map of the Middle East with Palestine in the centre that looked old enough, although it didn't appear to be dated. It caught my eye because of the intricate detailing and the distinctive brown, red and blue shading. It was unlike any my father had, and the sticker read £20, which was at the upper end of my budget, but what the hell. I gave the old man a twenty-pound note. When I turned back, the tracksuit woman was looking at me.

'All those places. It must be wonderful.'

'I'm very lucky.'

'Don't you ever get lonely? You know, travelling on your own?'

'Not really. I quite like solitude.'

'I'd get terribly lonely. I can never be on my own. Isn't that right, Trevor?'

Trevor nodded, with a smile, and squeezed his wife's arm. I smiled back, wished them luck with their living room, and departed. Behind me, the door to the hall swung shut, the dull bell clanging loudly.

I'd made one small mistake. Just one. Not out of malice, or laziness. Out of greed maybe, but not big greed, not the kind that makes you rich, but the petty kind of greed that makes you take small risks, like not admitting that a shop assistant has given you too much change. Or writing about a place you've never actually been to.

My trip to Venezuela had gone so well, until the end. I'd managed to get ten writing commissions, spread across four-and-a-half weeks' travelling, earning me my biggest one-trip haul yet – roughly £6,000 net. I was almost done, into my last week, when I slipped getting off a bus in Mérida and broke my ankle in two places.

I sprawled in the rusty dirt, writhing in agony. The passengers stood around me, as if witnessing a death or a miracle. One Japanese tourist snapped a photograph, before someone called an ambulance.

One slip. A second amongst countless seconds that have made up my thirty-one years on earth. It was so stupid, so unnecessary. Why do things like that have to happen?

I was furious. The broken ankle meant there was no way I'd be able to make my final destination – the sleepy seaside village of Choronì. I sat on a trolley in the cockroach-splattered waiting room of the small district hospital and fumed. My tenth and final article, the final element of my masterplan, was scuppered. I would have to say goodbye to £500, plus £150 expenses.

And Choronì was a good story – a tiny fishing port that attracted a quarter of a million tourists each year – flocking to see the weeping statue of the Virgin in the main square. The statue had in reality shed tears on only one occasion, on the November day that Kennedy was shot dead in Dallas (a 'coincidence' that had ensured a steady, and lucrative, influx of American catholics over the decades).

So far, in forty-one years, there had been no more Virginal sobbing. But this didn't stop the pilgrims coming, in particular South America's vast population of black-clad grandmothers under the height of five-foot-two. Many people, I thought sadly, need something other than themselves to believe in. Which was fine by me, as long as I could make money writing about it.

As I lay in the Mérida hospital while the plaster shackle set firm and solid, I decided to do something I'd never done before. I would write an article about Choronì without actually going there.

I limped to an internet café and printed out three recent articles on Choronì by other travel writers (one American, one British and one Mexican, whose Spanish I understood only sketchily). These sources, added to the extensive research I'd done before flying to Venezuela, convinced me that I could write a credible piece. I could make up a few funny quotes, attribute them to fictitious locals, and collect my £500, plus expenses based on receipts I'd already amassed.

It would be a gamble, I knew, and I was notoriously bad at gambling, but there was a high probability that I would get away with it. Wasn't there?

I wrote the article on my laptop from my hospital bed. The nurses kept me supplied with platefuls of sliced mango, whilst giggling intermittently at my clumsy Spanish.

The article appeared on page six of the *Daily Times* travel section the following week, just before my return from South America. It was this article that Father John

Norton, priest of St Peter's Church, Stockport, cut out and photocopied, shortly before he was due to lead a group of his parishioners on a two-week trip to visit the New Word missionary project they were supporting in the slums of the industrialized Venezuelan city of Maracay.

And it was this article that the thirteen devout catholics in Father Norton's charge (ranging between nineteen and sixty-seven years old) re-read with some disbelief when, after a gruelling seven-hour drive in a spluttering minibus, they arrived from the mosquito-infested, cloud-soaked mountains to the sea, only to discover that the '*santissima statua de la Virgen*' had been moved to the capital, Caracas, four months previously by the newly elected Venezuelan President, Miguel Tavarez. The thousands of pilgrim-tourists had vanished along with it, leaving 'the somnambulant strange little paradise' (as I'd lovingly described it) with a failing fishing industry, teenage prostitutes and an impressive crack cocaine problem.

Two of the Stockport catholics were mugged in the first hour, whilst the priest himself was offered oral sex and amphetamines before he got off the bus.

I knew this, because the *Daily Times* travel editor, Martin Foster had, this very morning at 9 a.m., read Father Norton's letter of outrage to me with barely contained fury. The catholic priest had included a photocopy of my article, adorned with sections highlighted in red, ecclesiastical pen.

' "The delicate little roadside cafes . . ." "the little old ladies who dream of God and long-lost teeth . . ." ' Martin Foster repeated, bitter sarcasm injected into each syllable.

"'. . . the gentle lap of waves as children sing folk songs at the feet of the Madonna . . .'"

I didn't try to defend myself.

At the end of the thirty-minute meeting, Martin Foster informed me that I'd never work for the newspaper again. He added that he would do everything in his power to ensure that I'd never work as a travel writer anywhere again. His secretary cut up my press card in front of me, with a pair of pearl-handled scissors that seemed reserved specifically for this task.

Standing in the middle of Gutter Lane, EC2, I realized I needed to call Molly. I needed to see her. I dialled her mobile.

'Hi, just wondering if you've time for a quick coffee?'

'I'm a little up to my eyes, babes. Something the bank calls work. I don't know if you've heard of it, but I thought I'd give it a go, you know, see what all the fuss was about.'

Normally my girlfriend's caustic jokiness made me smile. But not today.

'Come on. Just a quick coffee. I haven't seen you all week.'

I knew I was sounding whiny, and Molly was particularly averse to whining. This surprise call on her time went against the basis of our relationship, which was all about detachment, ease and a lack of demands. But for once I didn't care. Somehow, I knew, her smile would make me feel a little better.

I never planned to be a travel writer. I just loved travelling – the thrill of departure, the anonymity of flight, the freedom of movement. During my second year at university I started writing comic accounts of my vacation travels, one of which I submitted to the *Daily Times* on a whim. They called me back and published it the following week – a story about surfing with ex-Sandinistas in Nicaragua. I earned £250 and never looked back.

I was excited at first – the world was mine. It baffled me that airlines, hotels, car rental companies, even restaurants, gave me things for free because I was writing about them. I could call up airline PR companies and they would seem delighted to fly me to Rio de Janeiro, 'and of course we've put in a request for an upgrade'. It was the best job on earth. Once I flew KLM first class to Buenos Aires – I was undoubtedly the poorest person ever to have sat in the seat.

But as I visited places that I'd once considered so mystical – Marrakesh, Madagascar, Mount Fiji – I realized that everywhere was now accessible, nowhere was new. I began to wonder if this was a cause of our twenty-first century apathy – the sense that there is nowhere left to go, nothing original left to do. I got annoyed at some of my fellow travel writers, who tried to pretend they were real explorers. Much as I would have loved to have been born two hundred years ago, hitching a ride on the *Beagle* or Shackleton's sled, I was realistic. All I could do was to try and write about places in a different way, to present my own imaginative impression of destinations everyone had already been to.

I was good, I knew, because I was organized. I mapped out my trips, I planned them intricately, to maximize my chances of covering everything and getting a good story.

I created folders with maps, lists, newspaper clippings. I booked ahead, arranged for tourist boards to show me around. I ensured that everything went smoothly, allowing me space and time to come up with good descriptions, witty one-liners, and authentic sounding dialogue.

My 'talent', or so several editors told me, was capturing 'the quirky reality' of what a destination had to offer.

I'd never broken a bone before. I'd never made up a sentence. I was always careful. Honesty and authenticity were my trademarks.

Until now.

I stopped at my flat near Paddington Station. I'd been renting the small one-bedroom apartment for three years, with its fabulous view across six feet of concrete to the back wall of the Peking Garden Chinese Restaurant, run by a large Pakistani family from Lahore. Its major selling point, as far as I was concerned, was its cheapness and proximity to the train that could whisk me in fifteen minutes to my favourite part of London – Heathrow Airport.

I didn't like London. Apart from the fact that my best friend Gemma, my girlfriend Molly (Gemma's sister) and most of my limited social circle lived in London, and it was easy to get a flight from there to almost anywhere in the world, I would happily have lived elsewhere. London made my body ache. Maybe it was the incoherent mess of buildings, or the scrappy rubbish everywhere, or the embattled faces of the pallid inhabitants. Or maybe it was the dampness that gnawed at your bones like an old dog.

It's a tough city, there's no doubt about it. To survive

London, I thought, you had to map out your territory. I had my own landmarks – my flat, Molly's 'loft', Gemma's new house in the far-flung, newly cool breeding-zone of Victoria Park, and the Starbucks on Praed Road next to Paddington Station. It was like a personal *A to Z* street guide, containing only the pages you needed. Or in my case, an *A to B*.

A few years ago, I actually photocopied selected pages from the London *A to Z*, marking in a black felt-tip pen my personal landmarks and the short cuts between them. I debated for several days whether laminating these pages would be going too far, and then I did it anyway.

As I stumbled up the curry-spotted stairs, past the London Underground map (free from any London Transport office), my plaster leg clunking at each step like a punishment, I cursed loudly.

'Bollocks! Bollocks!'

I cursed my broken bone. I cursed my stupidity. I cursed the slippery buses of Venezuela and the Virgin Mary who pretended to weep in order to hook her deluded disciples.

While I was in the tiny cramped toilet, trying to zip up my trousers, the doorbell rang. In my hurry, I fell against the wall, my arm flailing out and knocking the neat line of mini shampoo bottles from a dozen luxury hotels around the world into the toilet bowl, one by one, followed by my last remaining toilet roll, which bobbed in the water like a drowned marsupial. I cursed again, then wondered, for an instant, if Molly was at the door. I was hopeful (maybe there would be a chance of quick afternoon sex). But I knew this was unlikely for two reasons:

Reason 1. When we first got together, Molly took one look, or more precisely smell, at my bedroom and told me that she wouldn't sleep within a mile of the place.

Reason 2. We'd been going out just over eight months now, but since I'd got back from Venezuela I'd hardly seen her. We hadn't even had sex. In four and a half weeks. If I was honest, it was starting to bother me a little. I wanted her. I needed her body.

Of course the person at the door was not Molly. It was the antithesis of Molly. Standing on the step was my landlord, the potbellied, gingery, chain-smoking Mr Vincent Henderson.

The news, as I quickly surmised, was not good. London landlords do not visit to offer flowers, glad tidings or bowls of fruit. Vincent Henderson was dogmatic.

'I gave you notice five weeks ago. In writing.'

I did remember the envelope, vaguely. It was lying in a pile of oppressive looking mail I'd been managing not to open since my return from South America.

'I'm selling, Mr Thompson. Clear and simple. I'll get two hundred grand for this place.'

'Two hundred grand? The flat isn't worth that.'

The flat wasn't worth that. It was worth a visit from Westminster Council Environmental Services.

I couldn't believe it. First the Choroní article, now this! You saw days like this at the beginning of films, in which screenwriters had only a few minutes to bring a character's comfortable existence crashing down around them, and thus set up the main thrust of the plot. But days like this didn't happen in real life. Real life was structured. You had control.

'You wanna buy it?'

Vincent Henderson viewed me with narrowed, fatty eyes that had undoubtedly seen far worse during thirty-plus years in London debt and rent collection.

'The flat?' I looked a little more panicked than I'd intended.

'Naw. You couldn't come close, could you?'

I glared at Vincent Henderson. Of course I couldn't come close. Sometimes I felt jealous of my contemporaries from university, who were far wealthier than me, thanks to jobs in the City or top London law and media firms. But the way I saw it, they were simply following someone else's map, down a route marked 'Job, Marriage, Kids, Retirement, Death' that welcomed a million visitors a year. I had other ideas. I was drawing my own chart.

'Travel writer, ain't you?'

I nodded, only half listening. I wouldn't buy a flat like this. I would buy somewhere nice, with a garden, where I could write and grow things. Like tomatoes. I liked tomatoes.

'The fing is, Mrs Henderson wants to go to Greece.'

I couldn't move. Not right now. I hadn't planned for this.

'You wouldn't know anywhere good in Greece, would you?'

I looked up. This happened to me a lot. As soon as people heard I was a travel writer, they'd start asking me where they should travel. Many of my fellow travel writers refused, like Hollywood stars declining autographs, 'I'm sorry, I don't do that, it's too messy,' they'd say. 'You'll end up blaming me if you have a shit time.' But I liked helping people.

I don't consider myself a miracle healer, but I know that holidays are important to people. Doesn't everyone dream of their next holiday? Isn't this dream sometimes enough to get you through the day, the week, the year? And when you've finally booked, isn't the countdown delicious, waiting, anticipating, purchasing dozens of things you'll never need? Isn't there both hate and love in the bittersweet return? Isn't there a final redemption to be had, basking in the glow that lasts for weeks afterwards?

'Greece in September is perfect,' I heard myself saying. 'You could do the southern mainland, the Pelóponnisos with some amazing ancient sites like Tiryns, Sparta and the epic theatre at Epidhavros . . . or maybe a more relaxed option like Paxos . . .'

I stopped. Suddenly I didn't want to talk to Vincent Henderson any more. I wanted things back to the way they were – a cheap flat where I slept and did laundry, a travel writing trip on the horizon, and the possibility of an imminent visit to Molly's loft for sex. I decided to cash in my travel advice.

'Look, I can get you all the details. I just need a bit more time on the flat . . .'

Vincent Henderson shook his head, sadly.

'Sorry son. You're out by Monday.'

I sat in Paddington Starbucks and watched the rain streak down the windows. I felt calmer here. Paddington Starbucks was my neutral zone, a 1920s Tangiers or 1960s West Berlin, disconnected from the hostile state in which it was located. In this coffee shop, with its standardized décor, multilingual menu board and international clientele,

I could be anywhere from Buenos Aires to Manhattan. Except for the summer rain that fell outside, in dark, dull drops. This, I thought, could only be London. The ragged reproachful London rain.

Where was Molly? I should never have asked her to take a break from her vast computer screen on the fifteenth floor of the Paddington Tower, where she collated and analyzed company data from firms in northern England. She was an investment specialist, a mergers and acquisitions maestro. One of the numerous things I admired about her was the way she seemed to waste very little of her time.

In many ways, I couldn't believe my luck. Whilst fellow travel writers complained constantly of their girlfriends/boyfriends, wives/husbands who didn't understand why they had to be away so much, who always wanted to travel with them, who on their return always wanted to talk seriously about their relationships and 'The Future', Molly didn't like travelling (more so since her divorce), and she had no desire to talk about 'our relationship', or where it was 'going'.

'It's fun, isn't it?' was her cheerful refrain, one that I echoed wholeheartedly.

Occasionally people (my mother) asked me if I ever thought about marriage, as if turning thirty-one was a trap-door you fell through into a pit marked 'Matrimony'. I would laugh it off, pointing out that Molly had recently come out of a divorce and quite understandably showed no inclination towards making our relationship any more permanent.

And besides, who was ready for marriage in this day

and age? Getting hitched had long ceased to be the major life aim of civilized people, coming way down the list after:

Making serious money.
Buying serious property.
Having seriously sexy relationship with people of
    various ages and nationalities.

In some ways, I reckoned, my generation had come to perceive marriage as the equivalent of nipple piercing, tofu or clubbing. Some people were into it, some weren't. No big deal.

I wasn't like Gemma, who'd rushed to tie the knot a year ago, at the youthful age of twenty-eight. In many ways, I admired her – she'd decided what she wanted, and went out and got it. Husband, house, children imminent. I respected her choices, and she, for the most part, re-sisted the temptation to encourage me to follow the same path.

'Thirty-five is the new thirty,' she told me from time to time, quoting from one of the numerous women's magazines her husband gave her subscriptions to each Christmas.

Over a second semi-skimmed latte, I considered my options. I needed somewhere to stay until I found another flat. The most obvious thing was to ask Molly, but this was risky – she'd made it clear when we started dating that she considered her expensive loft apartment in Clerkenwell her own place – separate from boyfriends, work colleagues and even family, 'a haven, an oasis in the urban jungle'. On the odd occasion I stayed the night, waking long after she'd departed for work, I would find a note saying 'Busy tonight, C U soon' on the kitchen table, next to my toothbrush which had been removed from the bathroom and pointed precisely towards the exit.

I could, of course, call Gemma. After all, she was the only one of my friends to have a five-bedroom, four-storey house in London. The problem was, she was in the middle of renovating it, according to her own design drawn up at the age of twelve, and funded by Raj's weighty bank balance. I'd been only once, a few months ago with Molly, when the place had resembled a bomb-site, only without the charm. There was no chance they'd finished it, but a couple of bedrooms might be inhabitable. It would only be for a few days.

The sad thing was, I didn't feel like calling Gemma. This was partly because I was now dating her sister, and things had been a little clumsy and awkward since Molly and I started seeing each other. But mainly it was because of her husband.

I'd tried to like Raj, ever since Gemma brought him to dinner that first time, red-faced, a little breathless with excitement and nerves. I was careful to tell her while Raj was in the toilet that I thought he was wonderful, because I knew that's what she wanted to hear.

I was still trying to like Raj, because I knew Raj was good for Gemma, offering her the security she'd been craving ever since her father died. It was just that Raj and I were so different. Raj was naturally conservative, having followed a well-signposted route direct from Oxford to the City (pick up a nice £100,000 signing-on bonus when you pass Go). Raj, in turn, would never understand why I loved to travel, why I lived in a dingy flat next to a mainline railway station, and 'how on earth' Molly and I managed to keep our relationship going, considering how little we saw of each other and our lack of official commitment to one another.

And Raj was clearly and visibly jealous of my friendship with his wife, even though I'd known Gemma for almost twelve years, since our first weekend at Sheffield University.

One day soon, I'd have to talk to Raj, to clear the air between us. I wanted the old Gemma back. I wanted to feel light with her again. I wanted to feel protective, and practical, I wanted to put up shelves and drive her to the supermarket. I wanted to laugh with her, and I wanted Raj to laugh with us.

'Hey, Hopalong. What's up?'

I looked up. Molly was standing over me, like a schoolteacher checking work, but no teacher ever looked this good, her shoulder-length brown hair pulled back in a coquettish pony tail. She was wearing a dark skirt suit, and her knee-high black leather boots with the small heels that never failed to make my loins stir.

'Hey. Thanks for coming.'

'I've got twelve minutes, buster. Sunderland's calling.'

I noted her smile, photographing it instantly in my mind, but to my surprise it didn't make me feel better. I fought my instinct to tell her about my Choronì article, Father Norton of Stockport, and Martin Foster's threat to my career. I wasn't sure how she'd react. She would be sympathetic, I knew, but it would put a significant dent in the fading aura of coolness I'd just about managed to maintain over the past eight months.

I decided to be matter-of-fact.

'I'm getting thrown out of my flat. The bastard landlord's selling.'

She sipped her double espresso and chuckled.

'Wow. That's a relief. It's a dump. You should get somewhere nicer.'

'Thanks, Molly.'

'Sorry. But you know I hate that place. When do you have to be out?'

'The weekend.'

'Oh. Shit. Unlucky.'

Her phone rang. She glanced at the number display and turned it off. This made me feel better. I was more important than work.

'Okay, Cowboy,' she murmured, more softly. 'What are you going to do?'

I loved the way Molly was so energetic, so headfirst. I had a sudden urge to take her in my arms and kiss her.

'I'm not too sure,' I replied, hoping in that instant that she'd offer to let me come to her Clerkenwell loft for takeaways and hot sex. When she remained silent, still smiling, still sipping her coffee (she looked great sipping coffee), I decided to try a new tactic.

'I was wondering about asking Gemma . . .' I remarked, coyly. I knew this was manipulative on my part, but small manipulations, ruses and gambits are the fabric of every relationship, aren't they? I was banking on my suspicion that even though Molly seemed to have no problem with

43

my close friendship with her sister, she would still rather I didn't spend my nights at Gemma's house.

I had used 'The Gemma Ploy' before, with previous girlfriends – to bind them more closely to me – even though I had no inkling of desire for Gemma, not even in my darkest, loneliest hours of the night. Any such suggestion, from myself or others, made me shudder. It was unthinkable. It would be incest.

'I thought you hated going there because of Raj?' Molly said, finishing her double espresso.

'No. I'm just a shallow person with too little patience.'

'You forgot to mention your tendency towards self-pity.'

'Thanks, Molly.'

'Well there's only one thing for it,' said my beautiful girlfriend, brightly.

'What's that?' I looked up hopefully. She was going to say it; she was going to invite me to stay.

'Your parents. It's your dad's birthday and you said last week how much they were dying to see you.'

CARING

My parents came to collect me. They arrived at 9 a.m., which meant they had departed Cambridge at seven-thirty in the morning, on a Saturday. I was relieved – at least I would now be looked after. But I was also a little ashamed – I was thirty-one and still reliant on my mum and dad.

I knew they'd be early, so I'd woken before seven, hobbling down to the news-stand at the station to buy the *Daily Times*. The retraction was smaller than I'd feared, just a paragraph in the travel section at the bottom of page three explaining that the article on Choronì was erroneous and written by a freelancer who no longer worked for the paper. It was possible most people would miss it, if they weren't in the business. Unfortunately, the people who usually commissioned me were all in the business.

I waited for my parents in the upstairs window, like my grandmother used to sit in her room at the nursing home. It had always made me sad, how lonely she looked, gazing down in hope and expectation. But she'd been eighty-seven. She, at least, had had an excuse for being on her own.

When I opened the door my parents hurried to me, excited and animated. To my relief, it seemed clear they'd not read the *Daily Times* retraction.

'So much traffic,' chirped my mother, putting her arms around me. I pulled away slightly.

'How's the ankle?' my father asked, shaking my hand.

'Getting better.'

'How did you do it again?'

'Slipped, getting off a bus in Venezuela.'

'A fall from grace?' my father smiled, pleased as always with a clerical quip.

'Yeah, Dad. Something like that.'

They packed my possessions – the futon, the books, my four framed photographs from Antarctica and Vietnam – into the back of the small Peugeot 306. I tried to help, but my mother insisted I sat and rested my foot. I felt like a child once more, watching my parents prepare for a holiday. I was never allowed to help; they had their system and I'd only get in the way.

I went to the toilet one last time, wondering if I'd miss this flat where I'd spent three years of my life. I doubted it. I pulled down the map of the London Underground from the hallway and crumpled it into the bin, where it languished alongside the bottles of luxury hotel shampoo.

'It's just like packing him up for university, isn't it John?' remarked my mother brightly.

'I think he's got even less stuff this time,' declared my father, slamming the back of the car firmly and locking it, twice, before taking my arm to help me into the front seat.

'I'll take the crutches, I'll take the crutches,' shrilled my mother. I handed her the crutches and buckled myself into the front seat. Suddenly I wished I'd never called them. It felt so familiar, this suffocating bustle. I looked

46

around, afraid that someone would see me being cosseted by my mother, but the only passers-by were a group of Japanese tourists in matching yellow raincoats. They seemed sympathetic (the Japanese all lived with their parents until marriage, didn't they?).

The Peugeot pulled away from the dingy flat. I watched the grey front door disappear in the wing mirror. One more landmark removed.

'Ah, London,' my father said, overtaking a red double-decker bus.

'So many people,' said my mother fearfully, staring out of the passenger window as if seeing more than ten people together in public for the first time in her life. I followed her gaze – to me the streets around Paddington seemed comparatively quiet.

'Did you get the *Daily Times* today?' I asked, as innocently as I could.

'Oh no. Are you in it?' replied my mother, a little panicked. I breathed out.

'No. I thought I was going to be, but I'm not.'

I was safe. They didn't know. My father, as a committed liberal, was a *Guardian* reader, and only bought the more conservative *Daily Times* when I called him to say one of my articles was going to be in it (to the delight of the local Muslim newsagent, Mr Gupta, who looked forward to such Saturdays when he could murmur 'closet fascist!' as he handed the change to his old friend, the Vicar of St Phillips).

There was still an outside chance that one of his parishioners might show my father the page at Sunday Communion, but I was prepared to take that risk. Most of them were more than a little scared of the Reverend John Thompson and his strict edicts about 'casting the first stone', so it was unlikely that they would openly accuse his son of being a fraud and a liar, at least not on the Sabbath.

'We read your last article, about that statue and festival in Venezuela. It was so good, I sent copies to the Joneses and the McGuires,' my mother chirped proudly from the back seat. 'When's your next trip?'

'I don't know, Mum,' I replied, a little too tersely.

'Your mother was just asking, Ian,' my father reproached me as he turned onto the North Circular.

'I don't understand why they don't publish you more often,' continued my mother. 'You're a good writer.'

'Thanks Mum,' I muttered, pretending to be fascinated by the passing trees.

We ate at six-thirty, as my parents have done as long as I can remember.

'No nuts,' joked my mother as she passed me a plate of stringy rust-coloured lamb and vegetables that oozed liquid as if wounded. My father rolled his eyes; I winced and my mother laughed quickly, the triangular ritual that has been mapped out between us over twenty-five years or more.

I hate my allergy, as some people hate their nose, bottom or bald spot. I hate the way I've been given it, without any reason, without having any control over it. It's bad enough that there are a thousand things out there that can kill you, from falling trees to anthrax in your Christmas card, without having to fight a constant and wary battle against nuts. It's crazy. It is, as Gemma used to joke, nuts.

Because of a quirk of genetics, a defect installed at conception, whereby my body reacts in a spectacularly adverse way to proteins in all nut oils, any nut – from pecan to peanut – can dispatch me to my maker. Walnuts are the worst. Just a crumb of this innocent, friendly round husk, so prized for its nutrients and healthy fatty acids, causes my lips and mouth to swell, my throat to close and my body to go into anaphylactic shock – the blood pressure plummets suddenly, you can't breathe, you pass out and bingo . . . the end of the journey.

So far I've come out on top. I carry lists, carefully laminated, of the words for different nuts in the world's ten most common languages. It's difficult, abroad, to avoid them. Only twice have I suffered badly, once in Italy (chocolate ice-cream, cunningly laced with hazelnuts), once in Boston, (ravioli with ground walnuts not mentioned on the menu). I never told mum and dad – they worry about me enough, every time I go anywhere they've never been to themselves, which is just about everywhere.

Ever since the Boston attack, I've carried an epi-pen (a syringe pen that you jab into your thigh, releasing an immediate dose of adrenalin into the system). I've never had to use it 'in the field', but I've practised occasionally, on innocent oranges, as the doctors showed me; jab, jab.

Dinner passed quickly, with my parents chatting about their routines and asking vague and unobtrusive questions about my future projects. By the amorphous egg-suet-sultana pudding, I was beginning to wonder, for the first time in several years, whether I might actually be able to spend more time with them.

'So do you think there's a chance Molly might come for Christmas this year?' my mother asked abruptly, breaking a short silence. I choked on a sultana.

'It's August, Mum.'

'We've only met her once. I know she has a high-flying job with the bank, but it would be nice to get to know her a little bit better . . .'

'Come on, Mum . . .' I groaned.

'How's Gemma doing?' asked my father hurriedly, aware of his wife's reddening face. 'Is the new house finished?'

'Er . . . I don't think so. I haven't seen her since I got back.'

'Her husband must be wealthy,' my mother chirped, as she rearmed for another assault on the 'Molly Situation'.

'Well, he's a lawyer in the City.'

'Indian, isn't he?' continued my mother, scraping the discarded Spotted Dick back into the bowl from whence it came.

'He's British, Mum. He was born here. His parents are from India.'

My mother nodded, as if understanding this concept for the first time. She stood, pushing back her chair.

'I still don't know why you didn't ask Gemma to marry you. Really, sometimes Ian, I think you're too introverted for your own good.'

I glanced at my father, who was busy studying the label on the back of the Sainsbury's claret bottle. My mother disappeared into the kitchen, from where clanking noises announced she was no longer in a good mood. My father looked up, sudden concern on his face.

'We'll do the dishes, Margaret!' cried the Reverend John Thompson, standing to his full six-feet-three and shoving the chair so firmly under the table that it struck a leg and vibrated with shock for a moment. 'Leave it to the men!'

I eased my own chair gently under the oak table, irritation bubbling through me. They both angered me in their own unique way. I wished my mother didn't have friends whose children had all got married before they were thirty and were popping out offspring at a rate that should have the World Health Organization on their doorsteps with free condoms and leaflets about population control. And I wished my father didn't treat my mother like one of his congregation, someone for whom all things could be assuaged, reordered and generally fixed.

As a child I had always clamoured for the responsibility of dish-washing, lording in the raised height of the plastic footstool, deciding which piece of crockery would be washed when; speeding up, slowing down, like a General marching troops. But now I was happy to be a lowly conscript and sit wiping away the soapy water, rubbing the glasses clean.

As I watched the Reverend Thompson pull on the yellow rubber gloves, one finger at a time, a surgeon preparing, I was surprised to see my father's hands tremble, just a shiver. I thought about asking him if anything was wrong, but our habitual stance when alone in a small room together was silence.

This was my father's routine. Glassware first. Then

cutlery. Then crockery. Then pans. You could not deviate, nor alter the divine pattern.

It didn't take long. Soon we had got to the plates, and then finally to saucepans that hadn't changed since I was old enough to turn on the hot tap, the dearth of words between us punctuated by tough little ticks of the plastic wall clock.

After I'd counted twenty-one clicks of the clock, I asked, finally:

'Looking forward to retirement?'

'It's not for another eight months,' my father replied, without looking round.

'Really? Eight months. That's, what, thirty-two more sermons?'

'Thirty-eight. I've written most of them already.'

'Wow. Prolific.'

'Not like you. I don't know how you can churn out those articles like you do.'

'I don't exactly churn them out, Dad.'

'I know, I know. It was just a figure of speech.'

When I was a teenager I used to daydream that my father was a farmer and that I, the son, would return from college to take over the family smallholding, treading in my father's muddy Wellington boot steps. As a boy, I tried to imagine being a Vicar, sneaking into my father's office on several occasions and pulling on the giant cassock that seemed like a parachute (in later years, this image served to fuel my contempt for the Revered Thompson, a man who needed a parachute, a safety net in life, who peddled this need to others). But I never felt comfortable, pretending to stand at the lectern delivering my Christmas sermon. I was like a cattle farmer's son who was allergic to cows, or a teacher's offspring who loathed children.

'So, everything's looking okay?' I found myself stumbling over the words. 'The pension's all in place?'

My father placed the dripping dessert bowl on the table in front of me, and swiped his brow with the back of his bright yellow hand.

'We'll make do. You don't have to worry, Ian.'

I nodded, with a smile I hoped was sympathetic. My parents were the poorest sixty-year-olds I knew. Molly and Gemma's mum had made a couple of hundred thousand selling her Tesco shares. Her house in Surrey was worth at least a million. But the Thompsons claimed they didn't care about wealth. Unlike every other sixty-something couple, they had no real savings, no big house to sell, no investments to cash in. As long as I'd been conscious of their attitudes, my parents had made a virtue of their relative poverty.

'The sparrows of the hedgerows possess nought yet want for nought.'

Heaven makes most sense to bankrupt saints.

'Make sure you rub them hard, Ian, I don't want any stains,' my father intoned as I took the knives and forks. Suddenly, my big toe at the end of the plaster cast started to itch. I tried to lean forward, the chair creaking, to scratch it.

'What's the matter, Ian?' my father asked, turning, soap suds dripping to the floor.

'Just an itch. It's hard to reach sometimes, with the plaster.'

I wondered, just for a moment, whether my father

might lean over and scratch my toes for me, healing the afflicted. Instead he nodded, turning back to the sink once more.

'I remember when I broke my arm falling off that ladder when you were little. Very inconvenient.'

I rubbed my toe, breathed out, and finished wiping the bowl. I looked to place it in the cupboard above the kettle, where it had lived for the last twenty years.

'It doesn't go there any more.'

My father took the bowl from me, his hand quivering gently, and placed it on a shelf below the boiler.

I couldn't sleep. I watched television late into the night, flicking through the channels in a half-thrilled attempt to find some female nudity. An infant longing to be somewhere else, far, far away, invaded me once more. I needed to escape. Any feelings of comfort and solace that had come from returning to the bosom and care of my family had vanished. I felt the walls of the darkened house closing in, as they had done so often in my childhood.

In my mid-twenties I began to wonder if my desire to travel, to escape to places where I was a complete stranger, had something to do with the pressure I'd felt as a child, being the Vicar's son. From an early age I'd loved the anonymity of transport, the places of departure and arrival, and the grimy, neutral way-stations in between.

One of my earliest memories of being completely happy was of sitting at a grease-stained table in a Little Chef restaurant, at a service station somewhere up the M1. The bright fluorescent light which cast no shadows seemed to wash away the diners, granting each complete anonymity.

No one looked at each other, everyone was caught up in thoughts of where they'd come from and where they were going to. I loved this state of limbo, of flux and uncertainty. It seemed so far from the stark certainties of Right and Wrong at the 1960s concrete manse in Cambridge.

'Bollocks!' I said, a little more loudly than I intended.

I was thirty-one and back with my parents.

I woke at ten the next morning. I lay, eyes closed, listening to silence. I couldn't remember a time when the small box house had ever been this peaceful. During my childhood there were always people coming and going – parishioners, bishops, local business leaders, schizophrenics, teenage mothers, Alzheimer widows, the good, the bad and the lonely. There were times when I felt like I was an intruder in my own house, with my atheist tendencies and my lack of personal tragedy to merit my father's soft advice and my mother's glutinous Shepherd's Pie. I would creep away to my bedroom and hide in my bed, reading tales of travel and derring-do, from The Hardy Boys to Jules Verne. Under my bedclothes at least, in the midst of a High Seas Adventure, I felt important and worthy.

At once, the bell in the church tower opposite began to chime, as if admonishing me. I wondered, for a moment, whether I could get out of bed and hobble over to the Church, but there were people there who still knew me as the Vicar's son, who would judge me whilst they cooed over my broken ankle. They had long mistrusted me, ever since I stopped going to services at the age of sixteen. They reproached me for breaking my father's heart.

It wasn't that I hated Christianity. I understood why

people adhered to such forms of organized religion. And Christianity was, give or take a few yearly massacres in Northern Ireland and India, a fairly peaceable faith, at least in its contemporary incarnation. In fact I quite liked the buildings that Christians excelled in – the lofty intricate architecture, the spacious tranquillity, the way light shone through stained glass. It was just that I didn't really believe in God. Unlike my mother, I watched the news, I read the papers. From the age of six, I'd been aware of the terrible, horrible things that happened in the world. I'd seen proof of man's ultimate power over the divine, the street beggars, the prostitutes, the drug addicts.

Holding a universal, unseen and omnipotent force responsible for everything might appear easier in the short-term, but the long-term implications are too terrifying to imagine.

Once again, I was caught by an overwhelming urge to call Molly. My reference point. My Greenwich Meridian. What else did I have? Some savings, my friendship (faltering) with Gemma, a few university friends, all married, who increasingly reminded me of my parents. Molly was different. She was like me.

I wondered if she knew how important she was to me, and how that would make her feel. I was terrified, suddenly, that if she sensed my need, she would pull away.

I decided to take a shower in the downstairs cubicle, used by the homeless people my mother invited to dinner, and young mothers needing to change babies' nappies during church services.

The water was lukewarm. I washed my hair quickly, my plaster-cast lower leg sticking out of the rickety shower door. Then, as I was about to rinse, the water cut off, abruptly. Soap streamed down my face, filling my eyes.

'Ow!' I bellowed. This was too much. This was an insult.

I cursed the ugly '60s house, I cursed the Church of England, I cursed my father's ineptitude with home maintenance and his creed of poverty. I stumbled out of the shower, eyes screwed shut, feeling for the towel. But it was mysteriously absent. I grappled for the doorhandle, turned and lurched out into the hallway, slipping slightly. I knocked into something hard and angular.

'Bollocks!' I exclaimed, loudly.

'Oh my!'

I blinked. There appeared to be someone else in the hallway.

'Ian?'

I opened my eyes against the searing soap. My mother and two middle-aged women stood in the doorway wearing floral summer dresses. One of them was Mrs Atkinson, the wife of the part-time organist, whose daughter Cynthia once wrote a typed letter to my father, complaining that I'd tried to kiss her during a Young Pilgrims sponsored walk (I had, I was bored).

I was naked in front of my mother and two female Parish council members.

I became aware of something crumbly by my naked right foot. I looked down. A cake lay crumbled into several pieces next to my hairy toes. My mother's voice cracked with anguish and distress.

'My Victoria sponge!'

*

At lunch I present my father with the map of Palestine.

'Happy Birthday, Dad.'

'Thank you, Ian. It's very pretty. Very delicate shading.'

'I'm sorry I didn't have time to get you a frame. But I will . . .'

'Thank you.'

'Sorry about the cake,' I mumble.

'Next time, Ian, perhaps you could try and keep the towel close by,' says my mother, as we munch the replacement malt loaf.

'Next time, perhaps there could be some hot water . . .' I reply, a little too harshly.

'Ian! Please don't talk to your mother like that!'

We fall into silence. I am a bad son, I know, but I can't take much more of this. I need to escape. I stare at the plastic wall clock, the thick black hand clicking inexorably to the right.

My mobile rings. I snatch it out of my pocket.

'Hello, Ian?'

I wonder, for a moment, if I'm imagining this, if I have created Gemma out of my boredom.

'Hey, gorgeous, how are you doing?' I stand awkwardly from the table, mouth the word 'Gemma' at my parents and hobble gratefully into the hallway.

'Sorry to trouble you . . .' she says, falteringly.

'No, it's fine, I'm at my parents, they're driving me mad. It's great to hear from you. Sorry I haven't called, it's been a bit crazy since I got back.'

'Yeah, me too. I've been meaning to call, but . . . you know . . . Where are you off to next?'

'Er . . . I'm not sure yet. France, maybe. I've got to sort it out.'

I pause, the lie sticking in my throat. She's silent. I wonder what to say next. Our telephone conversations have been like this in the last few months – stilted, disconnected. I'm worried we're drifting too far apart, like satellites whose orbits change by millimetres each day, until all at once, they're too distant to communicate. I know both of us feel it, and both of us regret it, but we seem powerless to prevent it. Once again, I wonder if it has something to do with me going out with her sister.

'So what's up with you?' I ask, brightly.

'I'm . . . er . . .' stumbles Gemma.

'Are you okay?' She doesn't sound okay.

'Yeah, I'm . . . oh God . . .'

'Gem?'

'It's Raj . . .'

'What? Is he okay?'

'I'm sorry . . . I didn't mean . . .'

Gemma chokes; once, then twice. She's trying not to cry.

'What's happened, Gemma?'

'He left. Raj has gone, Ian.'

My pulse quickens. I know I shouldn't feel excitement, but I can't help it. I feel alive, suddenly invigorated.

'I . . . don't know . . . what . . . to . . . do . . .'

I stand from the hallway chair, unaware of my ankle for the first time since Venezuela.

'Don't worry, Gem. I'm on my way. I'll be there by five.'

DESPAIR

Draw up the plans, calculate angles, stress points and maximum load-bearing. Figure it out.

> *The differences between Gemma and Raj*
> Raj uncaring. Gemma compassionate.
> Raj television. Gemma theatre, museums, new restaurants, clubs.
> Raj 32. Gemma 29.
> Raj sleeps on his front. Gemma sleeps on her back.
> Raj apple juice. Gemma orange.
> Raj work. Gemma relationship.
> Raj Phil Collins. Gemma Eminem.
> Raj beach. Gemma backstroke.
> Raj door open 'to see where the opposition is coming from'. Gemma door shut. To keep her safe.
> Raj intellectual and determined. Gemma reserved, and sometimes confused.

How could it be that the very things that attract you to someone become the things that drive you away from them? At the outset, I loved his slow, cautious step. He'd built strong, old-fashioned walls around him, so different from the insubstantial construction in which I lived with its paper-thin divisions, and fragile reflecting glass. I was delighted to discover his solidity, the protection and solace his building offered. So how could it be that these same walls have become a prison to me?

What's changed? What do I need?

I need to feel something. Something I've felt only at bright, sharp moments in my life – my first kiss with Matthew Vincent, when he grasped my arm behind the wheelie bins by the science block, Neil's look from the Student Union bar, his huge fingers brushing my breast two weeks' later, the phone call to tell me I had the job at KPSG, Raj's quiet insistent voice in my ear on our second date, his soft dark hand on mine the night he proposed.

Is it too much to ask? The bright sharp flash? Because I need it more than ever.

'How about pizza?' asks Ian, uncorking the wine he's purchased at the off-licence on the corner.

'I'm not hungry, I told you.'

'You have to eat. You're looking so skinny.'

He thinks I'll take this as a compliment; he's waiting for a smile. I remain stone-faced. He orders a pizza. I haven't the energy to protest.

'Come on, let's watch a film.'

'The machine's in a box somewhere.'

'Where? I'll find it. Look, I've got all your favourites, some Clooney, some Brad Pitt, *Gladiator* with the burly yet strangely irresistible Russell Crowe . . .'

The mention of Russell Crowe makes me think of Raj and I start to cry again. Ian looks panicked.

'We don't have to watch any of them . . .'

I glance up at him, eyes swollen.

'I don't know what to do.'

He puts his hand on my shoulder. I want him to grip it firmly, but he seems unsure, embarrassed.

'Look, give it a few more days, then who knows. Maybe I can talk to him?'

'Please don't try and solve this, Ian . . .'

'Sorry.'

The ache gapes open once more. I wonder if I can tell him, my oldest friend.

'What's wrong with me?' I ask, a question I've been wanting to voice out loud for two weeks.

'Nothing's wrong with you.'

Ian doesn't seem to believe his own answer. He likes reasons, he wants an explanation of why his friend, who has always seemed so sorted, so bold and stringent in following the path she's drawn for herself, has lost her way.

'I like security. I'm not adventurous or carefree like you . . .'

Ian opens his mouth to protest, but I continue, hell-bent.

'. . . So I chose Raj. He was easy. Convenient. He fitted my perfect little plan.'

'Has the plan changed?' Ian asks, gently.

'I DON'T KNOW!'

My empty wine glass flies across the room. It hits the brick wall and shatters. I'm impressed. It's a good throw, for a girl.

'Gemma . . .'

I turn on him, eyes wide now.

'Don't Ian! Please don't use that tone, don't patronize me. Just listen to me, for once, will you?'

He holds up his hands in defence and supplication.

'I'm sorry . . .'

I start sobbing again. It's as if I'm possessed by some spirit that comes and goes, passing through me at intervals and sucking out my strength and flooding me with misery.

'I've fucked up everything. I'm one big fuck-up.'

Ian sits down on the sofa beside me. The deeply upholstered cushions breathe out lusciously, as if on the verge of orgasm.

'Bollocks. I'm the fuck-up.'

I ignore him. Ian continues.

'Yes, I am. I'm more of a fuck-up than you.'

I shake my head, in admonishment rather than negation. Ian repeats himself, his voice becoming increasingly childish.

'Really. I'm the biggest fuck-up.'

'Ian . . .'

'I'm the biggest.'

He tries a quick, thin smile, hoping I'll take the bait. Something in his eagerness softens me.

'No . . .'

'Am.'

'Not.'

'Am.'

'Jesus . . .'

'I'm the fuck-up.'

'No. I am,' I say quietly, offering a hint of a smile.

'Nowhere near. You've just fucked up your marriage. At least you've a roof over your head. I'm homeless, I've fucked up my career, and I haven't had sex in weeks.'

I hit him sharply on the arm, as I've always done in the past whenever he says something that I consider out of order. I try not to imagine him and my sister having sex.

The pizza arrives and Ian tells me about his broken ankle and how he made up an article about a village in Venezuela. I manage a couple of short sharp laughs, and by the end of his full and fairly frank account I'm sitting upright on the sofa once more.

'Okay. You win, Thompson. You are a fuck-up.'

He nods, sagely.

'I thought you never made up anything in your articles, Mr Reality Report?'

'Ironic, isn't it?'

'So what does Molly think about all this?'

He glances down at his hands.

'You haven't told her?'

'I will. I just haven't had time.'

'You should tell her,' I say, aware at the moment of saying it that I'm a terrible hypocrite. When am I going to tell my sister anything? Hopefully never.

'I'm sorry, Ian. It's none of my business. I'll keep it quiet.'

He doesn't reply and I'm worried I've touched a nerve.

'Thanks for coming to my rescue like this. I appreciate it. Really, I do.'

He nods, more happily.

Suddenly, the phone rings. I grab it, snatching up the receiver to analyze the caller display. It's my mother. I don't press talk. The answering machine clicks on. My mother's voice trills loudly.

'Hello dear, calling for our Sunday chat, I haven't heard from you in a while. Hope all is well. Love to lovely Raj. Call me soon. Bye-eee!'

I shake my head. The machine clicks off.

Ian looks at me. Now he knows that I haven't told anyone about Raj. He looks a little scared. I realize that I've been a dreadful coward. I've made him responsible. I've summoned him to be the audience for my bad news, in the knowledge that he will have to break it to my sister, and by extension to my mother.

'Does anyone else know about Raj?' he asks, quietly.

I try to meet his gaze, my fingers kneading my forehead.

'Not really.'

'Your sister?'

I shake my head.

'We're both big chickens, aren't we?'

I nod.

'Do you want me to keep quiet?'

'I can't tell her anything until I know what I'm going to do. Where I'm going.'

'She'll understand.'

'No. She won't!' My voice is more strident than I'd intended. 'She'll tell me that I'm being selfish and it's about time I realized I can't have everything in life. She'll want answers!'

He looks down, uncertain. Suddenly I want to hide away.

'Look, I'm sorry the place is such a mess. There's a duvet on the bed in the back bedroom. Do you mind if I try and get some sleep? I'm knackered.'

'No problem. Wake me if you need anything.'

'Thanks Hopalong.'

'That's what Molly called me.'

'Oh. Well. I've never been that original.'

Before he can reply, I turn and disappear up the rickety wooden stairs, stepping quickly away.

I can't sleep. Again. It has crossed my mind that perhaps I'm getting depressed, a thought which depresses me. I've never considered myself a candidate for melancholia – such people are weak, or infirm, or living in conditions a thousand times worse than mine. I can't feel depressed. As my mother is fond of pointing out, I'm too well-off, too comfortable. But here I am, feeling awful, an emotion that just won't go away. I feel heavy, as if wearing lead. My stomach is as tight as a wrung towel.

I think about Raj, about how he might be coping with the hotel, whether he's getting any sleep, how his work is going, his 'highly complex case'. I wonder, with a pang of panic, whether he's told his parents yet.

His mother won't be surprised. The formidable Geeta Singh was tacitly against him marrying an English girl in the first place, even though, to her credit, she softened during our engagement (in no small part due to my stead-fast and energetic attempts to learn and perform all the right Hindu ceremonies, and meet every single aunty and cousin in the family – there seemed to be hundreds). Raj's father, the venerable Panjit Singh, was more overtly welcoming. A dentist in Croydon, he considered good teeth the mark of a good character, no matter what race or creed, and since my incisors have been praised by dental experts from Brent Cross to Bradford, he warmed to me.

'Fluoride pills, very responsible," he nodded merrily, as I explained how each childhood morning our father ensured that Molly and I supplemented our Rice Krispies with a small orange tablet.

I like Mr Singh. He always smells faintly of sandalwood and tobacco, and smiles when I enter the room. I feel sick now, curled on the sofa, thinking about his reaction to what I've done. I have proved him wrong. Despite my excellent teeth, I am a bad person, after all.

Oh God. Have I just made the biggest mistake of my life? Have I just thrown something away, because of all the pressure I'm feeling, that will turn out to have been the most precious thing I've ever possessed? I imagine myself watching the *Antiques Roadshow* programme my mother loves so much, seeing a middle-aged woman showing the experts her household treasure.

'Oh my,' the expert would say, looking at the woman's item with brightening eyes. 'It's a Raj Singh. Very, very rare . . .'

'How much is it worth?' the greedy little woman would ask, avariciously.

The expert would take off his glasses, then place them back on the end of his nose once more with an impeccable sense of timing, and declare, solemnly:

'Well, I'm glad you're sitting down, my dear. Because I have to tell you that your Raj Singh is nothing short of priceless!'

I want to hurt myself. I wonder if I have the courage for self-harm. But I'm afraid of blades and needles and the glowing ends of cigarettes. I want to scream, but I have no voice.

Why did I say those words? Some things are meant to remain locked away, aren't they, spinning through cerebral voids, churning amidst whirlpool dreams and daytime eddies, never to be rescued from the water.

But I've been keeping quiet about so much. It's inevitable something would seep out, break free.

'I don't love you.'

It started nine months ago. I remember the day, or at least the day I've chosen to represent the beginning, plotting it on the chart in my head. It was getting late and I was waiting, yearning for Raj to come home. Eventually he came in after eleven, only to start his usual thirty-minute diatribe against his boss and general working conditions. The difference, on this night, was that I had my own news – the contract for the Soho bar redevelopment, project leader Gemma Cook, which had been announced that afternoon (I'd been unable to get my husband on the phone to tell him how excited I was). When he'd finished his monologue, I took a deep breath and informed him of my thrill and pride in being awarded my first solo project, to which he'd smiled, said, 'That's wonderful, darling. Maybe my office could book its Christmas bash there when it's all completed,' before loping upstairs to run himself a bath.

My anger boiled up, steaming spite, but I kept it in, because he'd had a terrible day and I knew he'd continue to have terrible days for the coming weeks and months, and my work was not as important or well paid.

I lay in bed that night, on the edge of the mattress, blood simmering.

Looking back on it, I think this was my fatal mistake.

The small malignant anger from that evening, diminutive, unnoticeable almost, grew (a fury of cells dividing and multiplying), until it had infected both my mind and body. If only I'd cut it out at the outset. Perhaps I could have saved Raj. Perhaps I could have saved myself.

'You keep things pent-up inside,' my mother told me after my father's death, 'and they will kill you.'

Outside, a car engine coughs, dies and is resurrected once more. A man shouts. I sneak to the window and glance outside, pulling the wedding present sheets and duvet around me, for warmth and protection.

When we first moved in, I used to love curling up in this old window seat, surreptitiously spying on the comings and goings in the street below. It was a new area of London to me, the notorious East End, which, if I was honest, I found a little intimidating – the many different ethnic faces, the hard skinny teenage boys smoking cigarettes in expensive tracksuits, the old men sitting on park benches sipping cheap beer, the police cars wailing in the distance. My mother, West End woman number one, thought we were mad moving east, but as I watched from my fourth-floor spy hole, I began to realize that this was just like any other part of London, with its proximity of rich and poor, beautiful and ugly, inherited and self-made: the welfare and Range Rover families, the champagne and Special Brew alcoholics, the lonely of every creed and colour.

As I'd sit in the window seat watching the middle-class mummies pushing their prams into the park across the road, I'd imagine Raj returning in the Audi, with two little girls skipping from the car up to our front door. They would look up, see their mummy in the window, and wave.

I used to imagine.

I glance out of the window but the street is empty, which is perhaps unsurprising considering it's 2.42 a.m. I focus on number 22, two houses along the terrace, with black railings and a newly painted black front door which shines luxuriously in the soft light from the streetlamp. Raj is obsessed with this house, or more accurately with the man who recently moved in there. He's in his forties, thin as a rake, with slicked back dark hair and sunken eyes. He usually appears on the doorstep to greet the postman or early morning couriers in a silk dressing gown and white bare feet. At night there are always people coming to the house – wealthy looking men and women in suits and expensive streetwear. Some drive large SUVs, others gleaming new Minis. What goes on in the house is unclear – maybe he's just a popular man, with plenty of cool, well-heeled friends. After all, this is one of the capital's up-and-coming areas. Yet the blinds always remain down. There's never a chance to peek inside.

'The layabout,' Raj calls him. I remember how annoyed I was with my husband; he was so judgemental – anyone who's a bit different ends up condemned by the scathing prosecution of Mr Raj Singh LLB. Partly because of Raj's disapproval, I became covertly intrigued by the rakish man in the silk dressing gown. He was different. He did things his own way, following his own inscrutable plans. I admired that. Secretly I hoped he was running some sort of sex club, or upmarket brothel. It excited me to think that behind that stately door, all sorts of debauchery was being performed.

But tonight, the black front door remains resolutely closed. The street is silent, just a dull hum from traffic in central London where people are still drinking, dancing, fighting, fucking. Here the dark, empty park is still. It begins to rain, streaks of drops like veins down the window pane.

As the minutes become half, then full hours, I try to banish the thought that nags at me like a bluebottle buzz, that I married Raj because Molly made me dump Neil Farrelly.

Neil Farrelly. I still enjoy saying the words, lingering over the syllables. He was studying Veterinary Science at Liverpool, the career he'd dreamed of since his childhood on the family farm in the Scottish borders. We met two months into our first year at university, during rag week, and started a trans-Pennine relationship that seemed to me as exciting and dangerous as *Wuthering Heights* or *Tilly Trotter*. We met up every weekend, enduring train delays and motorway traffic jams to spend thirty-six hours in each other's company. It was exhilarating, to begin with. I craved the weekends like a desperate office worker rather than an indolent student. In the face of derision and gloomy predictions from friends and family, we survived Christmas, then the spring term, Easter and the first few weeks of exam preparation.

Then, one June night, Neil did not return my call and I panicked. It was as if a huge crack had appeared in a newly finished building. He called the next day, apologizing, saying he'd fallen asleep because he was exhausted from rugby and revising. We agreed not to speak for a couple of weeks, until exams were over.

On the day of my last exam my sister came to stay. While everyone else was celebrating, I sat with Molly in a pub and told her of my concerns and fears for my relationship with Neil. My sister listened carefully before informing me that her one big regret of student life was having continued to date Mike Peters in her first year, travelling between London and Manchester, when she could have had a much more 'interesting and wild time' being single at UCL.

'The whole distance thing, Gem, it's just not worth it.'

I came away from this conversation very worried – less about my own need to 'explore' student life in Sheffield, and more about Neil and what I was doing to him. Men were different, I told myself. Maybe he was just stringing me along, waiting for the right moment to dump me for someone else, just like my sister had done with poor Mike (I recalled his tearful phone messages, his six letters in one week, and his eventual appearance on our doorstep one Friday evening, when Molly hid under my bed and I was instructed to inform her now ex-boyfriend that she'd gone to Dublin for the weekend).

It was a miserable beginning to the summer holidays for me, as I battled in my mind with my insecurities and sense of morality. What was the best thing for Neil? Should I give him his freedom, if he wanted it?

We booked a holiday together to Turkey, backpacking around the southern coast. It started out well; we got drunk, talked about our childhoods, skinny-dipped in the sharp bright waters, had sex on beaches and hill tops. But as the dog days brought scorching unbearable heat, so I began to notice Neil's increasing irritation with the things I did – the way I ate honey straight from the jar, the way I wanted to swim before breakfast each morning, the way I folded the corners of the pages of my books to mark my place. Each time Neil seemed annoyed with me, I became convinced that I was holding him back.

By the time we returned to England in the middle of August, I had decided on a plan of action. At Heathrow bus station, I informed Neil that I thought we needed a break in our relationship. We should spend some time apart, and if the inclination came, we should see other people. I suggested that he didn't call for the first two weeks of the new term. He was surprised, but didn't I detect a hint of relief in his protestations?

I returned to Sheffield full of fear but with a strong sense that my strategy would work out for the best. Because I didn't think for one moment that Neil would turn his back on me, that he would abandon me. I was convinced that this was simply a small test of his love. It was only a matter of time (days, maybe hours) before he'd call me, breathlessly, and tell me that he didn't want to have a more interesting and exhilarating time with someone else, that there was none other than me, Gemma Cook: I was the one. It was painful, waiting, but it would be worth it – soon I would have final, conclusive proof that Neil didn't feel about me like Molly had about Mike Peters. I would know that he loved me like no other.

After nineteen days of chewing my fingernails to the core, I called him, and asked why he hadn't phoned. He was quiet, evasive and stumbling in his replies. Following a particularly unpleasant silence, during which I heard music playing in the background which sounded suspiciously like Prince's 'Kiss', he admitted he'd slept with someone in his first week back, and he thought I was right, maybe we did need to make the most of our short time at university.

I was distraught, and demonstrated so by slamming down the phone. I sought out Ian in tears and asked him what to do. He told me to go straight to Liverpool and talk to Neil. I did, but Neil would not look me in the eye. He informed me that he'd been hurt by my rejection of him, and had slept with the other woman out of spite. But now, having broken the taboo, he'd come to think it would be better to be single for a while, to see what was 'out there'. I pleaded with him, saying that I hadn't meant it, that it had been a test of his love. He looked at me with his deep blue eyes and replied:

'I don't want to be with someone who feels she needs to test me.'

It took me the next three years at university to get over Neil. I had sex with only two men during this time, hardly the wild student experience touted by my sister. As the emotional pain grew less I became more convinced that in the future I would need to show unflinching love. That I couldn't afford to waver, even for a moment. When I finally fell in love again, I told myself, it would be for ever.

ELECTRICITY

Who walks a dog at five in the morning?

I watch the figure (old, young, male, female, it's impossible to tell in the big hooded coat) pace along the pavement, the little white terrier shuffling slowly alongside, as sleepy as its owner.

I try to imagine the sort of person who gets up at 5 a.m. to walk a small dog – insomniac, new parent escaping screaming baby, old person? Or woman rapidly approaching thirty who's wrecked her life by telling her handsome but work-obsessed husband that she doesn't love him any more?

The hooded coat and the terrier disappear into the park.

I think about making coffee, but I haven't the energy. I sit in the downstairs window – my new spy-hole, wrapping the cashmere blanket around me, and make a firm decision not to move for several hours.

I am the outsider who gazes out at the world as it turns, never interacting. The crazy old spinster whom children will point to as they hurry past the dark foreboding house that schoolyard whispers say is haunted. But I don't care. Not any more.

I stare into the empty street. The windows of number 22 are dark. I wonder if the hooded coat is in fact the thin man, Raj's layabout, walking his prize terrier before returning to an early morning yoga meditation session. Or orgy. It comforts me slightly to think that we are the only two people awake. I need to believe that I am not alone.

But the person and the terrier do not reappear.

Ian clunks downstairs at 8.30 a.m. like a one-legged pantomime pirate, carrying Raj's DVD player. He yawns and smiles, weakly. I know he's got up early to be with me. Ian hates the mornings.

'Shall I make some tea, then?'

We sit without exchanging more than single words until the teapot is empty. The large clock I found at a retro stall in Camden Market ticks inexorably towards 9 a.m. For a moment, I think about ripping it from the wall.

I can't go to work, even though we're approaching the project deadline. I feel helpless, empty, drained. It's as if I've been holding out, being strong, until Ian arrived. He has enabled me to let it all go. I wonder, not for the first time, why I've always needed the company of men more than women. My mother still chastises me for not having any real 'girlfriends', as if this deficit is indicative of some shortcoming in the way Susan Cook raised her daughter. I know my mother was always a little jealous of my closeness to my father. But this doesn't stop me worrying, wondering whether my lack of female friends is due to an insecurity about myself that makes me unable to show the vulnerability which everyone tells me is the necessary bond for close female – female relationships.

I like Ian because he's uncomplicated. Even though I cried my eyes out in front of him last night, I know, as a man, he won't store up this knowledge of my weakness and use it against me at some point in the future. Not like some women would. Not like Sophie at the office.

I can't call. I think about asking Ian to call, but he would have to explain who he is and that would give the evil Sophie-monster too much ammunition. I just want to cover my head with the blanket and remain like that for a very long time. I hear my mother's voice, admonishing me, telling me there are people in the world far worse off than myself, but this only serves to expand and consolidate my misery.

'I'm not going to work,' I say gruffly.

'Definitely not,' Ian replies, cheerfully. 'Take a mental health day.'

We sit in silence, whilst children pass by, screeching their way to school.

'This is strange, isn't it, Gem?'

'What? That kids around here sound like they've had speedballs for breakfast?'

He smiles at my poor joke. I know 'what'. The strange thing is, it doesn't feel strange. It's like being back at college, that mixture of cheerful apathy and vague anxiousness, knowing there are things to be done, but coming up with no pressing reason to do them.

The clock ticks. I glance at him, noticing a couple of grey hairs at his temples. He hasn't shaved recently. He looks older than I remember – Brosnan in *Remington Steele*. I don't want Ian to get too old (*Die Another Day* Brosnan). It means I'm next.

'What are you going to do about your career?' I ask suddenly, my tone deeper and more strict.

'Jesus, Gem, it's only nine o'clock.'

'You love your travel writing.'

He shifts slightly, sliding his bare feet under the sofa cushions, for warmth or security.

'When the ankle's better . . .'

'How did you fall off the bus?'

'I slipped. I didn't exactly plan it. It was an accident.' He looks pained. I nod slowly, realizing I've confronted him with his failure because it makes me feel less of one.

I call work from the bedroom. To my dismay, Sophie answers. As quickly and efficiently as I can, I inform her that I'm not feeling well and won't be coming in today.

'Flu, I think,' I add, matter-of-factly.

'Really? I didn't know there was anything going around.'

'Summer flu. It's quite common.'

'Well . . . I'll tell Duncan.'

'I'll know more when I've been to the doctor's.'

'I hope you feel better soon.'

'I'm not pregnant, Sophie,' I say crossly, and put down the phone. I lie down on the bed, pulling handfuls of sheets around me, tucking my feet behind me, making myself as tiny as I can. It's my cave, my nest. I pull the Frette sheets tighter still, as I used to as a little girl, for my protection and punishment.

All is quiet, except the angry pump of my pulse. I haven't washed the sheets since Raj departed; not for any emotional reasons, I tell myself, but because I couldn't be bothered. In the midst of my expensive cotton cocoon, I try to locate his smell, his musty masculine scent with the faintest hint of his father's sandalwood. But all I can smell is myself, the sweet whiff of the Gucci Envy that Raj gave me last birthday, which I've been wearing recently, even though it seems too grown up and wanton compared to the gentle Ralph Lauren scent I've been wearing since I was fifteen.

I feel my tears damp and warm against my cheek. I just want to be alone, cut off from everything and everyone.

'Are you okay?'

Ian's voice. Words he's spoken so many times in the past, my guardian angel. Yet this morning, for some reason, his solicitous tone irritates me. It's as if he's hoping I'm not okay.

'Fine.'

I try quickly to unravel myself from the ball of sheets, but my legs are caught somehow, and I feel immediately claustrophobic. I breathe in quickly, but it's too hot, too tight. I panic, tearing at the material as if it's on fire, rolling forwards, kicking, cloth in my mouth and eyes. Rage rushes through me and I rip at the sheets, the expensive cloth tearing surprisingly easily and I'm jettisoned from the cocoon like a cannonball, falling heavily onto the floor.

'Ouch.'

So much for our wedding sheets. I look up at Ian. He grins.

'Nice move. Been practising that one?'

'Shut up.'

'Sorry.'

I hear the sound of my small breathing, which curiously reminds my of my panting during sex. I pull myself up.

'I think I could use a glass of wine.'

'At ten in the morning?'

'Who's counting?'

I feel a little better after the first bottle. We watch *Die Another Day* (my choice, due to the Brosnan connection) and I enjoy the sound of explosions and gunfire that remind me of childhood Sunday evenings watching television with my father. Next it's Ian's choice, and he thumbs along a line of Raj's DVDs like a tailor fingering silk.

'*When Harry Met Sally*?!' Ian roars in disgust.

'I like it. It made me cry when I was fifteen.'

'No wonder Raj hates me,' Ian says with a chuckle.

'What? He doesn't hate you . . .'

'Of course he does. He thinks I'm Billy Crystal.'

'What?'

'The film, Gem. They spend two hours saying they're just friends and then they end up together.'

'No they don't. They stay just friends, that's the point of the film. It proves a man and a woman can overcome the whole sex thing.'

'No, that's what everyone remembers, but actually they end up married. It's a romantic comedy.'

'Just choose something else then, Ian!'

I sense my anger bristling. I want to forget about Raj, about relationships, about everything.

'*The Life of Brian*!'

'Oh please, no.' Raj loves Monty Python, as do his few Oxford friends. I hate it, the comedy seems so old-fashioned and laboured.

'It's my choice, it's my choice!' chimes Ian, enthusiastically.

'All right, Tigger.'

'It was the first time I saw a grown woman naked,' he offers, by way of explanation.

'What?'

'I was twelve and me and Brian Pugh snuck into the Victoria Cinema in Cambridge. It was a 'Double A' certificate, you had to be fourteen, and there was a naked woman in one of the scenes.'

'How artistic.'

'We thought so. Hey, are you hungry?'

'Not really.'

'I'm starving. There's all this pizza left.'

'No thanks.'

We watch the film. As usual, I find the humour puerile and leaden. As I pretend to watch, a memory steals into my head. I wonder about sharing it with Ian – Raj has long since stopped pretending to listen to my ramblings about my childhood. But Ian's my best friend, isn't he?

'What was your worst holiday when you were little?' I ask, by way of introduction.

'Easy. Scotland, er, nineteen eighty . . . three. Rained every day and the car broke down. Yours?'

'This one Easter when we went to the Lake District, I must have been about ten. It rained all the time too. We ended up getting lost up some mountain or other, it felt like the bloody Alps . . .'

I pull my knees into my chest.

'So my dad gets his map out – he always had a map – and as he and Mum are arguing about which way to go, and Molly's whining, I see this path . . .'

'To true enlightenment?'

'Shut up. I remember having this sudden overwhelming feeling that this path was the right way to go. So I said we should go that way . . .'

'Gemma, Queen of the Mountains . . .'

'But it wasn't on the map, so Dad said we couldn't go that way, we'd get lost, but I stamped my feet and insisted; I said I knew it was the right way, I felt it, and Mum ended up humouring me, I think to piss Dad off, she said she was going with me, so they all followed me up this path . . .'

'This story's going one of two ways . . .'

'And it was a dead end. We ended up at this ravine, it was really steep and dangerous, Molly almost fell. We couldn't go on, Dad was hopping mad, he shouted at me. I was devastated, I really wanted to impress him, but I was completely wrong.'

'Did you get to the top of the mountain?'

'No. We had to go back to the car. Dad didn't speak to me for the rest of the day. Molly just laughed at me.'

I shake my head as if trying to rid myself of the image. As I move, the sun cuts my eyes, a quick sharp slice.

'That's how I feel now.'

'What's that?'

'I feel like I've followed my instinct and taken the wrong path. I should have looked at the map. But now it's too late.'

We watch the film in silence for a while, as Ian munches pizza. The wine is helping, I think, numbing me to time and emotion. I feel more tired than ever. I wonder if I should go and sleep.

Ian fills my glass again and smiles.

'If it's any consolation, I'm sort of enjoying myself.'

He hands me the glass.

'I mean, I know it's a bad time and everything, but I

guess I'm just enjoying hanging out like this. We haven't done this in a while.'

I nod slowly. He's right. There is something reassuring about sitting here, getting drunk watching movies, while the rest of the world strives for advancement. Perhaps I have a choice – I can decide to wallow in it, or decide to break free.

On the screen, the scene changes, and a naked woman appears, fleetingly.

'See! Full frontal. Fantastic!'

'That's the highlight of your pornographic youth?'

''Fraid so.'

'Wow. That's pretty sad.'

Ian nods again, and stands up from the sofa, picking up the oil-stained pizza box.

'Leave it!' I bark, with a sudden vehemence that surprises even me. He puts down the box. I kick out, sending the box zipping across the floor, the lid leaping open in shock. Ian looks at me. I smile, mischievously, aware that this is a smirk from my under-ten past.

'Okay . . .' he says, quizzically. I pick up a cushion and throw it towards the pizza box. Then I throw one at Ian. He catches it and tosses it back at me. I look at him, seize the cushion by the corner and swing it. Ian ducks to his left, snatches up another cushion, and swings it at me, slapping me on the back. I shriek, a childish squeal, snatch my cushion in both hands and smack it hard against his arm.

'Hey!'

Ian hobbles backwards, and I advance, raising the cushion once more.

'Prepare to die!'

He starts to laugh, unable to move quickly enough to avoid my blows, while I pound him with my cushion, laughing too. I thump him, six times, in quick succession, on the last swing catching the vase of lilies I bought two weeks ago to brighten up the half-finished house, now dead. In what seems like slow motion, the vase sweeps majestically off the mantelpiece, crashing to the floor and smashing in to shards. Ian stops, tottering on his single crutch.

'Whoops!' I cry.

I feel joyous. The smashing of the vase has released something in me and I want more. I look around, locate a glass of water on the coffee table, reach down and in one movement throw it over Ian. Water shoots everywhere, soaking the sofa, splattering the worn wooden floorboards.

'Right!' he cries, and lumbers towards the kitchen.

'No!' I scream in delighted fear as he whips on the tap to fill a saucepan he's plucked from the drying rack. I throw myself at him, attempting to wrestle his hand away. He holds firm, beating me away with his crutch. He's stronger than I am and therefore fair game, so I bend down quickly and sink my teeth into his wrist. This is gratifyingly effective. He yelps 'Arrgghhh!' and pulls away rapidly, leaving the tap open, and I wrench the saucepan out, half full of water and in one fluid movement I turn and toss its contents towards Ian's limping retreat. The airborne wave creates a beautiful arc in the air before it crashes in to his haunch, just as he turns to avoid it. As water sprays everywhere, the laugh bubbling from my throat, another voice rings out.

'What the hell is going on?'

I freeze. A last slip of water dribbles from the saucepan to the floor. Ian stands, dripping wet, his plastered leg raised, crutch in the air like a flag pole. He swivels, swiftly. He looks scared.

Raj stands by the sofa. He's wearing his black Armani suit, carrying the small, expensive tan briefcase I bought him in Milan. I see his eyes flick quickly around the room – the open pizza box, the broken shards of glass vase and strewn dead flowers, the wine bottles, the cushions flung here and there as if by some demented bowling machine, his favourite DVD still playing on the television.

I cannot speak. The clock ticks. We remain immobile, the three of us, hardly a muscle moving, as if playing some children's game in which the first to tremble will lose. Then Ian coughs quickly and raises his hand, smoothing down his drenched hair.

'All right, Raj?' he says, in that voice men use to other men when they're embarrassed about something.

This vocal interruption seems to galvanize Raj. He turns quickly (quite gracefully, I think), and disappears up the creaking, uneven staircase. I listen to his light footsteps, vanishing higher, away from me and the mess I've created.

FIDELITY

I try to hear what they're saying from the safety of the landing. I dragged myself there thirty seconds after Gemma followed Raj upstairs, counting carefully, one, two, three . . . hauling my club foot up each creaking step like a large Amazonian sloth. What I hear through the closed bedroom door is this:

'I'm so sorry, Raj.'

Silence.

'I never intended to hurt you. I'm just really confused at the moment.'

Silence.

'I washed your shirt, the grey one.'

'Which one?'

'Your Friday shirt.'

Sounds of rummaging.

'I'm really, really sorry, Raj. Can't we just talk about this?'

'There's nothing to say. Perhaps it's for the best.'

'We don't know that. It's just me, everything's so mixed up right now . . .'

'I'll call you. We can arrange to discuss matters fully. Now if you'll excuse me, I have a meeting to get to.'

The door opens and I turn, the heavy plaster cast swinging round with a momentum all its own; my left leg buckles, and I fall down the stairs on my backside, ugh, ugh, ugh.

I land, on my back.

'Ooof!'

As I wriggle my toes for signs of life, I think that it's a good thing my ankle's already broken.

Raj steps off the last stair, adroitly rounding my prone body. I look up, and attempt a smile. Raj holds out his hand.

'Are you okay?'

I take the warm, soft, damp hand and Raj yanks me up with surprising ease. I wonder if he works out.

'Er . . . thanks.'

Raj lets go of my hand, and takes a step back. I look at him.

'Take care of her,' Raj declares, curtly, before I can open my mouth. 'She shouldn't be alone at the moment.'

With that he's gone, striding from the building site paid for by his £350 an hour billing fee. In his right hand he grips a large full holdall bag, no doubt containing enough clothes and possessions to enable him to stay away from the house for many weeks to come. The front door closes gently.

Painfully, I ascend the rickety stairs once more and knock on the bedroom door. No answer. I open the door. The lights are off, the curtains drawn. As I squint into the darkness, I can just make out her form curled tightly onto the bed.

'Hey, Gem.'

Nothing.

'It's going to be okay, it'll all work itself out . . .'

Nothing.

'Can I get you anything?'

'Go away! I need to sleep!'

I turn and leave the room.

I hobble up again twenty minutes later, painstakingly touting a cup of camomile tea. I whisper further queries about her emotional and physical state, but there's no reply, so I leave the tea by the bedside. When I return after a further thirty minutes of worrying, she appears to be sleeping. Gentle snores emanate from the small mound of sheets at the far side of the large double bed. I remain for a while by the door, listening to the murmur of her breathing. Intermittently, a diminutive high-pitched nasal whistle punctuates the small sniffles. I smile, remembering how this trait drove all her room-mates at Sheffield mad. Only Neil professed to appreciate it. He said it reminded him of a kettle his grandmother once owned.

I sit in the unfinished kitchen for a long time, admiring the fan of shattered vase on the floor by the wall. I like the way the sliver shards catch the light, spraying shimmering flecks on to the dark brick. It's random, but strangely beautiful. I have no desire to clean it up.

The pizza box lies open, as if recently robbed. I feel a little queasy. Everything is off-kilter, like a picture tilted at an angle.

I wonder, in this moment, whether Gemma is thinking about Neil at all. I know from my own limited experience that the first thing men do when they break up with someone is to think about their exes. They take out the old map from the bottom of the drawer, with its well-worn creases and loving fingerprints on familiar landmarks, and fondly retrace old journeys.

On Gemma's map, Neil isn't just any old ex. He was her first love.

I smile at the memory of the two of them in Sheffield that first Christmas, cuddled up on my sofa in the house on Eccleshall Road. I asked them, with weary undergraduate sarcasm, when they thought the wedding would be. Gemma took Neil's hand quickly in her own, and replied sarcastically:

'I'm only in it for his money.'

Neil nodded, and added, more earnestly:

'We've only just met.'

I liked Neil. He was Scottish, from a Borders farming family, studying Veterinary Science at Liverpool. Gemma met him during rag week when the Liverpool students invaded Sheffield and there was an almighty party in the Student Union. He was about my height, but with the epic chunkiness of a man bred from bull-rearing ancestors, with thick rugby-playing shoulders and thighs the size of children. He and Gemma were inseparable when they started dating, meeting every weekend, doing essays together in the library, campaigning in London against student fees, going to obscure foreign films in which nobody spoke and everyone was naked.

Neil never seemed jealous of me (not that he had any reason to be). He was always friendly, always good-humoured.

If I were Gemma, I'd be thinking about Neil. But fortunately, women aren't that shallow.

I call Molly from Gemma's fancy charcoal phone. It rings and rings before cutting to her answering service. I leave a quick message, not mentioning Raj. At the end of the message I find myself mumbling 'Love you, babes . . .', before hanging up hurriedly.

I panic. I should never have said that. I wasn't thinking, I'm tired. I'm worried that she will take those three words and construct in her mind a tourniquet that will tighten around her, suffocating her. She doesn't want to hear that I love her. I don't love her. They were just words.

The problem is, women behave differently with words. They treat words with far more respect and seriousness. Men hold little value in language. From an early age we don't communicate with words, we don't learn their nuances and subtleties. We kick our footballs, cycle our bikes, punch our best friends, and construct a physical language for ourselves. Words are never as important as actions to the male mind. So in adult life, we cast out words like francs in a world of euros – women think they're worth something, that we value them in the same way they do. But we don't.

It annoys me that Raj left Gemma because of words. It doesn't seem very manly.

I wonder if I should call Molly back and explain this theory to her.

My ankle hurts. I push open the large glass door that leads out onto the garden. The rain has stopped and the evening air is cooler now. In a few days it'll be September, and there's already an autumnal crispness. I stand, looking out into the encroaching dusk. I wonder how big the garden is, and whether there are any tomatoes. I think that perhaps, now that Raj is gone, I could plant some for my friend. Then I feel guilty. It's still not clear if Raj being gone is a good thing.

I look out into the shadows and shapes start to form amorphously as my eyes adjust – a few trees, a cement mixer, a spade.

I don't understand why Gemma hasn't told her sister about Raj. As an only child, I dreamed of having a sibling to share confidences with, to unite with against parental tyranny. But I was always on my own. I had an imaginary friend when I was six, but the Astronaut was a useless confidant, only interested in taking rockets to Mars, or exploring the molten core of the earth on my tricycle.

If I were Gemma, I'd tell Molly everything. It wouldn't be difficult spilling the beans to such a beautiful woman. Just looking into those eyes would make you confess to everything. To anything.

If I'm honest I've always fancied Molly. You'd have to be gay not to. I first met her while Gemma and I were at university, but I was careful to be nothing more than friendly towards her. I'd always wondered about us getting together – she seemed to like me – but then I started travelling, and I was dating a series of foreign women who flew to England at the weekends, and then she got engaged and married Will, the dashing stockbroking genius.

I hardly saw anything of her during the three years she was married. Then Gemma told me on the phone one night that her sister was getting a divorce, and to my surprise an electric spark of desire flashed through my stomach.

We got together at Gemma's office party. We all got badly drunk and ended up back at Molly's loft playing drinking games. Raj was absent, for some reason I can't remember, and Gemma drank too much and threw up. Molly and I helped her to bed, and ended up talking, sitting outside the door to the guest bedroom on the premise of keeping an eye on Gemma. We drank vodka from the bottle, and chatted about music and films and people we fancied, and it seemed so easy, vodka-talk, and I noticed the small crow's feet at the edge of Molly's eyes when she smiled, and her long slender fingers.

Despite being adverse to instinctive acts of passion, I took another swig and leaned over and kissed her quickly on the neck. Her flesh was hot. She hesitated, and I was terrified in that instant that she'd slap me. Then in a miraculous moment, she moved her mouth against mine, soft-hot, and we kissed for a while. I pinched her nipple, then moved my hand to her lap where I undid her Levi's.

She breathed in, I pressed my damp hot hand against her flat stomach, still kissing, it was easy, good and right, and my spread fingers smoothed down, the first soft bristle of pubic hair, and I slid my middle finger further down, to touch the crease of her. She was wet. She moaned and shivered.

I shifted, delicious agony, finger moving deeper, closer, wetter and she exhaled my name 'Ian' and with both hands pushed me away gently, wriggling back, taking my hand and slipping it upwards out of her, casting it to one side as if severing it from my arm.

We went for breakfast, just the two of us, the following day, and at the tube station she kissed me, the kiss that started everything.

'Can I call you?' I asked, my heart thumping. She looked at me, head cocked slightly to one side and whispered:

'Why not.'

I danced all the way home.

The next morning, when I come downstairs, Gemma is sitting once more in the front window of the semi-derelict house. She looks wrecked – her eyes puffed as if she's recently finished crying, her nails bitten low, her body seemingly shrunken overnight, skeletal beneath the loose pyjamas and hooded sweatshirt.

She's in a terrible mood. She declines my offer of coffee or tea, or any other form of beverage (which is fortunate, because the only other form of beverage is a third of a bottle of gin, which is going to do neither of us any good).

I make some Lavazza, and propose sitting out on the unfinished patio.

'Make the most of the sun?'

Gemma shakes her head, without looking up.

'It's a lovely day.'

'For fuck's sake, Ian, I just want to sit here and do fuck all! All right?!'

When Gemma uses two fucks in a sentence, it's time to leave her alone. I open the glass doors and walk out, slyly leaving one of them open, to allow a sliver of fresh late-August air into the house that I hope will blow in and dispel the unhappy scent of decay.

I stand in the bright sunshine, sipping my coffee. I wish Gemma could be enticed outside, to be cured by the end-of-summer morning sun and a cup of Italian Arabica. I try to put myself into her head, but I can't imagine how she's feeling. Unlike my own, Gemma's travails are, as she noted so bravely the previous day, her own doing. Whereas I can blame others (Venezuelan bus companies, ginger-headed landlords, the Virgin Mary) Gemma has to wake up each morning knowing that the reason she feels so miserable is because she's made herself feel miserable.

The sunshine liberates me and I realize I've been feeling cooped up. I don't understand why, when she lives next to a park, Gemma won't leave the house. I've never liked interiors, preferring the open spaces of the great outdoors, even in London. I like to move (hence my career choice). The broken ankle is a severe strain on my psyche, on my basic nomadic need to relocate. Only another couple of weeks, I tell myself forcefully.

I look around the sixty-foot-long garden. It's big for London, an advantage, I suppose, of moving to one of the more extraneous boroughs. It is, like most of the house interior, a mess. A hole has been dug for some uncertain purpose, which is now filled with rainwater. Concrete slabs lie like gravestones in the far corner. The only feature of any discernible beauty, as far as I'm concerned, is a mature tree by the back fence that must have been planted when the houses were originally built, sometime at the end of the nineteenth century.

I love trees – they seem so stable, so sure of themselves with their confident spreading branches and unseen solid roots – so unlike people in their steadfastness when faced with adverse elements. I often mention them in my travel articles:

The majestic plane trees line the Cours Mirabeau like ancient courtiers saluting the Sun King.

A hillside of ochre aspens, nodding lazily in Colorado's early autumn breeze, is more beautiful than any Van Gogh.

I sat beneath a venerable palm tree, laden with voluptuous dates, and wondered how many sheikhs, spies and scorpions had sat in its benevolent shade before me.

This tree, I notice on closer inspection, is a walnut, laden with green fruit. I imagine the legions of meaty testicular nuts, lurking inside their fleshy feminine cups, and shiver slightly. I have a sudden urgent desire to see Molly. I want to have sex with her, to feel her, to hold her close to me, despite my comedy ankle plaster.

But I can't be selfish. First, I need to cheer up Gemma. Such is my role, I feel – somewhere between Activities Counsellor and Court Jester. I hobble back inside.

'Fancy some brunch?'

I open one of the newly installed cupboards. It's empty, apart from a couple of small screws that seem lonely and lost in the large vacant cabinet.

'There's no food,' she says in a monotone voice, as I open the next cupboard.

'I could go and get some. Eggs, bagels, smoked salmon. You love smoked salmon.'

She doesn't reply.

'Where's the nearest shop?'

'I'm not hungry, Ian.'

'You need to eat.'

'No I don't.'

'Just some scrambled eggs, *à la* Thompson . . .'

'I don't want anything, thank you!'

A phone rings. It's my mobile, coming from my jacket. I want to answer it, in case it's Molly, but I don't want to make Gemma feel unwanted. The phone continues to ring.

'Well, fucking answer it!'

I snatch for the jacket and extract the phone. To my disappointment (which I try to conceal), it's my mother.

'I'm a little busy right now, Mum.'

'Oh.'

I glance at Gemma, who is gazing out at the empty street.

'Can I help with anything?' I ask my mother, feeling guilty.

'No. I just wanted to see how you were doing, you went off in such a hurry . . .'

'I'm fine. I'm at Gemma's, she's just not feeling very well.'

'Oh, poor love. Nothing serious, I hope?'

'No, no, nothing like that . . .' I wonder when I stopped telling my mother the truth about things. Probably when I told her I fancied Maisy Gardiner in Class 3C, and she told me I should concentrate on my five-times table instead.

There's a small silence.

'How's Dad doing?' I ask, as flippantly as I can.

Another pause.

'He's fine. You know Dad.'

We say our goodbyes and I put down the phone, sensing that small leaden emptiness that I feel whenever I come off the phone with my mother these days.

I stand, uncertain what to do next.

'I'll go and get some food then.'

Gemma doesn't look up.

'Whatever.'

*

I buy two bags of expensive groceries from the Londis in Victoria Park Village, and start back towards Raleigh Street. But something slows me. I feel relief that I'm outside, and guilt that I'm enjoying these few minutes away from the friend I've come to help. It's a beautiful late summer's day, and I don't want to return to the stifling atmosphere at number 26. I pause by a sweet-smelling oleander bush and take out my phone. I punch in the number for Geoffrey Walters, a prize-winning travel writer I know from press trips and Christmas parties over the years.

'Dear boy,' Geoffrey Walters chuckles from his shed in deepest Richmond. 'That was quite a stunt you pulled. Ha, ha, ha . . . Choroní, ha, ha, that silly statue, ha, ha, ha, the good pilgrims of Stockport, ha, ha, old Foster blew his bloody top, ha, ha . . .'

'I wondered if you had any ideas about what I could do?'

'Leave the country?'

'Come on, Geoffrey . . .'

'It's a tough one, dear boy. Foster's a fella who bears a grudge. I remember when he got a bee in his bonnet about old Barnaby Fredericks. Barney wrote about some luxury hotel in Italy that turned out to be run by Neo-facists; he should have known from the décor, but anyway Foster fired him and he couldn't get a job for yonks. Ended up going to Canada, became a coal-mining correspondent or some such slow death.'

'Thanks, Geoff.'

'It'll blow over, dear boy. Keep your head down, do other things.'

'Like what?' I ask, gruffly.

'Dear boy, please don't take umbrage with me. I wasn't the one who committed journalistic hara-kiri. You'll find something. Now, if you'll excuse me, I must get back to my book. Tashkent beckons.'

I feel despondent. I have to start earning some money. Molly has expensive tastes, and to be honest I'm having trouble keeping up with the restaurant dinners, takeaways, taxis, theatre tickets and everything else that is supposed to make modern metropolitan living so fulfilling. I could always dip into my savings, but that would further delay the purchase of a property, which is the only true mark of success in the modern British world.

The sun is hot now. I really don't feel like going back to Gemma's house, which makes me feel guilty once more, but I can't help it. I need to regain composure, stoke up my strength to stop worrying about myself and look after her in her time of need.

For the first time in weeks, my ankle isn't hurting. I think of going into the park, where some teenagers are playing football, but for some reason the dry summer-scorched grass and tired-looking trees seem a little depressing, so I continue past Raleigh Street, crossing a main road. It's lunchtime and the streets are empty, people sheltering from the lethargic dog-day heat that seems to mark the end of something, without the hint of a new beginning. It makes me feel vaguely philosophical.

The houses here are built in blocks of three or four, unlike the serried ranks of terraced houses on Gemma's street. They're probably late-Victorian, with fat bay-fronted living rooms and neatly clipped hedges – the area, like Gemma's street, is a ruffled mix of wealthy renovation and indigenous neglect, Old and New Labour. On one street an ugly 1950s-style brick cube house has been inserted into the middle of a stately Victorian row, as if by a malicious child, the two older houses rising a full storey above it on either side.

The 1950s block house seems incongruous, but I have a good idea why it's here. I remember my father telling me about streets in Liverpool that were bombed in the war, where one house was obliterated whilst its neighbours stood firm. I imagine the German bombs, swooping like deadly angels from the sky to flatten the East End and destroy the plucky will of London's most proud and industrious citizens. The original house was blown up. The houses on either side survived. The block house was built in its place, a perfect symbol of the absurd randomness of life and death.

As I stand, staring at the brick cube house like an architecture student or burglar, wondering how my father could still believe in God when all around him are examples of Godless happenings, I take out my phone and impulsively dial Molly's work number.

'Hi Molly.'

'Oh. Ian. How's Cambridge?'

'I'm back in London. I've been seeing Gemma. At her house.'

'Oh.'

Silence.

'So how is little sis? I haven't seen her in weeks. You've got to love London, I mean we only live a couple of miles away . . .'

I know I'm going to tell her about Gemma, even though I'm pretty sure Gemma doesn't want me to tell her about Gemma (not having siblings of my own, I think, might be a valid defence, if it ever ends up in court).

'Look, Molly . . .'

To be honest, it's a relief. As I tell her, I realize I've been worrying more than I've wanted to admit that I was the only one who knew Raj has left, the only one with the responsibility.

Molly listens carefully. I wonder what she's thinking, and feeling. Is she experiencing purely sorrow and concern for her sister? Or is she relieved, in some way, that she's no longer the only Cook daughter to have fucked up a marriage? How do sisters work? Do they thrive on peace, or adversity?

'Poor Gem,' Molly murmurs, when I've finished recounting what I know about the break-up. 'God. Poor Gem.'

'I don't know if she wanted you to know,' I proffer, hoping to be contradicted.

'I'm sure she didn't. But she shouldn't be alone.'

'I'm there.'

'Yes, of course, I didn't mean that . . . It's just, I've been through it. It might be good for her to talk about it.'

'She doesn't seem to want to talk about it.'

'I know. I didn't. But she needs to. Look, I went through hell, but I'm happy now. Okay, Mum can't understand it, but it's like I tell her, I know plenty of miserable 32-year-old married women with kids. Better alone than a clone.'

I grimace at this clumsy Molly-crafted aphorism.

'I'm on my way.'

'What?'

'She's my sister. She needs me.'

'But . . .'

'I'll take the afternoon off, see her, try and get her to talk.'

She sounds business-like. It's very attractive.

'Can I see you afterwards?'

Shit. Am I whining? I continue, hurriedly:

'I mean . . . I haven't really seen you properly since I got back . . .'

That's better, more in control. I wonder if she detects the blatant insinuation contained in the word 'properly' – that I'm desperate to have sex with her.

'Gemma's in trouble here, Ian. This is her marriage we're talking about.'

'I know, I know. I'm sorry . . .'

'Look, maybe we can meet up later. I'll call you. I've got to run . . .'

Before I can apologize any more, Molly puts down the phone.

GUILT

June 1982. Gemma is eight, Molly nine-and-a-half. Molly discovers Gemma wearing her bikini, the one with red roses on it. Molly pushes her younger sister into a patch of stinging nettles at the bottom of the garden. Gemma is badly stung, causing welts all over her back, three of which leave permanent scars.

Christmas 1987. Gemma steps carefully downstairs in Christmas Eve darkness, slips into the shadows cast by the quivering Christmas tree, picks up the wrapped box with her sister's name on it, and slams it against the wall. The next morning, upon unwrapping, the Wella Catwalk Professional hairdryer and curling tongs are found to be cracked. Molly has to wait six weeks for a replacement shipment to reach the shelves of Dickins and Jones, too late for Jason Morrow's fifteenth birthday party.

August 1994. Gemma and Molly go on holiday together for the first time. They both agree they need to be closer, to be more like sisters. Gemma plans the trip to Corfu. Molly complains about the hotel and the distance to the beach. They go to the local disco – Zorba's, in Kérkira. Molly is wearing a Diane von Furstenburg wrap dress bought for her graduation a month previously. Gemma is wearing a Marks and Spencer skirt and top. Molly buys several rounds of drinks as her way of apologizing for her complaints about her sister's travel plans. They down White Russians and Molly encourages her sister to list the boys on the dance floor she considers snoggable. After some grilling, Gemma admits she fancies a tall German boy with a nice smile. To Gemma's horror, Molly goes and talks to him. He looks over at Gemma, approaches, they dance, his English is good. She's excited, flushed with cheap cocktails and sexual attraction. He excuses himself to go to the toilet and she searches for him for the next hour. Later, Gemma glimpses her sister and the German outside by the fountain of Zeus, kissing. The German has his hand on her sister's arse. Gemma goes back to the hotel, throws up in the shower and the next morning she greets her sister with a smile. At the beach, Molly tells her the German was 'nothing special'.

Molly slaps down the orange juice carton on to the old Formica worktop.

'You just said it, like that?'

'It slipped out.'

'How could "I don't love you any more" just slip out?'

'I don't know. I suppose I'd been thinking about it for a long time.'

We both look away. I feel, with rising irritation, that this is all too familiar – the older sister's condescending, exasperated tone, the younger sister's irritated defiance. It makes each of us uncomfortable and annoyed. It's clear we both believe we've moved beyond childhood a long while back, and we're silently blaming the other for letting the zombies of our past out of the crypt.

'So you meant it? You don't love Raj?' my sister reiter-ates crossly.

'I think so.'

'Do you want a divorce?'

'I don't know.'

'Do you think you could ever love him again?'

'I don't know.'

'Do you love somebody else?'

'No. It's not that.'

'What is it?'

'It's . . .'

But I can't say.

'What?'

'Nothing.'

'Wow. You've really got it sorted out, haven't you, Gem.'

'Piss off, Molly!'

I pull my legs into my chest and bury my face into the small cleft created by my knees. I sense tears coming, but I don't want to cry in front of my older sister. It's an age-old feeling, trying to be big and strong in front of Molly. It's a little sad that at the age of twenty-nine I'm still attempting it, but there you go. It feels both childish, and reassuring. At least, with this emotion, I know where I am.

Time passes, the clock ticks its seconds. My sister is silent. I keep my eyes closed. I wonder, as I stare through the red and golden dust flickering around my shut-eyed galaxy, whether I can tell my sister everything.

I want to. I want to be taken care of.

But something holds me back. I listen.

Silence.

Perhaps Molly has departed, slipping away without a sound. Or perhaps she's standing above me, fist raised, waiting for me to open my eyes before she gives me a big sisterly slap.

In some ways, I admit to myself, I'm glad that Molly now knows about Raj. Because my sister will be my fiercest critic, she will chastise me like a mother, with extra venom stemming from the pain still lingering from her own short but torturous divorce. As I sit there, cheek against patella, I realize that I want my sister's admonishments. In some ways I am craving them. I want Molly to berate me. I want to feel punished. It will make me feel less responsible.

I open my eyes. My sister is sitting on the floor, four feet away, looking at me.

'I'm sorry, Gem. I didn't mean . . .'

The punishment will not be coming. Unless I seek it out myself.

'You never mean to, Molly. But you do it anyway.'

I await the bellow of wounded outrage, maybe even a curse or a blow to my shoulder. But curiously, Molly is nodding sympathetically.

'I'm sorry. It must be really hard for you . . .'

'Hard? Why? I've done it to myself. Nobody forced me into it, I told him I didn't love him, he left. Who else is to blame?'

'Raj.'

'What?'

'It's his fault too.'

'Why?'

'One, you don't storm off like a teenager unless there's been actual infidelity, and even then you should be the one to kick the guilty party out. Two, he should have known something was up and asked you what the problem was.'

This is not what I want to hear. I want to hear that I am to blame, that I am too demanding, that I live too much in the future, that I plan for things, then get disappointed and destructive when my plans don't work out. I want to hear that what I have, what I've been given, this unexpected and dreadful gift, I deserve.

'How could he have known?'

'By opening his bloody eyes!' Molly sounds genuinely outraged. 'You haven't been happy for months!'

'What? I have been happy.'

'Come on Gemmi. Even Mum's noticed it.'

'What? When?'

'She said the other day that you seemed to have lost your old spunk.'

'Spunk?'

'Yes, well, Mum's vocabulary did stop developing around 1969.'

'I'm fine!' I declare, a little too ferociously.

'It takes two to ruin a relationship. He shouldn't work so bloody hard!'

'It's not Raj's fault!'

'Yes it is. He needs to pay more attention to you.'

'I'm not you, Molly! I don't need what you need!'

I pull myself from the sofa and stride to the kitchen area, not caring that I'm wearing my shabby old pyjamas and the Gap sweatshirt Molly gave me last Christmas. I rip open the carton of orange juice and pour myself a glass without offering any to my sister.

'Aren't you meant to be at work?'

'I'm taking personal time.'

'Personal time? What fucking corporate nonsense is that?'

Angrily, I push open the glass doors to the garden and for the first time in three days step out into the late-August sunshine.

I sit on one of the plastic chairs that the builders use at lunchtimes to drink their tea and smoke roll-up cigarettes. My sister maddens me. In some ways she is so like our mother – she always applies her own criteria, her own feelings and experiences to judge others. Molly's blame of Raj reflects her feelings of culpability over her own marriage break-up. Her insistence that Raj pay more attention to me stems from Molly's own cravings for attention, which she voiced to Will only after it became far too late.

Almost immediately, my sister appears, carrying her own glass of juice. She pulls up another chair. Her tone is text-book conciliatory.

'You know, Gem, you're welcome at mine any time. You could stay for a while. Until things sort themselves out.'

I don't answer. In one of the numerous plans I've drawn up in my head, I've envisaged just such an occurrence – a protracted stay in the vast contemporary loft-space in hip and trendy Clerkenwell, during which time the two sisters will head to numerous bars and be chatted up by countless dashing young men, thus becoming the friends they never were in childhood.

'I could cook. I'm getting better, those courses I took were really good . . .'

But it's all fantasy. We will never be friends. Maybe, at one stage we could have been, in our early teens when the world was new and thrillingly intoxicating, but then my father died and Molly clung closer to Mum and I retreated into solitude.

So, rather than leaning on each other for support during that horrible time when we needed it most, we kept secrets, ignoring each other's tacit pleas for love, and the silence between us swelled rapidly, like air rushing into a vacuum, until it became a solid immovable barrier. Since then, we have tried many times to open up, to be vulnerable with one another. But it's too late. We're divided, and guarded.

Perhaps it has always been too late. We are so different. Molly, squeezed first into the world, is more outgoing. She's sociable, impetuous, brash on occasions. I am wary. I always paused first to analyze what my big sister was doing before committing myself. I like to plan, to structure. I'm no good at being impetuous, I like to know the ending before I embark on anything. Which makes my present situation all the more ridiculous.

We sit in the sunny building site that is the garden of number 26 Raleigh Street. We sip orange juice, one after the other, in silence, like colonial wives awaiting our husbands' return on some soporific Ceylon afternoon. It's such a familiar silence, reminiscent of the wordless hours we used to spend before bedtime, when we read books without talking, only whispering goodnight as Molly turned off the light. It was Molly's rule, she was the eldest, she needed her 'Book Time', as she called it. We sat in our twin beds, reading, like an old married couple – me always flicking to the last page before commencing the first, so I'd know what would happen, so there would be no unpleasant surprises. This 'cheating' used to infuriate Molly, but I stood firm, telling her that it was 'just a different way of doing things' in the most pompous voice I could muster.

Over the top of the juice glass, I sneak a glance at Molly, who's squinting against the bright sun. She looks good, I think, her hair cut shoulder length. She's lost weight since the divorce. Her face is pretty, but I feel no jealousy in that department, we've both been granted our mother's delicate symmetrical features and nice full lips. What annoys me the most are Molly's legs. They're beautiful limbs, long and toned, with definition in thigh and calf. Not like my own, the tree trunks, the meat slabs, the horrible lumps of clay. And then there are my sister's breasts, which have always been bigger and more fulsome, the lucky cow.

I wonder, for an instant, whether I can tell my sister my innermost fears. I play with words, lolling them around my head, as I did with the spell that made Raj vanish from my life. But I can't utter them. After a lifetime of concealment it's impossible to expose myself now.

We sit in awkward silence for a moment. Then I look up at my elder sister.

'So, are you going to tell Mum about me and Raj?'

'What do you think?'

Molly smiles. I attempt a smile back at her. We sit in silence again. Somewhere, a police siren wails. Then Molly speaks.

'It's okay, Gemmi. It'll work itself out.'

'I wish I could turn to the last page. To know what happens.'

'That would be cheating.'

I smile, despite myself. Can you ever escape the past, I wonder? Or are we born with the characters we will die with? I breathe in, anxious to be different with Molly, brighter and more confident.

'Is Ian coming back?' I ask, gaily. 'Or have you stolen him away?'

'I asked him to give us an hour or two.'

'He's been really kind.'

'I'm sure.'

'He's a friend, Molly.'

'Yup.' Molly's expression oozes amused disbelief.

'He's my best friend.'

'Of course.'

I shake my head. We can't break free.

'Why is it, darling sister, that you find it so hard to conceive of a relationship between a man and a woman that doesn't involve sex, or the potential for sex?'

'It's impossible. It's always there.'

'For you.'

'You too.'

'What do you know, Molly? You don't have any male friends.'

'Yes I do.'

'Greg and Simon? They're ex-boyfriends.'

'So?'

'So, your "friendship" is based on a complex sexual history. It's not pure friendship. They still want to sleep with you.'

'No they don't.'

'Come on, Mother Teresa. Have you seen the way Simon looks at you?'

'Yeah? Have you seen the way Ian looks at you?'

'Ha, fucking ha.'

'I'm serious, Gem.'

I wonder for a moment whether perhaps Molly might be re-opening this stale old argument on purpose, to make me feel angry enough to forget my present wretchedness. But it's unlikely – Molly is no master of pop psychology.

'Can I ask you a question, Gemma?'

'No.'

'I don't want you to get mad. Just think about it . . .'

I stand, taking both empty glasses. The sun is hot on my face.

'So? What?'

'Did you tell Raj you don't love him because deep down you want to be with Ian?'

I look at my elder sister. Her face is open, gentle even, not accusatory.

'Molly, Molly, Molly . . .' I reply, each word intoned more wearily than the last as I walk away into the house, placing down the glasses and marching upstairs to the bathroom where I take a lengthy shower, smoothing down the cellulite in my thighs again and again with the fat yellow loofah Raj bought me for Christmas.

I'm not angry with my sister. Merely tired. Molly has always been prosecutor, judge and jury. Yet this time I have brought judgement on myself, I've slipped up and given the prosecution a key piece of evidence. I should never have said that thing about Ian being kind. I saw Molly's eyes. There was jealousy glinting.

Is she scared of losing Ian? It seems unlikely – neither of them seem to be taking it too seriously. Is she annoyed that I chose Ian (a man!) over my own sister when it came to seeking solace and solutions? But I have no reason to feel guilty. It's horses for courses. In my time of need I simply chose Ian's male bustle over Molly's emotional bludgeoning.

The thing is, they are similar in some ways, Ian and my sister. They share the oldest and the only child's blend of confidence and insecurity, of calm intransigence and turbulent self-doubt. They are both above average in the food chain of attractiveness, they are both stubborn, both prone to random acts of selfishness.

Shit. They're perfect for each other.

I feel a sudden sickness grip me, like the onset of cramps. Ian and Molly should be together. Mr and Mrs Similar.

Not like Raj and me. Mr and Mrs Opposite.

The water turns cold. I dry myself quickly, patting my body gently, feeling, not for the first time in the past two weeks, as if I'm dabbing flesh that no longer belongs to me. I wrap myself in the towelling robe and begin to take all of Raj's remaining toiletries from the cabinet, stacking them neatly on the floor by the door. I line up the razor blades, the aftershave I bought him a year ago that he never wears, the half-empty bottles of contact lens solution, and I curse every novel, play, sonnet and Hollywood blockbuster that perpetuates the foul myth that differences can be overcome, and that true love will see it through.

Romeo and Juliet? Bollocks! Superman and Lois Lane? Screw them! Bogart and Bacall? To hell with the trouser-wearing pair of them!

Differences don't work out. They can't be overcome. Two opposites can fall in love, but they can never love each other for ever if they don't share the same taste in films, food, morning swimming or gentle gestures of everyday love!

When I come downstairs an hour later, I'm pleased to find that my sister has gone, without leaving any trace that she's ever been here.

I stare at the black shining door. Below the 22 is a large silver knocker. All I have to do is reach up and take the cold metal and swing it hard, three times, against the door. The thin rakish man will open it, and I will ask him who he is and what he does, and then I will call Raj and tell him.

I take a deep breath. A child's voice shrieks from the playground in the park. I turn quickly and walk away down the steps, hurrying to my own front door, unlocking it swiftly and disappearing inside.

HAPPINESS

I catch a taxi from Mare Street, feeling a modicum of guilt that I'm deserting Gemma for a few hours, but filled with that wholly male certainty that almost anything is justified if there's a chance of sex. Anyway, Gemma probably needs some space. She'll take a nap, replenish her energy. I'll see her later this evening, a new man.

I am going to wait for Molly to return to her refuge after seeing her younger sister. I'm prepared to wait for a long time. This might sound romantic, noble and chivalrous even. The truth is, what else have I got to do?

In Boots I buy a sixteen-pack of Durex Ultra Thins. There's nothing wrong with being prepared.

I sit in the coffee shop opposite the converted printworks on St John Street, with Gemma's groceries by my side. As I sip my latte, I consider the two sisters.

Molly is more attractive. There's no doubt that I got the sexier Cook girl. She's probably not quite as bright as Gemma, if I'm brutally honest, but sometimes Gemma's over-analytical side can be tiresome. I like the way Molly can switch off and leave her work behind, the way she dedicates energy to enjoying herself. She might lack Gemma's great sense of humour, but any Molly deficiencies in the funny bone department are easily compensated by the rest of her body, which is breathtaking, a magazine figure. I love her confidence and style, which seem to open any door in London. Molly engages, with that devastating smile. Gemma pulls away in social situations. She's more awkward. Like me.

If there's one thing I would change about Molly, it would be to make her a little sweeter, a little more caring, like Gemma. Molly's frequent need to be on her own, the way some mornings she asks me to leave her apartment, her ability to be away from me for weeks and then greet me without any outward sign that she's missed me greatly – these are characteristics that occasionally bother me. But she is a banker after all. And I recognize that in many ways these very traits make our relationship possible. They allow me to jet off around the world, safe in the knowledge that there's no resentment festering back home.

It's perfect. Too perfect?

I exhale quickly when I see the taxi pull up and Molly get out (oh, the legs, the arse, the breasts) and smile at the driver (she can be sweet, can't she?). I am strangely nervous, as if on a first date. It is, I realize, as if I've been waiting for this moment since my return from Venezuela, as if this is the culmination of something. After this encounter, I know I will be able to move forward, to formulate a plan and take control of my life. After sex with Molly, I will become me once more. And we will move on to the next level in our relationship.

Suddenly I wish I'd changed into something more sartorially seductive, not the Adidas jogging trousers that slip easily over the bulky plaster cast, and my black Nike sweatshirt. But Molly isn't going out with me for my sense of style, as she's pointed out on more than one occasion.

I wait five minutes, not wanting to appear too eager,

then hobble as fast as I can across the street, grocery bags flying, thrusting the crutches on to the asphalt like super-robotic limbs and pushing down so hard I almost fly through the air, my feet leaving the ground. I am a limping, grinning, winged god of love.

She opens the door to her apartment after a couple of rings.

'Ian. What are you doing here?" she says, without taking breath. She's wearing work clothes – a striped shirt, wool knee-length skirt, calves long and naked below the hem.

'I just wanted to see you . . . It's been too long . . .'

I lean in and kiss her. It's not a bad kiss, I'm pleased to say, on the lips. She doesn't resist.

'How's Gemma?' I mumble, my erection already rigid in my trousers.

'She's okay. It was good to talk.'

Molly glances down at the bulge in my Adidas trousers. I turn slightly, trying to hide my obvious arousal.

'Sorry. I should have called you. I just thought . . .'

Suddenly, Molly leans down, whips down the elastic of the trousers and boxer shorts and takes my penis in her hand. I drop the grocery bags. I think I hear eggs breaking.

'Molly . . .'

I try to push her gently back, but she holds my penis hard, with an expert grip, as she jerks her hand rapidly. She leans in against me. Her hair is warm and very soft.

'The bed . . .' I mumble, as I glimpse egg yolk and white seeping across the floor. 'I bought condoms . . .'

But she's not listening and then I'm not listening.

I come.

Molly stands, turns swiftly and hurries to the bathroom. The sound of running water.

I am standing with my tracksuit trousers around my thighs, in a pool of raw egg. I collapse on to the bed. Molly returns shortly afterwards.

'Better?'

She buttons up her blouse. I'm annoyed, because this is a sure sign that sex is over for the time being, and I want to touch her. I want to take control of her, to make her squirm and gasp as she's just done to me. She sits down in the armchair opposite the bed, crosses her legs.

'I've got a new account.'

'That's great, Moll.'

'I've got to go up to Scotland in a couple of weeks.'

'Okay . . .'

She sits in silence for a few moments, as if contemplating something. I decide to wait, to let her speak. Which she does almost immediately, in a soft and stammering voice.

'If you wanted, you could get a writing assignment, come up for the weekend.'

I look at her, and I'm surprised to see something in her eyes that I've not noticed before. It's . . . what? Vulnerability? Fear, even?

A strange and novel sensation floods through me. It feels like the rush before the onset of tears, from stomach through chest to throat and eyes. A surge, almost electrical, unforeseen and virulent. It's surprising.

'I'd love to Molly . . . it's just . . .'

She cocks her head slightly to one side, analyzing.

'Just what?'

I tell her everything. I tell her about the Choronì article, about my firing from the newspaper. I tell her about my anger and my disbelief and my shame. I tell her about my insecurities, about how I feel I should be somewhere else in life at the age of thirty-one, and she listens without laughing.

'Wow. Unfortunate,' Molly murmurs. 'So, what's your plan?'

'I'll get work. I'll call around the papers tomorrow. I can bounce back.'

'Up, up and away,' she says, smiling, for what seems the first time since I arrived.

'I'd love to come to Scotland,' I say, quickly.

'Great.'

I smile, and reach out to touch her hand. She squeezes my fingers gently, then stands from the chair.

'I need a shower.'

I look up at her. She does have a wonderful body. I sense my erection stirring again, which surprises and delights me (usually I need a short nap). I want to join her in the shower, but she's never offered such a step in our relationship, and anyway I can't get my plaster cast wet.

'Maybe you should call Gemma, check she's okay?'

'Yeah. Okay.'

As Molly disappears into the bathroom, I pull my-self up, feeling an overwhelming sensation of joy. I pick up the ultra slim phone and joy flips to confusion, and panic. I came to Molly's apartment hoping for sex and good tidings, but not this. This is bigger. This is huge. These are feelings. Feelings I hadn't planned to have for ages, until some distant, undecided time in the future.

I'm relieved when Gemma doesn't answer the phone. I leave a short, heartfelt message, instructing her to call me on my mobile as soon as she can. Then I haul myself up the bed, lie back and close my eyes, listening to the sound of the power shower, wondering how cheaply I can get a flight up to Edinburgh. Maybe I can find some publication to take a piece on the Scottish capital, perhaps one of the supermarket mags or credit card magazines which seem impervious to economic downturns. New shopping? Edinburgh markets? Post-devolution chic? I will find a way. I am Ian Thompson.

I pull off the Adidas trousers and my boxer shorts, enjoying the warm summer air on my naked body. I drift into sleep.

When I wake forty-five minutes later, Molly is just exiting the bathroom. She's wearing a pair of blue striped flannel pyjamas, her hair pulled back in a pony tail. She asks if I want anything to drink. I ask for some juice, she returns with two glasses. The late afternoon sunlight cuts through the blinds, streaks of gold. I wonder if I will remember this moment for the rest of my life.

'Ian, I've something to tell you . . .' Molly says suddenly. I look up. Her voice is shaky. She continues quickly. 'I don't know . . . I don't know how to say this, so I'll just say it.'

I sit up as quickly as I can. I think I see tears in her eyes.

'What? What is it, Moll?'

This is new. I realize that in eight months of dating

her, this is the first time I've seen her cry. It is both terrifying and wonderful, like a sudden wave or a freak hailstorm.

'I don't know why, I don't, but maybe it's what I needed, maybe it taught me . . .'

I push myself up from the bed and hobble, naked, towards her. I sense my erection, surging, I want to take her right there, fully, properly, right now. I move against her.

'No, Ian.' She steps back.

'It's okay baby, whatever it is, really.'

'While you were in South America, I saw my ex-husband.'

I look at her.

'Saw?'

'We had dinner.'

'What?'

'Dinner.'

My breath catches in my throat. Yet my erection remains, large and towering. My hand tries to push my penis down, but like a remnant of an old machine that has outlived its purpose, it continues to thrust upright.

'It was just dinner.'

'Really?'

She nods, although not fervently.

'Just dinner. Nothing else?'

Molly doesn't respond.

'Anything else, Molly?'

'No.'

I don't believe her. Something in her eyes, the way they flick away when she answers. I want to shout.

'I don't believe you.'

'It's true.'

We look at each other like gunslingers. I want to believe her, but I don't. Suddenly, I see Will Masterson's arse, thumping above Molly's naked body. I hear his laughter, which I imagine to be huge and manly. My fist clenches. My erection dwindles.

'You slept with him, didn't you?'

'What?'

'You fucked your ex-husband.'

Molly stares at me, as if looking at something in a foreign country that is both shocking and baffling, like a dying bull or a plate of snakes.

'Jesus Christ, Ian!'

She shakes her head once, then turns swiftly, marches to the bathroom, and slams the door behind her. The lock clicks. I lumber to the bathroom and hammer on the door.

'Molly!'

I can't believe what's happening. I can't focus, I can't take it in. My heart is racing, I am breathless. It's horrible, a pain, sharp and whole in my stomach. And the pain is spreading swiftly, from my abdomen outwards like an ice flame.

I hammer hard, again. It feels good to hammer.

'Did you sleep with him?'

Silence.

'I asked you a question. Did you?'

A small voice emanates from behind the heavy door.

'No. Of course not. Don't be so fucking childish.'

I snatch up my clothes, pulling on my trousers and

sweatshirt, then grab my crutches and propel myself towards the door. I don't know what I'm doing, where I'm going. I know only that I have to leave.

'Where are you going?'

Molly is standing in the bathroom doorway.

'Don't leave, Ian. If you leave . . .'

I whirl, a bristling bundle of anger.

'If I leave, what?'

'Just don't.'

'Why not? What are you going to do?'

I glare at her.

'Just don't go!'

'Fuck you, Molly Cook!'

I open the door and hurtle out into the hallway, thumbing furiously at the elevator button. She will follow me, she will try to pull me back inside. I wonder in that instant if I will go with her, to listen to what she has to say. That would be right.

A ring. The lift door opens. I look around. Molly's door is open, but she's nowhere to be seen.

There are no taxis. I start to walk, as hurriedly as I can. I don't look back, I won't give her that satisfaction.

I realize I've left Gemma's groceries behind. Some friend I am.

Passers-by look alarmed at my velocity, an invalid rocket, a robotic mutation with partly ripped Adidas Goretex trousers thrusting down Goswell Road like something from a badly designed production of *War Of The Worlds*. By the time I get to the Barbican, I'm exhausted. I look around for a taxi — this is the City, there should be dozens.

But it's just before six, everyone is leaving work, hundreds of people pouring into the tube stations, cramming onto buses, thinking of home and loved ones waiting for them. All the taxis are taken by commuters.

'Shit!' I bark out loud, not caring who hears me, the secretaries and money traders and investment bankers. They're all shits, they're all like Molly. They're all laughing at me, the Vicar's son who can't get laid. Maybe I am the biggest fuck-up, after all.

I look around me at the besuited men, with their expensively gelled hair and minutely checked shirts, and I want to see Will Masterson, the Master of London town, so that I can hit him. I want to do some damage to someone, to something. I wonder if I'm near the bank that he works for, where is it, Moorgate or somewhere? What would I do? Charge in there? Scream and shout, throw a few punches? He's bigger than me, judging from the pictures. He'd probably knock my head off.

I look up, trying to regain composure. I must orientate myself, get my bearings. Maybe I should go back to Molly's apartment? Should I apologize?

I'm standing at the entrance to one of the corporate offices with its modern glass frontage, its fish tank and abstract modern art in the lobby and its pretty, smartly dressed receptionist. I glance at the shiny silver plaque by the revolving doors.

Price, Chambers and Grosvenor.

I know the name. What is it?

A law firm. The company that Raj Singh works for. Gemma's husband. Who screwed up her life, just as Will Masterson is trying to screw up mine. Who reacted to a few words like a girl, not a man, and left her without looking back.

The bastard.

Before I have time to think, I find myself pushing through the revolving doors ('I'm not taking the fucking invalid door!') and marching up to the receptionist who smiles at me with the poise and ease of someone who smiles up at a hundred and sixty men a day.

Ignominy

No one at the office knew that Raj Singh was living in a cramped room at the Holiday Inn Express in Holborn. He could not afford to show any signs of weakness. Peter Saville was on his back about the Vickeray deal and Stephen Chambers himself had looked in a couple of times, inquiring as to how things were shaping up. It was Raj's biggest project yet, a $25 million franchise leasing deal with a US coffee shop chain. The pressure was high, with the deadline looming for final contracts. He had to perform.

It wasn't easy. He wasn't sleeping (the hotel room seemed terrifyingly stark at 3 a.m.), he wasn't eating (he bought greasy late night takeaways that he threw away the next morning, barely touched), he felt as if his liver, kidneys, lungs, heart and intestines had been ripped to shreds by something cold and mechanical, and yet he had to keep up with the reports, the emails, the calls, the documents, the research.

He arrived at the office early and stayed late. Anything to avoid being alone, to avoid thought and feeling. The work was his outlet. He needed the focus, the routine. It scared him a little, the ease with which he was able to just get on with it. There was something robotic about his methodical application. In his work he could avoid any flicker of emotion.

But now he'd lost a vital email from Vickeray's attorney in New York, and the unpleasant emotions that he'd been protecting himself from were swooping in like dragons. It wasn't anywhere in the system, even though he was sure he'd filed it. He couldn't tell Josephine, the secretary he shared with the two other less senior lawyers in the department. Not yet. She would make a fuss, and Saville would be sure to hear of it.

Why was he so unlucky? Misfortune always befell him. At school, he'd slipped on a newly mopped assembly hall floor and broken his arm the day before the fifth-form ski trip. At University College, Oxford, his block had been the only one to be damaged by the fire in the college kitchens. He'd never won anything in his life – raffles, scratchcards, bets. Raj Singh never played the lottery. He never filled in boxes in newspapers to win cars, holidays or Christmas hampers. When he read about large cash wins, or fortunate escapes from the jaws of raw danger, he nodded slowly to himself. God smiled on others, he knew, not on Raj Singh. Because God had given Raj Singh too much at the outset.

He looked at his finger, wrapped in toilet paper. It was remarkable how easily and effectively a simple piece of paper could cut into flesh. He'd just been pulling documents from the New York file, in his desperate bid to find some evidence of the email. And now it was bleeding again.

Was this another punishment? Was it true, as he'd suspected at moments in his life, that such frequent afflictions were God's way of penalizing him for being born into a life of such consummate ease and privilege? 'The luckiest boy in Britain, my son!' when compared to the travails of the average infant in India, especially those unfortunates in the impoverished region of Kashmir (from where his mother proudly hailed).

Where was the bloody email? It could not have simply vanished.

'Keep looking. It'll turn up.'

Gemma's voice. It was unmistakeable. He'd been hearing it at intervals over the previous ten days. It made him want to scream in rage, and sob with endless tears. She'd betrayed him. She'd told him that she didn't love him. What could he have done? He'd had to leave. Man not a mouse.

Anger returned once more. It was bullshit that he hadn't paid enough attention to her. Did she not realize how hard he was working? There were people at the office (women as well as men!) who saw much less of their partners than he did. He made an effort. He always had. But it wasn't enough for her, she needed more, always more, even though his hard-earned money was paying for her dream house, for the ridiculous expensive fittings, the reclaimed oak floors, the hand-crafted steel staircase, the pseudo-Japanese garden (how his father would cringe, if he ever saw so much concrete, in a country renowned for the greenness of its grass!). Even though his salary allowed her to follow her poorly paid path up the ladders of B-league architecture. Why couldn't she accept that for him to pursue his own (more illustrious) dream, he had to graft a damn sight harder than she did?

'She doesn't know. She's had it too easy. They don't know what it is to work hard.'

His mother's voice, shrill and absolute. He did not agree wholeheartedly with her (Gemma's upbringing had not been necessarily easy, in its own lonely way, despite the west London affluence). Yet he did resent her, his soon-to-be ex-wife. He'd done all he could to be there for her, at the same time as working hard to succeed in his own career, which let's face it would be beneficial to both of them. He'd told her more than once how much even a junior partner earned, and he'd enjoyed seeing her eyes grow wide with surprised delight.

What did she think? He had to work hard. Didn't she understand that? He had to work harder than anyone, as he alone knew that he would never get any help from any quarter, especially not from a deity with omnipotent powers.

Sitting at the computer, wrapping a clean Kleenex around his bleeding finger, he clicked on to the file in his Drafts folder. The outline contract he'd been writing during lunch-breaks and on his laptop at the hotel in the grim dark hours before dawn appeared. The divorce contract. Singh versus Cook-Singh.

It was fair, he thought, nodding to himself as he scrolled through the points. She would get the house, but nothing more. She'd have to raise finance to finish the work, or sell it somehow. That was not his problem. She was an architect, she could figure it out. She was getting assets approximating to £850,000 once the work was completed. Any judge would consider it more than equitable.

He clicked to close the document. From somewhere cold inside him, he sensed tears welling. Bloody hell! He had not cried in days, not since the last sobbing session alone in the hotel room in front of a repeat of *Friends* at 2 a.m. He turned his wedding ring round and round, as if it might produce magic, conjuring a happy solution to both the New York email and his marriage from invisibility.

All around him men and women proceeded purposefully about the office, talking quickly, moving with alacrity and sureness. None of them were feeling the emptiness that invaded him now. They were filled with direction and resolve. He hated how lonely they made him feel.

It was an anguish he knew well, from school to university and beyond. It wasn't the early chants of 'Paki!' or 'Brown arse!', or the way white people eyed him on the buses in Morden (after all, his ethnicity and background were none of his own doing). Such comments and looks made him feel strong, made him feel part of something (the 'coloured' community). It was the more personal individual rejections that were clearly snubbing him, rather than his skin or his parents' country of origin, that hurt Raj most.

Last to be picked for football (two other Indian boys were star centre forward and goalkeeper respectively).

Mocked by mini-skirted slacker girls for his thick glasses.

Dumped by Sarah Jenkinson, out of nowhere, the night of the sixth form Christmas party, because she said he was too dull and couldn't dance.

Chastised by his Oxford tutor for 'not capitalizing on your undoubted strong intellect and pushing yourself beyond what you feel is achievable, into realms that challenge and expand your existing knowledge!'

And now, finally and most spectacularly rejected by his

wife, the beautiful, artistic Gemma. Not because of his race, or his looks, but because he was Raj Singh. The lawyer. The workaholic. The failed husband.

'I don't love you any more.'

Shame gilded shame. He could not tell his parents. He could picture his mother's face, hear her soft, biting words.

'Oh, Raji, what did I tell you?'

No one in his family had ever divorced before. But then, as he was sure his mother would point out to every mamma-ji, mammi-ji, masi-ji, massar-ji, chacha-ji, chachi-ji, thaya-ji, thayi-ji, bhua-ji, phuphur-ji, cousins, second cousins, nephews, nieces, family friends and anybody with relatives within the 1,222,243 square miles of sovereign Indian territory, no one in his family had ever married a *ghoree* before. A white woman. Raj Singh had been the first. He'd finally pushed himself beyond, to realms that had challenged and expanded his existing knowledge. And look where it had got him.

He wondered for the sixty-third time if the washing machine incident had started it. Perhaps if he could pinpoint the moment of inception, when everything had started to go wrong, he could retrace the steps and somehow set them right. That was what he was trained to do – to go back through the documents and see where the wording first became ambiguous, or hostile, or just plain confusing.

He'd done the laundry one Sunday afternoon, having been made to feel guilty about his lack of participation in the general household chores (why didn't they get the cleaner to come more often, was his question, one which had been rejected immediately by his wife, who'd informed him he was, as usual, avoiding the real issue!). He'd put in a bundle of clothes, including items of her underwear, the lacy panties and bras that he still marvelled at, even though he'd lived with her for over two years, lingering to touch the finely stitched lace and silk before placing them reverentially in the 6 kg Siemens drum. Such finery, such delicacy – it seemed a miracle that he, the clumsy, introverted bore should be permitted to fondle such beauty. He'd set the dial to the cooler wash (Raj Singh remembered orders) and left the machine to spin.

He'd forgotten about his red socks. They'd been a present from his mother the previous Christmas. He'd forgotten to separate his wife's white La Perla bra and knickers and her white slips that she wore in bed. When Gemma pulled out the washing from the machine after her bath, she'd called him downstairs. He knew something was wrong, from her quiet, deliberate tone.

She was holding the pink underwear like the entrails of a dead pet. The look of disappointment and disdain on her face was clear. She did not shout (that would have been so much easier to deal with). She was quietly resigned. Sad, even.

'You're like a leopard, Raj . . .' she muttered, almost to herself. 'You just can't change your spots, can you?!'

He had turned without a word and hurried back up the stairs to his computer and the refuge of the latest contract, not angry at her, but feeling the familiar deep despair with himself that he'd got it all wrong, again.

Still he could not find the New York email. He resolved to lay his concerns to one side, to re-focus, to take control once more. He opened the Vickeray contract and tried to focus on the problematic clause 7. iii, with its deliberately ambiguous position regarding ancillary distribution rights. He read and re-read the lines carefully, allowing himself to be drawn into the exactitude of the terms, delighting in the lengthy, multi-syllabic words that seemed almost mathematical in their placing, so meticulously, so daintily positioned to balance and contrast, a formula conjured by the brightest and most steadfast of British and American legal intellects, until the small black letters in their neatly configured lines seemed to him a perfect riposte to the turmoil in his heart and mind – a chart forged out of chaos.

He changed a couple of words, erased a comma, added a semi-colon, and sat back, momentarily satisfied. Then Josephine strode up to his desk and announced:

'There's someone here to see you Mr Singh. He says he's a friend,' in a tone suggesting rampant disapproval.

He was shocked and angered to find Ian Thompson sitting in the waiting room. He looked like he'd just stepped from a gym or some suburban shopping mall, in tracksuit trousers with a rip in the side, and a sweatshirt. He was holding a pair of crutches awkwardly, as if embarrassed by them. His right leg was encased in thick white plaster.

'Hello, Ian. I'm rather busy, I've a deadline. What do you want?'

Raj had an inkling of what Ian wanted and it angered him further. Who did he think he was? Bloody Ross, or fat old Chandler from *Friends*? This wasn't some bloody sitcom, in which cheery buddies shared problems and partners. This was real life. And Ian had crossed an important line, just by stepping into Raj's office, his sanctuary. By sticking his bloody nose in, where it really was not wanted.

'Er . . . I thought we should have a quick chat.'

Raj remembered all the reasons he didn't like Ian. The man seemed to have an old-fashioned sense of *noblesse oblige* about him – it was as if he thought he could go anywhere, talk to anyone, and somehow people would welcome him, and listen. Raj knew such blind bravado well – many of the public schoolboys at Oxford had possessed a similar imperviousness to surroundings, in-stilled as they were with the belief, from an early age, that the world was indeed their oyster, lobster, clam – in fact their whole all-you-can-eat seafood platter.

'What about?'

As if he didn't know.

'Gemma. Your wife.'

Suddenly, Raj had a surge of desire to punch Ian Thompson. It was just a flash – a feeling he'd had only very rarely in his life – a bully at school who'd picked on a small, thin Ghanaian student, a member of the Keble College rugby team who'd stolen his bike at a party, his cousin Sarchin when he broke Raj's Pacman when they were ten. But he'd never hit anybody. His father had always preached restraint over revenge, reflection over reaction. And Raj wasn't going to lose his job just because Ian Thompson hadn't the decency and tact to use a telephone instead of invading his sacred ground.

'I've got five minutes. Come on.'

They sat opposite each other in the small conference room. He'd noted Josephine's glare as he'd hurried Ian through the door. He'd have to come up with some explanation. Maybe he'd say this was his wife's cousin, who needed advice about medical malpractice. That way he could appear both caring and knowledgeable.

Ian seemed in a belligerent mood. He sat down slowly, then leant his elbows on the mahogany conference table and glared across at Raj. Raj felt uncomfortable, as he did whenever there was a hint of aggression in a room. He tried to think of something to say to break the tension. Between them sat a bowl of dried fruit – Stephen Chambers's addiction to healthfoods was well known (and ridiculed) in the office.

'Raisin? Almond?' Raj tipped the bowl towards Ian.

'I'm allergic to nuts. Remember?'

Raj didn't remember. He withdrew the bowl quickly. He sensed the blood flushing to his neck and cheeks.

'Sorry. I forgot.'

Ian nodded, once. Raj breathed in, trying to feel like a lawyer.

'So . . .' he began, pleased that he sounded measured, yet concerned, 'what would you like to discuss, Ian?'

Ian laughed, bitterly.

'You're not being fair. You need to talk to her. You can't just walk off. You've really hurt her.'

Raj could not believe what he was hearing.

'Let me get this straight? I've hurt her? Have you forgotten, in your misguided attempts to support your so-called friend, that she was the one who told me she doesn't love me, probably never has, and doesn't want to be with me any more?'

'She didn't say she doesn't want to be with you!'

'She doesn't love me. Why would I want to stay with her?'

'Because you're married.'

'How quaintly old-fashioned. Two in three marriages end in divorce, you know.'

'Talk to her.'

'I will. In my own time. I'm not the one being unreasonable.'

'Yes, you are. You need to go and see her. She doesn't know why she said what she did. I don't think she really meant it.'

'Oh. Of course you know her so well, don't you . . .'

'Yes. I do . . .'

'Why do you care, Ian? I'd have thought you'd be grateful to have her all to yourself again.'

Raj was aware his voice was raised. He was also aware the door to the conference room was not fully closed, and several faces were turned their way.

'What?'

'This way you get to spend quality time with your precious Gemma.'

'We're just friends, you know that . . .'

'You can be her confidant, her confessor, spend plenty of time with her in our house, and finally, maybe, you'll get what you've always wanted . . .'

'What's that, Raj?'

Ian's knuckles were white, clenched on the dark mahogany table. Raj looked at him, feeling strangely calm, as if he was outside of the room, looking in.

'You tell me, Ian.'

'Don't be a prat.'

Raj found himself smiling. There was something about the situation that he found overwhelmingly comic.

'What's so fucking funny?'

'You. The way you always try to be the knight in shining armour. It's very . . . Monty Python.'

'Piss off, Raj.'

Raj shook his head. He looked across at Ian, attempting to keep a lid on the swirling anxiousness and irritation inside him.

'Look, I appreciate your concern. I will see Gemma, when my deadline's done.'

With this, he stood and walked to the door, opening it further, hoping that Ian would be less prone to anger with the rest of the office watching. He waited, holding open the door. Yet Ian remained sitting, as if contemplating various courses of action. Raj wondered what he should do – advance or retreat? He sensed people watching, behind his back. Just as he had decided to re-enter the room and close the door, Ian pulled back his chair and pushed himself upright. Raj breathed out quickly. He let Ian pass him, out into the communal work space of desks and bookshelves. He closed the conference room door, and turned to follow Ian out to reception, when Ian stopped and turned to him.

'Why do you always put work first?'

'Please Ian. Not here . . .'

'I don't care who hears this. Why is work so important to you?'

Raj felt crushed by the gazes accelerating towards him from what seemed like the entire workforce of Price, Chambers and Grosvenor. Why was he so often caught like this, in the headlights, like a terrified mammal? He heard laughter, sniggers, but it wasn't real, he knew, just memories of past sounds, past voices – the girls outside the canteen, the boys on the football field, the pretty young women at the Oxford parties. He felt his fist clench, and it seemed for once that it was a large fist, a compact, bristling ball of flesh, bone and gristle, that could crush a mouth, a nose, a windpipe. He breathed out again, quickly, and spoke low and directly.

'I will call Gemma, Ian. Now I have to get back to work.'

'Why's it so important?'

Raj held up his hand, fingers slightly outstretched, palm towards Ian's face. It was, he realized, a gesture his father employed occasionally when trying to subdue an onslaught from his mother. Suddenly, he felt immensely powerful.

'Right now, my work is all I've got!'

Ian glared at him. Raj tried to relax his right hand, which remained tightly outstretched.

'Don't push me, Ian. I'm in a weird place right now.'

He wanted Ian to leave. He wanted to get back to his desk, to open a contract file and immerse himself in the neatness of language, in the precise nature of carefully inserted words.

'Yeah. Well. Call her.'

'Bye, Ian.'

Ian nodded, almost to himself, turned and hobbled away. Raj waited for a moment, knowing that faces were watching him. If he looked up, he knew they'd look away. He just needed the strength.

He turned. As predicted, his fellow junior lawyers

glanced swiftly back at their computer screens. Only Peter Saville met his gaze. He was standing by Raj's desk, just six feet away, holding a sheath of papers. Raj approached him.

'Well, well, Mr Singh,' said Peter Saville, before Raj could mutter an explanation for his absence. 'Quite a show.'

'It was a family matter. I'll stay late so I can make up the time.'

'Quite . . . forceful. It would be nice to see the same degree of passion in the work environment.'

'I'm sorry?'

'There's plenty of room for fervour in the law, you know.'

'Fervour?'

'Perhaps we could see a little of that Singh kick-ass in your future dealings with our adversaries?'

'I'll see what I can do.'

'Good.' Peter Saville smiled. Raj had never seen his boss's lips rise above horizontal before. 'Now, are we still on course for the deadline?'

At his desk, Raj hurriedly clicked through his files one more time, his thoughts racing like mercury. What had just happened? Had it been good or bad to show anger and resolve in the midst of the office? Saville had seemed to indicate that he'd been impressed. But was that just double-bluff, something the middle manager was famous for? Would it come out as a black mark against him in his next interim assessment?

He could not focus on the documents he was opening.

'Slow down.'

Gemma's voice again. He shook his head, to purge her soft conciliatory tone.

'Just concentrate. You can do it.'

His thoughts raced on. Was it possible? Was Ian right? Did Gemma really want him back? In that moment, he half expected the phone by his left elbow to ring. That's what would have happened in a film, he thought, in one of those romantic comedies she was so fond of. He waited for a moment. Silence, except for the hum of computer screens and the low murmur of legal voices.

Suddenly he had an idea. He clicked on the wastepaper basket icon on his desktop. He did not know why he hadn't thought of it before. There, nestling comfortably between two draft letters, as if hibernating, was the New York email. He smiled.

He opened the email, printed it and began to re-write clause 7. iii, for the thirteenth, and, he felt certain now, last time.

JEOPARDY

You big fat bollocks.

Sitting on the bus to Victoria Park I am afraid that I've overreacted. Maybe Molly was telling the truth about her ex-husband. I didn't exactly give her a chance to explain herself more fully.

You've blown it.

At Shoreditch I call her, but it cuts straight to her answering machine. I leave a message, apologizing, asking her if we could talk about things.

At Cambridge Heath Station, I call her again, but leave no message.

At Gemma's road, I call her a third time and leave another message, again asking Molly to call me.

Ringing the doorbell at number 26 Raleigh Street, I prepare to spill out my confession to Gemma. She will know what to do.

Yet Gemma's expression invites no spewing of guts. The priest is not in. She doesn't even look me in the eyes as she opens the door, merely turning and walking back into the shadows. When I get to the lounge area, she's curled up once again, on the sofa in front of the television.

I look around. There's something about the house, its temporary, incomplete, exposed shell, that seems so tired and ancient. The evidences of decay, the rotten floorboards, the wires dangling forlornly from cracked ceilings, the peeling remnants of woodchip, all speak of a settled hopelessness, a despair even. The evening shadows seem to cast a pall of melancholy across the floor and up the walls. I feel suddenly and irredeemably sad.

Gemma sits silently, knees pulled up to her chin, staring blankly ahead. I have to talk to her, to break the musty, uncharitable silence. I try to be normal. I tell her I'm sorry I revealed everything about Raj to her sister. Gemma watches the television impassively, and replies:

'It's okay. She was going to find out sometime or other.'

Slowly, with as much care as I can muster, I sit down on the sofa beside her, straightening out my right leg so the insolent plaster cast is as far from me as possible. I have a sudden desire to lean over, put my arms around her, and bury my head in her neck. Instead I breathe in deeply, and turn my attention to the cookery show on the TV screen.

After a minute or two, Gemma speaks again.

'So, did you get laid?'

I feel my stomach tighten. I do not answer. Gemma remains silent. I feel so ashamed. The anger boils.

'Come on Ian, you can tell me. How's it going between the two of you?'

It's as if she senses something, knowing my wound, and is twisting a knife deeper. Women can do this, can't they? They have extrasensory instincts, especially when it comes to matters of emotion and sex.

Gemma turns to me, eyes suddenly bright and focused.

'Are you nuts about her?'

'What?'

'Are you nuts about my sister?'

'Nuts?'

'Oh, Ian. I've been thinking that one up for the last two hours. I thought you'd laugh.'

'Oh. Sorry.'

'So? Are you . . . Nuts?'

Gemma is smiling now, as if expecting good news. I try to suppress it, but I can't help feeling irritated by her need for me to provide her with hope that somewhere in the world there are relationships that are still light and fun and happy. I sense my anger rising once more, but I have no desire or ability to stop it.

'I went to see Raj,' I say, pointedly, and am momentarily rewarded by her look of panic.

'What? How? When?'

Gemma bites her bottom lip. She looks like Molly. Which makes me want to continue.

'I went to his office.'

'Why?'

'I wanted to talk to him. To make him see reason.'

'Oh Jesus, Ian. Why did you do that? You'll only make things worse.'

A moment. Then she asks, meekly.

'How was he?'

'Angry. I thought he was going to hit me.'

'What? Raj?'

She snorts with laughter, the sort of embarrassing grunt that would usually cause her to put her hand to her mouth, and blush. But this isn't usually. She carries on, snorting again.

'Raj has never hit anyone in his life.'

'I guess I bring out the best in people.'

'What did you say to him?'

There's desperation and longing in her voice, as her hand grips her forearm.

'I told him he was being unreasonable and that he'd hurt you and that he should come and talk to you.'

'Oh Ian.'

My anger subsides. I reach out to touch her arm, but she pushes me away.

'You've ruined it. You've ruined everything.'

'Look, I'm sorry. I thought I could help.'

She shouts. I'm shocked by her vehemence.

'Why do you try to control me? Why do you get involved, and try and fix things when they can't be fixed?'

'I didn't . . .'

'Why can't you just leave everything alone? You're not my father, Ian! Not my brother! Not my fucking boyfriend!'

'Yeah. I suppose I should be grateful for that!'

Gemma looks at me.

'At least Raj acts like a grown-up!'

'What the fuck's that supposed to mean?'

We glare at each other. Gemma turns off the television and goes to sit in the window. I get up without a word, and limp up the stairs and lie down on the bed in the spare room and stare at the ceiling. I feel completely alone.

Two hours later, I come downstairs.

'I think I broke up with Molly.'

Gemma looks up. 'What?'

'She told me not to leave, and I did, because I was angry.' It sounds like someone else, someone who's trying to sound cool about something they're far from cool about. Gemma stares at me.

'Why? What happened?'

'She saw Will. Ex-husband Will.'

I am pleased with the shock on Gemma's face.

'I don't believe you. She hates his guts.'

Gemma's angry reaction emboldens me. Suddenly, I feel like I've done the right thing again.

'So she said. But she had dinner with him. While I was in Venezuela.'

Gemma is shaking her head.

'Wow. Talk about a Damascene conversion . . .'

'I think she slept with him.'

'What?'

Gemma stares at me, eyes wide, mouth open. I nod quickly, trying to convince myself as much as her.

'I asked her, and she didn't deny it.'

My voice sounds like it did when I was younger, trying to convince my mother with excuses as to why I shouldn't have to go to Sunday School.

Gemma says nothing, but beckons for me to sit in the window seat beside her. I recount what happened (omitting the sexual encounter). When I've finished, Gemma puts her hand on my arm.

'Oh Ian.'

I look at her. I feel sick.

'I don't know what to do.'

Gemma puts her arms around me. Her body is warm through the pyjamas. She smells soft, a gentle sweet feminine scent. I can feel her breasts against me. It feels nice.

*

The following morning, there's a note on the sofa.

Gone to work. I can't give up. See you later? Chin up.

I call Molly several times, leaving increasingly desperate messages demanding a meeting to discuss 'things'. I feel sick, my stomach hollow and aching. I wonder what's wrong with me, how I managed to lose my job, my flat and my beautiful, funny, successful girlfriend in the space of a week?

I limp back and forth, up and down the stairs, craving movement. On the second floor, I notice the door to Gemma's bedroom is open slightly. I hesitate for a moment, then enter the room.

The bed is made. On the bedside table are some women's magazines and her perfume. A skirt is strewn over the old armchair that she's had since college. Beyond, in the en-suite bathroom I glimpse a clothes rack, where several pairs of colourful panties and G-strings are dangling. These make me feel strange. With my girlfriends, the sight of lacy knickers has always been titillating – a glimpse of a wholly feminine world that every hot-blooded male wants to get his hands on. But this is different. I feel uncomfortable. Do brothers feel like this when they see their sister's knickers drying?

For some reason I can't fathom, I open the wardrobe. Inside are three of Raj's suits, and a neat series of shelves containing sweaters, socks and white cotton vests, all aligned perfectly as if measured with rulers and set-squares.

I wonder if Gemma and Raj can fix it. Or be fixed. Are they right for each other? Who is right for each other? I mean, Raj is okay. He's not the most exciting, adventurous soul on earth. I wouldn't marry him, unless I needed the money. But he's a decent person, and that is not a quality to underestimate. But I believe Gemma needs more than that. She needs . . . I don't know. A spark. Fireworks, from time to time. She needs to shout and scream, someone who can bring her out of herself. Someone more like her father. Or Neil Farrelly.

I wonder if she still has mementoes of her time with Neil. Is there a hidden drawer, like my secret cardboard folder, crammed with letters and photos of ex-girlfriends?

I look around the bedroom. I try the drawer in the bedside table. It's empty apart from some official-looking letter from her doctor. I glance at it.

RE: University College Hospital Women's Health Clinic
Missed Appointment # 372
Please book new appointment urgently.

I hate hospitals. My father went to visit sick and elderly patients in Addenbrooke's Hospital in Cambridge quite frequently, and at Christmas time he would take his young son along to carry the presents my mother had wrapped. I couldn't breathe, I thought I could smell the death. I don't blame Gemma for not going to her appointment. Especially to a woman's health clinic. Women's health always sounds so . . . messy.

Then I have a thought. What if Gemma is pregnant? What if this is the reason why she broke up with Raj? Perhaps the baby isn't his? Perhaps she can't decide if she should keep it? I wonder if she's waiting for the right time to tell me.

All at once I succumb, as usual, to a racing daydream, taking me from this point to the birth of Gemma's fatherless baby boy, whom I help raise, Hugh Grant to Liz Hurley, teaching her son about football, travelling and girls. I get to his first day at university (Sheffield, of course, to study French), when I realize I've been staring out of the window for fifteen minutes, watching two smartly dressed middle-aged women enter and then exit the black front door at number 22.

I find the picture of Neil Farrelly in the middle of an architecture textbook in the spare room.

In the photo he's smiling, confident and strong. I wonder what he's doing now. I wonder whether he's single. I wonder about getting online, Friends Reunited, or something like that. I bet there's a site for Liverpool University.

I'm not trying to meddle. But having screwed up my own relationship, I feel that the least I can do is try to help my best friend. After all, sometimes fate needs a helping hand.

KNOWLEDGE

I wait for my mother to finish fluttering her hands above the menu, like some pantomime geisha or the star of Horsham Women's Institute's production of *Madame Butterfly*. The tall, suave Hispanic waiter looks on with a friendly smile, which only makes my mother quiver more.

'Stop smiling,' I want to tell him, 'and she will cease this pathetic little girl performance that she believes is captivating you, because she considers it the role of an attractive woman of any age to express a high degree of helplessness in order to hook and reel in a man she considers good-looking enough to be worthy of her guile . . .'

Instead I sit, feeling the familiar and caustic embarrassment and the deeper more troublesome fear that I am now older and more mature than my mother, that Susan Cook does not understand the ways of the modern world, and that the daughter will as usual have to extricate the mother from another ignominious situation.

My mother's arrival at the office has capped off a terrible day, and it's only lunchtime. I woke once again at dawn, showering at length in a bid to wash away my dark feelings (ugh, thighs, ugh, belly, ugh, breasts).

I left the house (which, for the first time, felt like it might actually be on the verge of falling down) into an early morning August rain squall. I was wearing a denim skirt and H & M blouse, and I'd forgotten my umbrella. I should have turned round and gone back to the bedroom and pulled the blanket over my head. But I had to go to the office. I had to be strong.

For the first time since Raj's departure, I was worried about work. The final drawings for the bar project were due by the middle of September, and I sensed we were behind. It was silly, I knew, but under the circumstances the bar project seemed more important to me than ever. I needed to feel like I could accomplish something, before it was too late.

This is my first project as a team leader. Initially I was overjoyed at the mini-promotion, even though it was only a refit of a Soho bar called The Place, a £150,000 project which pales into insignificance in comparison to much that KPSG works on – big corporate headquarters, the odd internationally renowned museum, and several cutting-edge shopping malls in Europe and the Far East.

The company employs ninety-five staff, with three different departments – corporate, commercial and residential. I've been working on the commercial team since joining two years ago, and I know being made team leader, albeit on a small inconsequential project, has ruffled some feathers amongst those who've been here longer. I'm lucky that most of my co-workers seem to like me. I'm deferential and keep my head down. I know I've been given the bar project because I'm the commercial department boss's favourite, but everyone needs a lucky break at some stage in their careers, don't they?

I like these smaller commercial projects. My speciality, the talent that got me the job (so unexpectedly – KPSG is ranked in the top five most desirable architecture firms to work for in the UK, and I'm far from a genius, unlike some of my colleagues) is my ability with 3D Studio Max and AutoCad – the two computer design programs beloved by modern architecture firms. Whilst others in the office, who graduated five years before me still do drawings by hand, taking them days, I can sit at a keyboard and plot intricate designs on the screen in a matter of hours.

'Miraculous!' Duncan Archer proclaimed when he saw my first drawing, a rendering of a new restaurant in Fulham, south-west London. He took me out for a lunch-time drink and it didn't cross my mind that the way he looked at me had anything to do with factors beyond his admiration for my plotting skills. His attention to me didn't surpass 'friendly' for two years, although he once put his hand on my arm whilst talking about changes to a smoke vent design, but he was married to a pretty English teacher, the mother of his two small girls.

It wasn't until rumours began to spread that Duncan's marriage was on the rocks, that I began to wonder if his insistence that I move from a desk at the back of the office to one next to his at the front might not be purely influenced by work concerns.

I arrived at the office in Shoreditch shortly after seven, and let myself in. I'd been hoping to have an hour or so there on my own, to collect my thoughts, to review anything I'd missed during the two days I'd hidden away at home. To my surprise and dismay, Duncan was already in the office, alone. He looked as if he'd not slept much – his eyes were puffy and jaundiced and his hand trembled as he held a styrofoam coffee cup. He smiled widely on seeing me enter and insisted on making me a cup of coffee. As he flustered over the machine, I glanced at him from my desk. He wasn't so bad-looking for a forty-eight-year-old – grey only at the temples and he didn't have the belly of most men his age. He was short, but not stocky, there was a litheness to his movements. And he was talented, of this I was sure. Shortly after I started at the office, he showed me some designs he'd done when he owned his own company ('before we needed to make the house payments'). They were beautiful – glass and concrete living spaces which allowed the meagre London light to flood in as if in California, or Provence, much as I dreamed of doing at the house on Raleigh Street. Working within the confines of a big multinational company, in which he had to answer to two directors and six board members, was evidently a little trying for the great Duncan Archer.

As I flicked through my files, trying to get up to speed on things I'd missed the previous two days, Duncan sat on the edge of his desk and talked. And talked. He chatted about a tender for a new bar and dance complex in Manchester and a luxury shopping plaza in Frankfurt with impressive enthusiasm, considering the early hour. I tried to concentrate on my work, whilst giving the impression that I was listening to every word he said, but he kept finishing his sentences with a rising question mark that invited response.

'. . . And the floor is cantilevered on two levels?'

Then he asked to see my latest computer renderings, and pulled a chair close, and I could smell stale cigarettes and coffee and body odour, and I wondered if he'd been in the office all night.

I had no choice but to show him my drawings, and as I clicked on each plan and he seemed to shift closer to me in his chair, I heard Raj's voice:

'You just have to stand up to him!'

I felt a painful mixture of emotions, all at once: anger at Raj for his insensitivity in having repeated this to me so many times, irritation with myself that I was unable, once again, to do what he suggested, and a nostalgic yearning for the time when he and I used to talk about such things.

I wanted to be alone, but Duncan Archer continued to talk, praising my drawings, encouraging me to take 'as many creative risks as you feel you need to,' which I knew was his way of pretending to himself that all his staff were as adventurous and innovative as he was.

And then, without warning or encouragement, he put his hand on my naked knee.

I jerked away instantly, knocking the styrofoam cup of coffee, which spilled on to the computer keyboard.

'Oh. Sorry.'

I lunged at the keyboard, trying to dab at the coffee with my sleeve. With surprising alacrity, Duncan Archer yanked the cord from the back of the computer, whipped the keyboard from under my hand and turned it upside down so the coffee ran on to the floor.

'It was just an accident, Gemma.'

Was he referring to my clumsy spilling of the coffee, or his blatant grope of my knee?

I stood quickly, muttered another apology and hurried to the toilets, just as Sophie entered the office with two other architects.

I sat on the closed toilet seat, staring at the grey-white door for ten minutes. When finally I exited, make-up reapplied, breathing normally, at least half the workforce had arrived and the office was gratifyingly busy. Duncan Archer was in a meeting with Gwen, the Welsh office manager, and the other two department heads. He didn't look up as I passed his desk. At my own desk, my keyboard sat morosely in the bin. I spent twenty minutes asking if anyone had a spare one, which of course no one did. Eventually I was forced to plead with Sophie, who, true to her hoarding nature, had a spare keyboard at the back of her cupboard.

'What happened to yours?'

'Some coffee got spilt.'

'Really? Are you sure you're okay?'

'Fine. Thanks.'

I spent the rest of the morning reviewing my files, telephoning the bar's two owners in Dublin, going over drawings with the three junior members of my team, and taking a call from Ben Keane, the contractor who was working on the house in Raleigh Street. Keane wanted to know when more money would be available for the next phase of the work on the roof and the garden. I'd been dreading this call ever since Raj left, but I found myself telling him, calmly and professionally, that due to unforeseen circumstances the work needed to be postponed for a few weeks. The contractor started to laugh.

'Don't worry Ms Cook. We all have cash-flow problems.'

Cash-flow, I thought ruefully. Mine is more of a life-flow problem.

Trying to keep my annoyance in check, I returned to the

file on my desk. I picked out the letters from Westminster Council Planning Department, from Bob Wright, Assistant Planner, who was refusing to accept our proposal for an all-glass frontage to the bar, saying it would set a dangerous precedent for other commercial property on the street, and all the time I felt my anger expanding, billowing, like a balloon filling with toxic gas. Men were so arrogant. They never thought around a problem, they never attempted to put themselves in the position of others! And they never revised their decision, even if this refusal to change things meant harming the project, or the situation! I hated them, I decided.

Bob Wright, Duncan Archer, Raj Singh, even Ian Thompson.

All so stubborn, all so sure of their own righteousness, of their own position in the world. Why did I always feel so hesitant, in the face of male certainty?

For a moment, I entertained a brief fantasy involving all four men and a machine gun. It was as I was blasting the last one, Ian, in the stomach, blood and guts splattering in all directions, the rat-tat-tat of the gun deafening in my ears, that my mother appeared in front of me. I shook my head involuntarily, wondering, terrified, if I'd descended into twenty-four carat madness and was conjuring up more devils to torment me from the tortured recesses of my mind. But then the vision of my mother, dressed in a summer dress and wispy chiffon scarf spoke. The vision said:

'Molly said you've been a little down lately, dear. I thought we could have a spot of lunch . . .'

*

My mother finally orders – the special of Poached Salmon with Saffron Risotto. She smiles up at the waiter as if somehow he is the dish and she wants to nibble an extra special little bit of him. The waiter smiles back, the most professional smile I've seen in a long while. I can read his mind.

'Deluded old bag,' is what he's thinking, in Spanish.

Immediately, I feel bad. I'm being much too hard on my mother. Susan Cook is from a different generation, a different world. She was raised to believe in the goodly strength of men, in their constancy and ability to solve all the world's problems (she was born in Kenya, to a military father and a gin-addicted mother). To her credit, she found just such a man – Bill Cook, the steady-mannered senior accountant. She travelled with him to conferences around the world, studied cookery and languages, had two beautiful daughters exactly when she wanted to have them. If there was a plan, and knowing my mother, there was definitely a plan, it had worked out a treat. At least, until her husband died.

It's been fifteen years since Bill's death, but still I see that everything my mother does is influenced in some way by her loss. Susan Cook's desire to attract all men to her, is, I feel, an indication of my mother's fear of abandonment. She spends much of her time with one man in particular – Stanley Myers, a retired moustachioed lawyer, whom I've met, and liked, on several occasions. In many ways, I wish my mother would break free from her ridiculous notions of propriety and re-marry. But whenever I raise the issue, Susan Cook shakes her head, frowns and declares:

'There really isn't any need for that sort of talk. We're friends, nothing more.'

'So, how's life in the green pastures?' I ask hurriedly, deciding pre-emptive questioning is the best form of defence.

'Wonderful darling. Playing a bit of golf, you know.'

'How's the swing?' I smile.

'Coming along. It's all such good fun.'

My mother has taken to golf with as much passion as she can muster for something that doesn't involve Laura Ashley or recipe books. I suspect it has more to do with the fact that Stanley Myers is treasurer of Horsham Fairways Golf and Swimming Club than any particular passion for putting, but at least it gets her out of the house and doing some form of physical exercise that doesn't involve whisking eggs or handing over a credit card.

My mother starts on a lengthy monologue about her plans for Stanley's sixty-fifth birthday in four months time, chattering away about invites and marquees, and I nod, grateful to listen rather than to answer. I know that my mother has chosen her youngest daughter to off-load her concerns about the big occasion she's organizing because she thinks her youngest girl is still married and domestic, unlike her eldest child who is too nice for her own good and therefore a bit of a screw-up in the relationship department (at least when viewed from sixty-something Surrey) and is now working too hard and drinking more than is good for anyone.

'Oh, yes. I almost forgot. Stanley's asked me to accompany him on his birthday cruise. Separate cabins of course . . .'

'That's lovely Mum. Where are you going?'

'Antarctica!'

'Antarctica?'

'Yes, isn't it wonderful. I can't wait to see those lovely polar bears. I've always had a thing about polar bears, I suppose that's what comes of growing up in Kenya surrounded by all those lions . . . opposites attract.'

'Er . . . Mum, I don't think there are polar bears in Antarctica. Just penguins. Polar bears live in the Arctic.'

'No. Really? That can't be. I'm sure Stanley said there would be polar bears . . .'

'Well, maybe he's jetting some in especially.'

'Don't be facetious, Gemma Singh. It's the trip of a lifetime. I'm very lucky.'

'That you are, Mother. That you are.'

The food arrives and as we eat our salads and my mother chats away about rose bushes and the price of petrol and the scandalous misappropriation of the Chelmsley Village church hall fund by a retired Colonel of the Grenadier Guards, I find myself feeling detached and unmistakably relieved. Because it's so normal. It's as it ever has been. Evidently Molly hasn't told her about Raj. She's just meddled in her usual big sisterly way, hinting that I was feeling down and that a lunch with my mother would be just what I needed to cheer me up. And of course my mother has done what her favourite daughter suggested. They both win. Molly feels like a good sister. Susan Cook feels like a good mother.

Good mothers come up to town and buy their younger daughters lunch. Good mothers tell their younger daughters about their lives back in Surrey, so their younger daughters will feel connected to the older generation. And then good mothers ask their younger daughters one or two general questions about work (feigning enough interest to be able to move on to other queries relatively quickly), before getting to the real questions that need answering, i.e. how is the renovation progress going on the lovely town house, you lucky, lucky girl!, and when are you going to have children?

I can see Molly now, looking at her watch in the Paddington Tower and wondering when I'm going to tell our mother everything.

Well, tough shit, Molly.

I feel no compunction to fill my mother in on 'my situation'. It's as inconceivable as telling her about the first time I had sex, with Neil, when I'd been so alarmed by the large size of his cock. Or about the time, pre-Raj, when a man flashed at me in Old Street tube station. Or about the one thing that is really terrifying me.

Sitting toying with my tuna (I have no hunger, and, I feel, might never have again) I know questions about home life are coming, but I feel sure I can deal with them. I'm feeling okay.

True to the formula my mother has established over the last few years, she waits until we've finished our main courses before asking about her daughter's work. I am ready for her, sketchily describing my mini-promotion and the design for the new bar, while my mother's face flushes red with white wine and genuine excitement. It makes me feel warm to witness what is undoubtedly authentic pride emanating from her cheeks.

'That's so wonderful, darling! You really are very talented!'

'No I'm not, Mum, that's the problem,' I almost say, but instead I smile and mutter 'thanks'.

'And so, how is your dashing husband these days?'

My mother's eyes flash with hope and expectation. I sense my stomach constrict. But I can do it.

'He's fine. Busy at work.'

'Oh yes, I can imagine. A lawyer, in the City. He'll be made a partner before long, won't he darling?'

'Yes, well, I think that's the goal. He's certainly working hard for it.'

Susan Cook looks at me and ceases her fixed smile.

'Molly says he was working on a big contract . . .'

'He's busy, yes . . .'

'Is he working too hard, darling? Are you feeling left out?'

'No, Mum. It's not . . .'

'Because, you know, in every marriage there are periods of imbalance, when one has to give while the other takes . . .'

I listen to my mother's voice, which reminds me of that softly patronizing tone that so reassured me as a child, and then, despite every nerve, synapse and cell straining to maintain my detachment, I start to cry. I can't help it. And the more I cry, the more desperation I feel to stop crying, in the middle of this nice Mediterranean restaurant on a nice Wednesday lunchtime at the end of the nice month of August, with my nicer than nice mother.

'Oh darling,' declares my mother, jerking her hand into her handbag as quickly and instinctively as a Corsican fisherman snatching sardines from the sea, and whipping out a packet of Kleenex. 'What on earth is the matter?'

'Nothing,' I say. 'Nothing. I'm fine.' I take the tissue

and wipe my eyes and blow my nose and suddenly I feel so stupid for having cried, because I feel strong once again, a strength laced with anger – anger at myself for having broken down, anger at Raj for being the cause, and anger at my mother for being a woman I can never talk to about anything vital in my life.

'Are you unwell?'

'No. I told you, I'm fine,' I say, a little too forcibly. 'I'm tired, that's all.'

'Really?'

'It's quite a stressful project, Mum, at work. It's a lot of responsibility.'

'Are you sure you're feeling all right? There's not something you're not telling me, is there?'

I look at my mother. You can say what you like about her outdated views on men and summer fashions, but she's all woman when it comes to feminine intuition. She would make a fortune in the interrogation business. There'd be no need for electricity or running taps. Just my mother's Kleenex and constant verbal probing.

'No, Mum. I'm fine. I've just had a couple of late nights. Ian's staying with us . . .'

'Ian? Ian Thompson?'

'Yes, his landlord decided to sell the flat he was renting, so he's looking for somewhere else, but in the meantime he's crashing at ours . . .'

'Oh. Why isn't he staying with Molly?'

'You know how she feels about her space. And they've only been going out eight months.'

'Hmm. How does Raj feel about Ian staying in your house?'

'He's fine. Ian's my best friend. Why wouldn't he be fine?'

My mother shakes her head gently, whilst reapplying lipstick that she's plucked from her handbag shortly after the packet of Kleenex.

'It's not normal.'

'Oh Mum, please, not again. We've talked about this so many times.'

'I just don't see how a man and a woman can just be friends. Stanley thinks the same. There's always something else to it. Is he gay?'

'What?'

My mother sips wine, hurriedly.

'There, I've said it.'

'He's going out with your eldest daughter!'

'Was going out. It's over apparently, under somewhat suspicious circumstances . . .'

'Suspicious circumstances? Who are you, Miss Marple? Ian and Molly had a row, that's all . . .'

'Some men have plenty of female friends, even ones they call girlfriends . . .'

'What are you trying to say, Mother?'

'Stanley remarked the other day that you just can't tell these days, you know, who is and who isn't . . .'

'Ian's not gay, Mum! Jesus!'

'There's no need to curse, Gemma Singh!'

'He's a friend. All right? And he's not gay, not that there would be anything wrong if he was . . .'

'Did he ever try and kiss you?'

'What? No! What is wrong with you?'

'Nothing, darling. It's a perfectly innocent question. It's

just I would have thought that any normal man would have a hard time keeping his lips away from my beautiful daughter, if he spent any time with her . . .'

'Jesus, Mother, sometimes you are so medieval it makes me want to scream!'

I stand suddenly, push back my chair, pick up my handbag, stride quickly to the coat rack and snatch my coat before heading to the door. I won't, can't look back. I hear my mother call my name, once. I hear the waiter's Spanish voice asking if everything is all right, and then, finally, I hear my mother's voice declaring loudly and confidently, so the whole restaurant can hear her hypothesis, thereby absolving her from any responsibility for the scene that has just occurred:

'No, it's all fine. I'm sorry, but I think my daughter's pregnant, that's all!'

LOYALTY

When I hobble down the stairs brandishing my crutch at two in the morning, having been woken by noises from the living room, I'm surprised to see Gemma sitting on the floor, cross-legged in her pyjamas, surrounded by six or seven books with bright covers scattered like religious offerings around her. She has one book open on her lap, and appears to be reading avidly. By her left knee is a wine bottle, three-quarters empty, and a half-full glass of Rioja.

'What are you reading, Gem?'

'*Astrology and the Failing Marriage*,' she says, without looking up.

'What?'

'It's interesting. Apparently, I'm exhibiting all the characteristics of a true Capricorn. I have managed to turn my life upside down, and am swiftly regressing back into a teenage self that was never allowed to develop following my parents' divorce.'

'But your parents didn't divorce.'

'No. That's the only bit that doesn't fit. But I suppose my dad dying could help me qualify.'

I snort once and bend down to look at the other books. *Between Marriage and Divorce: A Woman's Diary.*
How to Cure Your Inner Imperfections.
Managing Stress For A Healthier Life.

Living is Tough: A Complete Guide to Understanding, Improving and Saving Your Marriage!

I grunt this time.

'You don't need these, Gem.'

'What harm can they do? I need something.'

She looks up.

'I need a map.'

We open another bottle of wine. Gemma continues to read, while I watch Argentinian football on television.

'I've been there,' I say, watching the crowds at the giant River Plate Stadium in Buenos Aires.

'So ... when are you going to get another writing assignment?' Gemma asks, skimming through *How to Cure Your Inner Imperfections*.

'I'm going to call around. Come up with a plan.'

I sit in silence for a few minutes, pretending to watch the football. I don't have the energy to come up with a plan. The most alarming thing is, when I think about getting on a plane to Argentina, or some such enticing far-flung corner of the world, I'm filled with dread. I feel as if I can't go travelling again, without Molly wanting me. They'll be able to read it in my face.

What's wrong with me? I'm a real traveller in this age of sofa-bound indolence. Yet now, for the first time in my life, I can't bear the idea of being alone in an unknown country. My strength has been sapped. My confidence shattered. My armour stripped.

I glance at Gemma as she swigs her wine.

'Should you really be drinking like that?'

She looks up, her small brow furrowed.

'Why not?'

I don't answer. Gemma takes another sip of wine.

'My mother's going to Antarctica.'

'Really? It's amazing. Good for her.'

'She's going to see the polar bears.'

'There aren't any polar bears.'

'I told her that. She wouldn't believe me.'

I laugh. Gemma takes another swig of wine.

'We had a row. I stormed out. She told everyone in the restaurant I was pregnant.'

I feel panic. It's true, as I suspected. Gemma is pregnant. My heart thumps. This means everything will change. And I don't want everything to change.

'Poor woman,' Gemma continues. 'She wants me to be just like her, the happy housewife.'

'So . . . are you pregnant?'

Gemma looks at me.

'Jesus, not you too!'

We sit in silence for a while.

Then Gemma speaks, her voice loud and more than a little drunk.

'Do you think I'm good-looking?'

'Gemma . . .'

'Come on, Ian. Play the game . . .'

'You're a stunner.'

'Do you think men will still want to shag me, even if I'm . . . ?'

'Pregnant?'

'Divorced.'

She looks away, pain on her face. I'm surprised how ugly and blatant the 'D' word sounds in this empty space.

'Don't be silly, Gem. You're gorgeous.'

She looks at me, and for a brief moment I'm terrified she's going to suggest that we have sex right here, right now, if only to prove a point. She shakes her head and waves her index finger at me.

'You, my friend, say nice things. But they aren't necessarily true.'

'Any man would give the lot to be with you.'

She looks at me, a little girl quizzing.

'How much?'

'A million quid . . . About two hundred million yen. I think you'd be very big in Japan, they like blondes.'

'Is that all?'

'All right. Ten million pounds. Plus VAT.'

She smiles. I'm relieved. She picks up the wine bottle.

'Yup. That's more like it. Gemma Cook, the ten million pound shag!'

She pours us each another drink, clinks my glass with hers.

'God, I hate this house!' she declares, with sudden violence.

I'm not too sure how we've ended up on the small balcony set into the slanted roof. At no stage did climbing up the ladder to the attic seem like a good idea, but then I ceased to have the ability to divine good ideas from bad about the time Gemma made me finish Raj's Caol Ila whisky.

Now, standing on the terrace, which appears to be missing only its most vital component – a metal rail to prevent you tumbling fifty feet to the concrete patio below, I feel sick. There's a strange quivering in my testicles – not a pleasant, sexual surge, but a fizzing discomfort. Is this vertigo, I wonder? Is it an instinctive, hard-wired fear of The Fall? My father could base a whole sermon on such a feeling of imminent obliteration.

Gemma was telling me about her plans for the house, about how she was so naive to think the renovations would bring her and Raj closer together. She threatened to go and find the plans to show me how over-ambitious and extravagant she'd been, especially with her idea to convert the loft space into a massive TV room, and then, before I knew it, we were climbing the worm-nibbled staircase to the fourth floor and then up a metal ladder (Gemma almost fell) and into the musty attic.

It was difficult with my plaster cast, but my drunkenness guided me as I crawled like a baboon across the joists, and out onto the three-foot-wide space the builders had just finished, before they stopped work to await more funds.

I have to admit, even through drink-blurred eyes, the view is pretty impressive. It's difficult to perceive from ground level, but Raleigh Street seems to rise up a small incline. From the roof level you can see out towards central London.

Beyond, the lights of the City flicker in the warm night like blue, white and red candles – the NatWest building, the shimmering dildo of the Swiss Re tower. To the left, I can just make out the ghostly white of St Paul's, and to the right the orange glow of Westminster, and the green shadows cast onto the wheel of the London Eye. It is, I think, a pretty nice view. It's not Paris or Manhattan or Hong Kong, but it's better than some. At night, London seems less sprawling, less randomly strewn.

'Nice view.'

'It should be, considering how much this stupid fucking balcony cost.'

Gemma starts to unscrew the top of the gin bottle she insisted on carrying up to the roof.

'I don't think that's a good idea,' I say sternly, placing my hand on hers.

'Fuck you, Ian Thompson, and your horse.'

Gemma smiles a wide sarcastic smile and I realize she's more drunk than I've seen her in a while. To my relief she places the bottle back on the balcony floor. She stands for a moment, perusing the London skyline.

'Why did this happen?' she asks, softly. I look at her.

'I don't know.'

'Did we do something wrong?'

I can't answer. It seems that somewhere in my alcohol-drenched thoughts, I am worried that we have done something wrong, that we have screwed up, that I've strayed too far from the path that everyone else is following. But I can't pinpoint the moment, or the action that triggered the split. And anyway, I decide, burping loudly, I'm used to being off the beaten track. It's my job.

At my side, Gemma gazes out at the darkened windows of her neighbours.

'Look at them all, sleeping so soundly. They've all complained about the work on the house. They hate us. We're too young to have a house like this, they think. We're too new. We're too . . . mixed!'

She bends down, and I wonder if she's going to be sick, but instead she picks up the gin bottle again and in one swift jerk of her forearm throws it, hard. It arches gracefully and sails earthwards, for an instant flashing with light caught from a neighbouring window, before crashing onto the concrete patio below.

'Bravo!' I say.

'Whoops,' says Gemma. Several lights come on along the row of houses, figures appearing at windows, curtains twitching.

'Hello, wonderful neighbours!' Gemma shouts, waving at the silhouettes, who vanish as swiftly as they appeared. She burps again and falls backwards into the attic.

I turn, hurriedly.

'Are you okay?'

Another burp from the shadows. Then a giggle.

'All right, Thompson. I've got a plan. You like plans, don't you?'

I reach down and she takes my hand and I pull her up, trying not to be afraid of tumbling backwards over the balcony edge. As Gemma stands, she begins to unbutton her jeans. In my blurred, dulled state, I wonder where this is going. I know I should be alarmed, but I'm too drunk and too tired to care.

'What are you doing, Gem?'

'Come on. You too.'

'Please, Gem, don't take off your trousers . . .'

But she's pulling them down, or at least trying to, as the denim struggles to make it down her thighs.

'Shit. Come on Thompson. We're going to moon the wonderful neighbours!'

I look at her.

'Come on, Ian. Be a mate. Come on . . .'

Reluctantly, I unbutton my jeans, wobbling briefly,

afraid that the plaster cast will unbalance me, but I spread my feet further, regaining control. I pull the denim down and shuffle to the centre of the balcony. We face the slanting roof, bend down, and expose our buttocks to the residents of one of the more affluent districts of east London. Gemma slaps her posterior and starts to sing.

'Blue moon . . .'

She shakes with laughter as she finishes the verse, and as she turns, her buttock flesh touches mine. It's cold, like marble.

'Oh . . .' She's reaching to pull up her jeans, but she slips and topples forward, hands out, falling against the balcony door frame, and clinging on for a moment, like a sailor in a storm. I pull up my own jeans. She stands there, legs apart, trying to balance. I try not to look at the dark shadow of pubic hair visible through her panties. She reaches down and tugs her jeans upwards.

'Wow. I think I'm really pissed.'

She sits down and then lies back in the balcony doorway, her feet reaching the end of the small terrace so her toes dangle into the black void.

'Come on Ian. Lie here. It's really, really comfortable.'

With difficulty, I shuffle back and lie down slowly by her side. The asphalted roof terrace is still warm from the day.

We stare up at the orange-glow night sky. I breathe in and out, seeking an oxygen antidote to the alcohol in my stomach. Then I hear myself asking, 'Do you ever hear from Neil?'

Gemma turns her head quizzically, suddenly more focused, more sober.

'Neil Farrelly? My Neil? Ex Neil?'

'Yeah. Do you know where he is?'

She waves her index finger, imperiously.

'No, no, no. Bad idea.'

'What if we found him? I bet we could.'

'I haven't seen him in . . . what? Ten years?'

She shakes her head again. I wait, wondering what she's thinking – is she excited by the idea, or will she accuse me of interfering once more, of trying to find solutions where none are available? I have a sudden image of Neil and Gemma, in a church, getting married. I would be best man and everyone would praise my matchmaking skills.

Gemma turns back to me.

'He's married. He's got to be.'

'We could find out.'

'How?'

'On the net. Friends Reunited, or something like that.'

Gemma burps loudly, then giggles.

'No. We shouldn't. I don't want to see Neily . . .'

'We could just look . . .'

'No, I said.'

It takes us five minutes. A site called www.oldunimates. co.uk allows us to register for free with an email address. Seconds later a password is emailed to us, we log on, then find Neil's year at Liverpool's John Moores University. And there he is. Neil Farrelly. With a short biography. It reads:

Following a couple of post-qualification years working as a vet in Canada's cattle country of Alberta, Neil returned to the UK to work in Bristol where he played a lot of rugby and lost a few more

brain cells to pints of scrumpy. He has since moved to South Coast
Vets in Brighton, where he is a partner.

Gemma is quiet.

'There's a picture. Do you want to see it?' I ask. She
doesn't reply, so I click on the icon. Neil's picture appears.
He looks older, more creased, just a little heavier in cheek
and chin. But he's smiling in a way that's familiar to me,
and, I know, to Gemma. It's a gentle, inviting smile, that
says, 'I may be six-foot-two and weigh sixteen stone, but
really I'm as soft as feathers.'

'He looks well,' I mutter.

'He looks like Neil.'

Gemma seems energized. On Google she types in
'South Coast Vets'. She clicks on the entry, the website
loads, and there's another picture of Neil Farrelly, in a
white coat, with three other vets, two men and a woman.
There's an address – and phone number.

'Do you think he's married?' Gemma whispers.

'I don't know. You'd have thought he would have
mentioned it on the uni website . . .'

'Maybe he hasn't updated it.'

'Maybe.'

She's silent once more.

'You could call him?' I suggest, quickly.

Gemma looks up at me, eyes wide, her face white and
glistening in the glow from the computer screen.

'I think I'm going to be sick.'

The next day, she returns to the house in the middle of
the afternoon, throws up in the downstairs toilet, tells me
she hates her job and that she's not going back, and that

she can't call Neil in Brighton. Just as I'm about to protest she nods her head once and says:

'I want to go there. I want to surprise him. If I see him, I'll know.'

'What will you know?'

'Everything.'

MODESTY

The day after a bad hangover is like the first day of spring. You wake feeling more refreshed than you've felt for weeks, as if all the lassitude and stress has been expelled from your body, along with your dinner. After a good fourteen hours' sleep you bounce out of bed, red wine and Chicken Tikka Masala replaced with joy and hope. At such times, you feel almost reborn. From this moment forth, you feel, you will do things differently (drink less, keep healthier, not worry about your body, men, or work).

I can't remember a post-hangover when I've felt more uplifted. Waking, clear-headed, shortly after eight, I open my eyes immediately and blink wide in the early bright sunshine. I shower, then make coffee and step outside onto the bare unfinished concrete, which is already warm under my naked feet. I feel like singing. It's a familiar, childish exhilaration, reminiscent of the joy that fills you at the beginning of school holidays. I haven't felt this happy in months.

It's as if none of the bad things happened. It's as if they have all been a bad TV dream, like Bobby in the shower in *Dallas*.

Now I have a plan. It's Saturday morning, the first of September, and I'm going to Brighton to see Neil. I'll meet him, and in the first few words we exchange, I will know everything. I will know my future.

The doorbell rings. I open the door, expecting the

postman. Molly stands there. Behind her is her new 5 Series BMW, bought with last Christmas's bonus.

'Hi.'

She looks tired. She's wearing a pretty black skirt and sleeveless T-shirt. I smile at her.

'Is . . . er . . . is Ian around?'

'I don't think he's up yet.'

'Oh.'

Molly looks flustered. I wonder about waking Ian and acting as a peacebroker in the Kofi Annan mould. Then an idea flashes brightly in my head.

'Have you plans for today?'

Molly shakes her head, looking puzzled.

'Well, you could talk to him on the way down to Brighton.'

It's perfect. If Molly drives us to Brighton, she and Ian will be stuck in the car together and will be forced to be civil, in deference to me and my potentially life-changing quest. And having the tension of their fractured relationship around me will help take my mind off my meeting with Neil.

'Brighton?'

'We're going to find Neil. Neil Farrelly.'

Molly looks confused, which is an expression I enjoy witnessing on my elder sister's face. At that moment, Ian appears in the doorway.

'Molly?'

I turn to my best friend with a big smile.

'Molly's driving us to Brighton. Won't this be fun?'

Nobody talks for the first hour, which suits me just fine. My heart is beating so loudly I'm amazed Molly and Ian can't hear it. Then the fear returns, the steel slice of doubt. I have to remind myself – the reality of my situation is complex and painful. It won't be easy or smooth. There's so much that needs to be untied.

I stare out of the passenger side window, at the people for whom this is just another Saturday. I look at the south London mothers with their children and wonder how they manage to look so normal, so in control, holding hands, scolding, shouting, laughing. How did they get to such a place in their lives, moving beyond the uncertainty of initial attraction, past the decision to commit to another person with secrets and troubles as yet uncharted, and through the insistent battles between personal ambition and relationship sacrifice? They seem so foreign, these smiling ladies with their scampering children, with thoughts, needs and rituals as alien to my own as those of Chinese hill-tribe women or Kenyan farmers.

It's then, somewhere on the A23 between Brixton and Croydon, that Raj's face appears. I wasn't thinking about him or my marriage, I was simply surveying the passers-by, trying to analyse and understand them. But he appears behind my eyes, inspecting me with a deep brown gaze that exudes confusion and hurt.

Poor Raj. He doesn't deserve this. He didn't ask for it. If he knew I was going to Brighton to see Neil Farrelly he would divorce me on the spot. Perhaps he'd do worse, striking me or hurling me to my death. Not that Raj has the temperament for such heartfelt violence. His aggression is purely passive – silence over shouting, withdrawal over surging advance.

He doesn't have the passion.

He's too controlled.

We turn onto the motorway after Croydon, and still Ian and Molly are silent. Ian has been staring out of the left-hand window for the entire journey. I wonder if he hates me for inviting Molly along.

But I can't help them. I'm separate, I have to lose myself in the hum of the tyres and the way the sun glints off the wing mirror. I put on my sunglasses. I have to prepare.

I imagine Neil's wide-eyed reaction when he sees me, his stammering greeting. We will go for a drink, the words will pour out as quickly as our thoughts. At some stage, an hour or so into our meeting, he will slide his hand across the table and take mine. He will suggest a drive up to the Sussex Downs, where we will stroll hand-in-hand. He will kiss me in the sunshine. I will feel electrified and calmed in the same moment. Perhaps we will book into a small hotel, hidden in the hills. Perhaps I will call in sick on Monday morning. Perhaps I will give up London and move to Brighton, for ever. Perhaps, in the mighty arms of the Scottish vet, I will recover and never feel pain again.

Then I see the first signpost to Brighton and feel breathless, then sick. My thoughts turn, the coin spun. Suddenly, I know that Neil will have difficulty even recognizing me after eight years. It will be so embarrassing, I will have to remind him who I am, blushing red, only for him to inform me, coldly, that he's blissfully married, with children on the way.

Suddenly, the plan that seemed so exciting, so novel and dangerously mature, seems tawdry and foolishly childish.

Brighton is so unoriginal. If this were one of the romance novels I used to read, I would groan at the heroine heading to the south-coast resort, renowned for a century or more as the English capital of 'The Dirty Weekend'. It's to Brighton that all Londoners head to embark on crude affairs with people they've met in offices, supermarket aisles or suburban health clubs, a place of shabby one-night stands and smelly guest-houses with sheets that are boiled every morning.

Am I a bad person? I never thought so in the past, despite my mother's insinuations. In fact I've been long convinced of my unique inherent decency, which, I realize now, has left me bordering on smugness. Perhaps this is how bad people live with themselves. They never see their own cruelty.

I wonder if I can ask Molly to keep driving on, past Brighton, keep driving along the southern coast of England until we get to the end, wherever that is, Cornwall, perhaps, and I can run from the car into the waves. All at once I want to flee; that's the word, isn't it, with its connotations of haste and lack of preparation? Flee like a refugee, taking nothing, destination unknown, simply moving because I need to escape from where I am.

I try to force myself to look at the countryside, the speeding green of hills and woods. England seems so spacious outside London. I wonder whether the capital, which I've not left for almost an entire year, is not really England at all. Perhaps it's a different country altogether. These white chalk hills and fields dotted with sheep are as distant to my everyday Hackney life as paddy fields or coconut palms. They're something I see on television.

Thinking about the hills and the sheep leads me to unpleasant memories from yesterday. Duncan Archer is a self-professed lover of the English countryside, and often exhorts his staff to take weekend trips out of London to see the 'great open spaces' which he feels influence so much of the country's urban architecture (no one does except the interns, who still believe, naively, that emulation might lead to promotion).

I don't know why I shouted at him. It was as if whatever is inside me is seeking my destruction on every level.

It happened so swiftly. He sidled up to me, reeking of deodorant and cigarettes, and asked whether the revised drawings would be ready by Monday at ten, because he wanted an hour or so to review the project before the lunchtime client meeting. Then he placed his hand on my arm, and I turned and pushed him away, screaming that he had no idea how hard I'd been working, that he was out of touch with his project managers, that there was a complete lack of respect for junior staff in an office that professed to promote equality and the sharing of ideas, and that he was a lecherous, pompous, deluded old bastard!

To be fair to the KPSG department head, he remained stoic-faced throughout the tirade. When I finished, my hands shaking, my face shining crimson, he nodded slowly, tugged his left earlobe and said, 'You look exhausted, Gemma, why don't you take the rest of the day off . . .'

He said it so softly, so sincerely, that I nodded, picked up my things and departed, feeling Sophie's victorious stare as I headed for the door.

As the BMW purrs to a stop at some traffic lights, I wish suddenly that I'd travelled to Brighton on my own.

I don't want anyone to witness my failure. I don't want Molly's covert satisfaction and Ian's over-attentive compassion when I fall short.

I feel stiflingly hot. I push the button to open the windows.

'Leave it! The air conditioning is on!' barks my sister, speaking for the first time in what seems like hours. This makes me push the button harder. All four windows speed swiftly downwards in a whir of German technology, and the car is filled suddenly with fat bursts of wind. In an instant, the map print-out that's been lying on Ian's lap is tugged from him. It shoots through the window and away.

'Shit!' Ian shouts, his hands pawing at empty air. 'The map!'

I glimpse the papers pirouetting like leaves over the car roofs behind us. It's a strangely beautiful sight.

'Shut the window!' hisses Molly.

'Sorry . . .' I mutter, and the apology seems to be for everything I have ever done.

'What are we going to do now?' Ian asks, and there's something in his tone, a whining, that irritates me. 'We don't have a map.'

'Why did you have it on your lap?' I ask angrily. 'It's not like we're even anywhere near Brighton!'

Ian doesn't reply, and we drive on in silence, each listening to the hum of the wheels on the newly asphalted road.

My first impressions of Brighton are not favourable. It seems to live up to my expectations of seediness. The outskirts are dominated by dull lines of Edwardian semis with net curtains, and sad little public parks with brick box lavatories splattered with graffiti, where old men walk old dogs. As we near the centre, the houses become shabbier, with broken windows and blankets where curtains should be, where numerous homeless people loiter in the sunnier doorways. In upper windows, figures lurk behind uneven blinds, no doubt making low-budget porn films on second-hand video cameras.

I want to plead with Molly and Ian to turn around and return to London. In two hours we could be home. I try to find the right words, the right tone in my head to convince them, and then, just as I'm about to turn and declare that it has all been a bad idea, and we have to go back home, Molly slams on the brakes and declares, 'There it is!', as if she's just discovered Tutankhamen's tomb.

It's a blur. We walk into the reception of South Coast Vets and Molly asks for Neil Farrelly. The receptionist looks up, gives us the once over, smiles and informs us that Mr Farrelly is out on his Saturday morning house calls but will be back after lunch. She inquires whether another vet might help, and Molly smiles like a big sister and explains that Neil is an old university friend and it would be great if our visit could be kept a surprise, until we return after two. The receptionist looks us up and down one more time, evidently amassing enough evidence to believe in our authenticity, and agrees that she won't say a word.

'Were you, er, close friends?' she asks, with a raised eyebrow. I look away. Molly glances at me and says:

'Close enough.'

The pub is surprisingly smoky considering it's only lunchtime, populated by old men and peroxided women in tracksuits. Outside, the late summer sun bakes the beaches and people are swimming in the English Channel without a shiver, but inside the bar, a fog of nicotine obscures time and climate.

Ian and Molly are not talking. Ian offers to buy drinks. Molly mutters 'diet coke' and I order a tomato juice, then change my mind and ask for a Bloody Mary. The palms of my hands are damp with sweat. Neil is married, I'm sure. He's the sort of man who would have sought out marriage like a woman, who would have craved the stability and compassion of married life. He likes to take care of things, whether people or animals. And he believes in the power of rings – he wore a signet that had once belonged to his great-grandfather. Whenever we talked about weddings, he'd always say that he would love his future wife to wear his grandmother's emerald engagement ring, as a symbol of the eternal power of love. I was thrilled by this idea, that a ring could connect the past to the present and the future. I pictured its sparkle, its smooth interior, polished by years of loving wear. I've seen it, felt it on my own finger.

I picture the ring now, on the finger of a tall redheaded woman, which is how I imagine Neil's wife. She's Scottish too, I think, with a pretty smile and pale freckled skin. They've been married two years, and are thinking about having children soon, although Neil is more keen on this idea than his wife. It surprises me how clear this image is. I wonder whether I want Neil to be married, so that I can forget all about him and return to the familiar country of east London where I can hide away for ever.

I wonder about calling Raj. I hate myself for thinking this, but I can't help it. It's my habit, learned over almost three years of knowing him. When things are bad, I call him, and if he has a moment he gives me a short lecture on how I have to put things in perspective, to get through the day, because tomorrow will be better.

I imagine he'd have a lot to say in this instance. When he came back down off the ceiling.

'Look, I don't think this is such a good idea . . .' I say falteringly, twisting my wedding ring round and round my finger. My sister frowns – a look that suggests she's been waiting for this moment. But she doesn't interject. Ian is silent, almost as if he's sulking in my sister's presence. I continue, 'I mean . . . he wasn't there. Maybe it's a sign. I'm not sure if I can . . .'

Molly puts a hand on my hand. My sister's palm is hot and soft. She was always a hot child, I remember. I used to cuddle up to her in the tent when we were little, instinctively seeking out her hand to hold against the darkness and chill of the Brittany night.

Molly does not speak for a moment, and I wonder if I should pull my hand away. But it is soothing to have my sister gently clasping my fingers.

'You know, Gem, I couldn't have done what you did, telling Raj what you really felt, even though God knows I should have done . . .' My sister's voice is quiet and measured. 'I couldn't be doing this now. I really admire you. You don't know how it's going to work out, but you know, deep down, that you have to give it a go.'

Molly releases my hand. I look at her. Somewhere behind me, a fruit machine jingles and coins spit into the metal bucket. I nod, slowly.

*

The receptionist seems pleased to see us.

'He's just with a client. I'll ask him to come out when he's finished.' Then she adds, with a grin and stage whisper, 'I'll tell him he needs to sign a drugs order.'

We sit in the uncomfortable plastic orange chairs and I want to be sick, or to scream, or to sleep, or to smash my fist through the glass door of the surgery. Molly and Ian sit there in stony silence. Suddenly, this seems like the very worst idea I have ever had, but it's impossible to move. I feel heavy and slow, as if in a dream where forces beyond my influence are controlling me. I want to pee, so I stand and ask the receptionist, who points to the glass doors, first on the left. As I step through the doors, looking for the toilet sign, I have a sudden urge to take off my wedding ring, so I pause and tug at it, desperate to rip it off, and a large figure steps into the narrow corridor. It's Neil. I stop, my finger on my ring. He stops. My heart stops.

'Jesus,' he says, his voice deeper and less Scottish than I remember it.

We stand there, silent, as if playing a childish game of statues. Minutes seem to pass. Then he puts his large hand to his dark curly hair and says, softly:

'Gemma Cook. What the hell are you doing here?'

NAUGHTINESS

At least Gemma seems to be having fun. As far as I can see over the large quiffs of six gay Elvis Presleys. There are probably close to fifty homosexual Elvis impersonators scattered throughout the large bar, along with their supporters, many of whom are sporting dazzling Priscilla Presley blonde wigs and sequin dresses. Brighton's one-and-only 'Gay Elvis Night', so Vincent the compere informed us, regularly brings in camp Kings from as far away as Winchester.

The Junction is a modern wood-floored place, dressed in creams and browns, which, despite its name, is the very antithesis of the way stations I appreciate, seeking as it does to make you feel at home (gas flame fire, comfy sofas, magazines) rather than alone and transient. It looks like any number of bars I've been to in the world's major cities over the past five years, from the shining pewter bar counter to the gaudy chandelier hung over the lounge area.

At least the Gay Elvis night is original. I'm no fan of the King of Rock and Roll, but you have to admire the dedication and ambition of the Elvis impersonators who've spangled and greased their way to Brighton town centre on this warm Saturday evening.

Neil chuckled when we saw the sign – 'Welcome Kings and Queens!'

He paused, smiling gently, and said:

'Well, we could go elsewhere, there's plenty of other places . . .' but Gemma was adamant that she liked the look of the place, and that a Gay Elvis Night in Brighton was top of her list of things to do before she died. Neil chuckled once more, touching her hand as they walked into the pub.

Now Gemma and Neil are sitting together across from the bar, Gemma in the burgundy leather booth, Neil opposite her on a small bar stool that seems to accentuate his large, implacable size. As far as I can tell, they've slipped back into the bantering I recall from their year together, leaning close, smiling and nodding.

It's remarkable, I think to myself, how reminiscent this is of the past – the raucous pub, sipping my pint of Guinness with Neil and Gemma deep in conversation at a table, and Molly and myself standing awkwardly at the bar. It's as if ten years have never happened. Rather than feeling reassured, this thought dismays me. I'm thirty-one years old. Have I not moved on?

I turn to Molly but she is studiously watching 'Malcolm from Hove' belt out 'Suspicious Minds' on the small stage. We haven't said a word to each other for almost ten hours since Molly pulled up in her fancy BMW. I try to think of a line to break the silence, but can't come up with anything after 'So, Molly . . .'

The sudden, familiar pang of loneliness stabs my lungs, like the niggling of an old injury in cold weather. I know I want to drink a lot tonight, and that drinking a lot will most likely lead me into melancholic self-pity, but I don't care. Self-pity is one of the few pleasures left to me.

'They seem to be getting on well,' says Molly, suddenly.

I glance at her. She smiles, briefly. To my surprise, I feel instantly better. I wonder, in this moment, whether women experience such a phenomenon, whereby a simple smile from an attractive man can obliterate all negative feelings as instantly and conclusively as an atom bomb. It's unlikely. Women are not that gullible.

I try to feel stronger.

'Fancy another drink?' I venture, softly.

'Go on then. Another vodka tonic.'

A slim Elvis in a red wig and sweat streaking down his foundation swaggers to the bar by our side and leans forwards, close to Molly.

'Priscilla darling, you look absolutely radiant tonight,' he croons, in a terrible American accent.

'Why, thank you Mr Presley. You appear somewhat slimmer than the last time I saw you,' she counters, with a large smile.

'Well darling,' says the bean-pole Elvis, reverting to a Liverpudlian twang, 'I've taken up shagging men. Keeps you trim!'

They laugh. I can't help smiling. Molly seems to have blatant knack for socializing with anyone – the very opposite of my own particular ability for detachment. Molly starts telling Jason from Newhaven the story of her sister and Neil. I listen to her exuberant explanation, trying to remain immune to her bubbling enthusiasm, the way she trips over words and repeats herself with cheerful insouciance, unlike my habitual focused, direct dictation. As I glance at Molly, telling her sister's story, I notice the small creases of crow's feet at the sides of her brown eyes, that I've loved ever since I met her in Gemma's first year at university.

'And now they're here, face to face for the first time in ten years!' Molly concludes with a flourish.

'Very Danielle Steele. I love it! What do you think they're talking about?'

Molly and Jason strain to hear words from the burgundy booth, but the music is too loud. I listen too. After a moment, Jason stands to his full height of five-feet-six in his platform heels and declares:

'I shall go and spy! My mama was in the KGB!'

'Elvis . . .' Molly rebukes him sternly, but it's too late – Jason is away to position himself by the booth with his vodka and Red Bull, pretending to stare intently at the stage where a large man with gold lamé flares and a naked chest adorned with a large medallion is launching into 'Hound Dog' to whoops of acclaim and ridicule.

I am uncomfortable. Listening in on Gemma and Neil's conversation seems like a betrayal of my best friend. As I gulp my pint, I wonder if I'm getting side-tracked, as I sometimes do, by my own thoughts. I need to re-focus on Gemma. After all, I'm here to help her. Molly seems less concerned about her younger sister, treating this excursion as a game, a jaunt. I wonder at the levels of jealousy and rivalry between them; emotions that I, the siblingless child, can merely guess at.

I'm not going to follow Molly's lead. I must be separate, objective – Gemma's best friend, looking out for her. I wonder about walking over and asking Jason to stop his covert surveillance, but I know this will seem prudish, and a part of me can't bear the idea of Molly thinking me uncool. At that moment, Jason returns to the bar.

'So?' inquires Molly, with a wry smile.

'In the proverbial Gucci darling,' states Jason, conspiratorially. 'They're talking about kitchens, like an old married couple. It's scary but true . . .'

'They haven't seen each other in ten years!' I say, gruffly. 'So what if they're talking about kitchens?'

Jason puts his hands on his hips.

'Well now, Mr Defensive! Anyone would think you were jealous of the bulky Scot!'

Molly laughs, a little too quickly, I think.

'Or maybe it's the lady you envy? Do you fancy a bit of Aberdeen Angus yourself, hey, Bigfoot?'

I lower my voice, trying to keep my cool. My toes itch at the end of my plaster cast.

'We should just let them get on with it . . .'

'Suit yourself. I'm off to create my own perfect love story.'

Jason downs the last of his drink and turns on his heels, flouncing away towards the dance floor.

'You didn't need to be like that,' says Molly, pointedly. 'He was just having a laugh.'

I don't answer. I stand, trying to think of a suitable rejoinder that would put Molly in her place, without resorting to a string of expletives. Neil laughs, leans across the table and whispers into Gemma's ear. Then he stands and turns to walk to the toilets. When he disappears through the door marked *Caballeros*, Gemma looks around, eyes wide, seeking us out, and Molly rushes to the booth. I follow, pushing on my single crutch, careful not to slip on the beer-stained floor.

'So?'

Gemma's face is flushed with red wine and elation.

'It's amazing. He's not married. He was seeing this woman, but they broke up six weeks ago. Can you believe it? He's thinking of going back to Canada to work. Oh God, this is so weird.'

An hour later I'm drunk. The pub is merrily riotous now – men with arms around each other, several pairs kissing. It's a happy, exuberant atmosphere that reminds me of children's birthday parties when I was young, with that same over-excited sense of fun, the same use of coloured lights and silver streamers and sparkling costumes, but without the bawdy hand gestures, men French-kissing other men and taking off their shirts to expose shaved chests and pierced nipples.

To my surprise, Molly asks if I would like a drink. I accept, a little too quickly, perhaps.

She buys our drinks as the latest Elvis finishes on stage. I look at my watch. It's 10.30 p.m. Suddenly I realize that after six vodka tonics Molly can't drive. We will have to stay in Brighton. We should get organized.

'Look, maybe we should be looking for somewhere to stay.'

Molly puts down her glass.

'Chill out, Ian. We'll figure something when the time comes . . .'

'But we should at least know where we're going to stay, you can't drive, you're way over the limit . . .'

'Yes. Thank you. I do realize that.'

She turns away, looking back at the stage where Jason is now standing, twirling the microphone. My stomach constricts with anger once more. We don't talk for several minutes, as Jason massacres 'Love Me Tender', gyrating energetically, to general acclaim.

'Wow. That's quite frightening,' says Molly eventually, in a tone that invites a rapprochement.

'I don't know,' I reply. 'It's strangely reminiscent of Nicolas Cage at the end of *Wild At Heart*.'

Molly turns to me, and at that moment her eyes are the most beautiful I've ever seen them.

'Oh, I love that film. It's so sexy, that actress . . . what's her name?'

'Laura Dern?'

'Yes, her, she's just so dirty . . .'

The way she says this word sends a thrill through my abdomen. My penis stirs.

As the bell rings for last orders, and Neil goes to the toilets once more – thereby proving that big men don't necessarily have big bladders – Gemma steps up, breathlessly.

'Look, I know this is kind of weird, but he wants to go on somewhere for a drink, and . . . well . . .'

Molly smiles.

'We can look after ourselves. Don't worry.'

'Really? I just think, I don't know, maybe it'd be good for us to have some quiet time, just the two of us . . .'

'It's going well?' I ask.

Gemma blushes once more.

'It's . . . good. Comfortable. Look, I've got my mobile, I'll give you a call.'

'We'll be fine,' says Molly, and I know that this is a tone she's used with her younger sister since childhood. 'You go and have fun.'

*

The air by the beach is colder. It's just stopped raining, and the bitter odour of wet asphalt mixes with the fresh rankness of the sea. I walk with Molly along the wide promenade above the shingle in silence. Several couples are also stumbling along the nocturnal wall, arms entwined, lurching occasionally to kiss or fumble. The hush of the sea is the rhythm of gentle yearning, back and forth across the pebbles.

'I want to see the sea,' declares Molly, with her usual vigour.

I hold out my crutches.

'Sorry, not too good at beaches.'

'Oh. Right. Yeah.'

'We could go on the pier?'

Molly looks at me. She nods, once.

'Okay.'

I know I'm wasted, but I have to admit that, at this particular juncture, with my plan for Gemma and Neil progressing nicely, and Molly seeming to soften, I feel surprisingly upbeat. I know I should be asking her again whether she slept with Will Masterson, but somehow, having her here at my side, I don't care any more. At the back of my mind I've made a deal with myself. If Molly will sleep with me tonight, it will be proof that she didn't have sex with her ex-husband, and I will forgive her and never think about it again.

It is, I'll admit, a very male bargain.

We walk on to the pier. The lights seem brighter, the sea louder, my body lighter. I want to put my hands on her thin white arms and lean down and kiss her hard, but I know that timing is everything. She starts to talk, almost to herself, a story about her childhood, as she stares out at the black oily sea. I try to listen, but all I can do is picture a moment in the following few minutes when I might be able to grasp her and crush her beautiful red lips against mine. I wonder if I should interrupt her under some pretext, say something that will melt her heart, and step up to claim my prize. Or just take her here against the cold metal rail. I nod and interject sounds of interest while she continues:

'I loved piers when I was little. We went to Clacton one year, I've no idea why, it was far too down-market for Mum, maybe it was Dad's idea, the old closet leftie that he was . . .'

I chuckle, and when she's finished her unassuming anecdote, we stand in silence, barely apart. The waves push and release. Once more, I imagine taking her in my arms, brutally, and kissing her again and again. Would she scream? Slap me? Or return my ardour like in a Hollywood movie?

'This is Brighton, not LA,' the voice in my head informs me, a voice which sounds not unlike Gemma's.

'Look . . . you were right,' Molly says suddenly, interrupting my planning. 'It's getting late. We should go and find somewhere to stay.'

She turns to me.

'I'm sorry about . . . you know. Will. I should have told you about meeting him earlier. I've just been so confused . . .'

'It's okay . . .' I lie.

She shakes her head in self-admonishment, a gesture I recognize from her younger sister.

'People think I'm this happy-go-lucky chick, but I'm not. I'm not that girl . . .'

She stops. Suddenly, she seems about to cry.

'The truth is, I don't know what I'm doing most of the time. I worry so much. I have to plan everything, secretly, so I feel in control, so I can appear impulsive . . .'

She glances at me. I nod for her to continue.

'The shrink said that I reacted to my father's death by becoming fixated on taking control. She said that was one reason my marriage failed, I could never just let things be . . .'

Her voice wavers. She takes a quick gulp of air.

'So I've been trying to . . . you know . . . let things be . . . and then Will called and . . .'

There are tears in her eyes. This is not the Molly I know. I'm a little shocked by how swiftly she's been transformed from an ebullient, forthright chatterbox into a thin, tearful trembling woman. I begin to wonder at the depth of emotion she's been containing, the residual pain that won't dissolve away. During the eight months we've been dating, we haven't talked about her divorce. To be honest, I haven't really thought about it.

Molly's lower lip trembles, and in that instant I see her as a teenage girl, trying to be strong in the face of her father's sudden death. I want to kiss her more than ever. And at once I have a revelation, a Damascene moment, that I can be there for her, like I've been there for Gemma – the head of the escape committee, tunnelling under prison walls.

I try to shuffle towards her, to bring myself within distance of her arms, but my leg is so heavy and awkward that

I feel like some nineteenth-century monster about to assault the beautiful heroine on the pier by the crashing sea. She looks at me. I hesitate. She steps to one side, gazing beyond towards the shimmering lights of the promenade.

'I'm cold. Come on. Let's go and get organized.'

The first two Bed and Breakfasts we try are full, and Molly starts to worry. As she becomes more concerned about where we are going to stay, I become increasingly fascinated at the change in her – she seems far from the cool *über-babe* I have always seen her as. It's empowering, seeing someone you've always felt a little intimidated by showing human weakness.

I feel like singing.

The third B&B, The Admiralty, is run by a middle-aged man with an earring and bleached blonde hair. He has just one room left, he says, with twin beds, the best room in the house. He looks from Molly to me, as if seeking an instant and complete history of our lives, and Molly nods and says, 'Great, we'll take it.'

The room is minimalist, but clean, with old-fashioned floorboards painted shining white. There's a small shower room which seems new and the towels are soft. It's not the Paris Ritz, but it's pretty nice. And affordable. I close the door behind us. Molly sits down on the bed.

'Do you think we should call Gemma?' she asks, before I can say anything.

'I don't know.'

'She'd call us if she needed to, wouldn't she?'

I nod, warmly pleased that she's deferring to my greater Gemma knowledge.

'Yeah. Of course. I bet she's just having fun . . .'

I sit down on the other bed nearest the door, facing her. The mattress sags suggestively. Our knees almost touch. I stretch out my plaster limb and wriggle my toes.

'Cold?' she asks.

'A little. You?'

She doesn't reply.

'Can I sit next to you?' I hear myself asking, like a child on the first day at school. She says nothing. I wonder if she can hear my heart pounding.

I stand slowly, as if stepping forth into some formal dance. I take one step towards her, turn and sit down beside her. Except that as I plant my plaster foot, the heel slips on the shiny white floorboard, my posterior misses its target, and I slice down the side of the bed until I hit the floor, thump, and sprawl at her feet.

'Shit!' I exhale.

'Are you okay?' she exclaims. I look up and from my horizontal position I can smell the leather of her boots.

'Shit, I'm so fucking clumsy . . .' I grin and reach up and rapidly take hold of her arms, pulling her down towards me. She does not resist. I kiss her. It's short, and sharp, and hot. She pulls away, about to say something but I reach up and grasp the back of her neck, kissing her throat and cheeks, and she doesn't protest. We turn on the floor, our bodies jammed against opposite beds, shoulders against the floor and I know my plaster foot is stuck under one of the beds but I can't tell which one and I don't care, I'll tear it off if I have to. We kiss again and my head is swimming, I feel suddenly drunk, and I press my face against hers, my tongue seeking to part her lips. Her hands push on my stomach, underneath my shirt, and then they're flickering up my naked chest, tiny hot wings beating.

'Ohhh . . .' I groan, and it seems too guttural and rude, but I'm hot, all heat, on fire, I need her to keep me burning, have to, must, must, must . . . My hand grasps hungrily at the back of her small thin neck and I pull her lips towards my face again and her hips push into me, instinctively seeking a mould, a fit, a home, her hard flat belly against my hardened penis.

'Ohhh . . .' I groan a second time, her soft hair dancing into my face, and in that moment Molly's mouth is hot against me.

'Ian . . .'

'Molly, yes . . .'

I reach down the back of her skirt seeking flesh, at the same time opening my mouth and kissing the curls of her hair and suddenly she yelps and pushes off me, bounding like a spring.

'What?'

'What the hell is that?'

'What is what?'

'Something in your pocket! It really hurt!' She pulls up her shirt, rubbing her hip bone, and I marvel at her pottery-white skin and the red blemish, in the centre of which is a tiny prick of blood. Molly puts her hand to her chest, her eyes wide.

'Oohh . . .' she mumbles. It doesn't sound good.

'Oh, shit . . .' I mutter, reaching down and foraging into my jacket pocket, snatching out the yellow tube the size of a thick marker pen. Sure enough, at the grey end where the plastic tapers is the tiny tip of a needle.

'My epi-pen. For my nut allergy. I hadn't put the top on properly.'

'What? It stabbed me?'

'Er . . . yeah. You just got a shot of adrenalin.'

Her face is wide with angry fear.

'I don't feel good . . .'

Her hands are fluttering, her eyes white and wide, her cheeks drained of colour.

'Look, it's all right . . .'

'Oh God, my heart is racing . . .'

Now I'm angry, my neck and face burning red. God-damn it! Bloody fucking hell! Why? Why, why, why?

'Look, lie down. It's just adrenalin, your heart will beat a bit faster for a while, then you'll be fine. Just try and breathe normally . . .'

She looks at me, her pretty face an ugly twist.

'What the hell were you thinking? You stabbed me!'

'It's for my allergy. Look, just lie down . . .'

'I don't want to lie down! God, my heart, it's hammering . . .'

'Try and be calm . . .'

'BE CALM?'

'I'm just trying to help . . .'

She turns, snatches up her bag and goes to the door.

'Where are you going?'

Molly turns and glares at me.

'TO THE FUCKING HOSPITAL!'

'I'll come with you!'

'Piss off, Ian!'

In an instant the door slams shut and she is gone. I hobble to the landing as the front door closes. I'll never catch her. I turn, in despair, and realize that I'm now locked out of the room.

Bollocks.

Opacity

I lie on the bed watching the shadows on the bare wall opposite. I wish now I'd accepted Neil's offer of pyjamas. I am cold and naked in my underwear and T-shirt, my arms and legs alive with goose bumps. A car passes, the flash of headlights like a searchlight sweeping. I feel alone, in a foreign country, where the beds are large and made of pine, with wooden balls crowning the bedposts like trophies, and the mattresses are lumpy and the sheets don't match, and strange, jagged silhouettes tip-toe up the woodchip wall.

What am I doing?

I'd expected everything to be clear. Standing there, frozen in the corridor of the South Coast Veterinary Practice like a rabbit about to be neutered, I'd waited for it to hit me. But there had been no lightbulb flash of certainty, no shattering realization.

Instead I'd felt a surge of attraction that I'd not felt since teenage years, followed by instant guilt and self-loathing. I was happy and furious and hugely sad. I felt like fainting. None of them exactly diamond-cut emotions.

After leaving Ian and my sister at the pub, we went for another drink in a city centre club, not a fancy place, but the sort of student hangout we used to frequent, where I felt older than the other drinkers. I enjoyed being led, not knowing where I was going for the first time in years.

At the bar we continued to talk and reminisce, and I remembered things about Neil that had been lost – his laugh, his habit of scratching his nose, the way he said 'don't you think?' at the end of every statement. These things made me feel secure, at least while we talked and drank.

I liked him still, that was sure. He was funny – he told a story about a colleague who'd tried to put down an old lady's budgie quietly by breaking its neck while she was in the kitchen making tea, only for the budgie's head to fly off under the television, out of his reach. He was gentle – he nodded and did not speak while I recounted a short and highly edited version of my break-up with my husband. And he was strong – he went to the bar each time, and people parted to make space and he was served almost immediately, which never, ever happened to Raj Singh, not since that first time I met him, at the bar in Hoxton.

Yet, as time passed, the clock on the wall flicking towards 1 a.m., I found that I liked myself less. Every anecdote I told seemed forced, I tried to make jokes, to be light, and Neil laughed each time, but I knew he was just being encouraging, sensing my discomfort. I heard myself say things that sounded like another person, like 'whoopee' and 'fantastic' and 'shoulder-to-shoulder'. It was as if I were watching a younger, more naive, clumsy Gemma make a great fat fool of herself.

At least Neil saved me each time I sensed panic rising, by saying something or making a joke that quelled my anxiety. At such moments, I had to admit, amongst the fear and the guilt, there were pangs of desire. I wondered, as he stood at the bar ordering our last drinks, whether I could just throw caution and my knickers to the wind. I wondered if I could let him fuck me. The sound of the word excited me. It was one I never used when thinking about Raj.

Yet when we walked from the club, out into the rain, and I heard the drunken shouts of Saturday night revellers and police sirens, and saw the takeaway boxes and vomit and a small pile of dog crap sitting insolently in the middle of the pavement, I felt irredeemably . . . dirty. It was a word that disgusted me.

We stood for a few moments in silence. Then Neil said, 'Maybe you should call your sister?' and I said, 'Yes, you're right.'

So I took out my phone and called Molly's number but there was no reply. I left a message. I called Ian, but similarly got through to voicemail.

'The bastards. I wonder if they're shagging?'

Neil laughed, a little too loudly.

'Do you think so?'

'I wouldn't put it past my sister. She screws her ex-husband while Ian's away, then decides she likes Ian after all. She never knows what she wants.'

'Really?'

I didn't answer, aware that I had only said this about my sister because I was feeling so dubious about myself. Then I started to cry.

He did not hesitate. He put his arms around me, and they were big and thick and strong and I wanted him to crush me, to squeeze until I felt my ribcage crack, keep squeezing until he crushed my lungs, my liver, my heart, my breasts.

'Tighter,' I whispered. But he didn't hear me.

'Come on,' he said. 'Let's head back to mine. I'll make us some coffee and you can try your sister again.'

I wondered as we entered the 1930s-style house a ten-minute cab ride from the city centre whether Neil was as innocent as I'd chosen to believe. I'd followed him so easily, so unconsciously. But I continued to believe in him, even if I no longer believed in myself.

We drank coffee (instant, but I needed the caffeine and the heat scorching my fingers) and I called my sister and Ian once more. Still the voicemails.

There was silence. A clock ticking somewhere.

'It's great to see you again, Gem,' said Neil softly.

I looked up and he was smiling again, gently.

'Yeah. You too.'

'Look, I don't know what brought you down here, but I think . . . maybe it's fate, you know, I was planning to go to Canada and . . .'

I nodded, although I was surprised at the way his words made me feel. Anxious. Fearful. Desperate to be elsewhere at an earlier stage in my life when I could have done everything differently. He looked down.

'But . . .'

I stopped nodding.

'What?'

'Look, it's great to see you . . . but . . . I think we should just start to get to know each other again . . . take it slowly. I mean, you've obviously got things to sort out back in London . . .'

'My marriage?'

'To put it bluntly.'

'Why don't I worry about my marriage, Neil?'

He looked away. I realized I was turning the ring on my finger, round and round, a newfound habit.

'Yeah, sorry.'

I started to cry again, wiping my eyes. When he came closer I stood from the kitchen chair, trying to be strong.

'I'm okay . . . thanks . . .'

I blew my nose on a piece of kitchen paper – not very sexy, I know, but I was beyond caring.

'You're right, Neil. I'm sorry. This must be really weird for you. I had no right to turn up like that. I should have called, or emailed or something. I just don't really know what I'm doing at all at the moment.'

When he said goodnight on the landing between the two bedrooms, he leaned down and kissed my cheek. His lips were warm. I wondered, in that moment, if I could tell him everything. He was a vet, after all. But then he turned in to his room and shut the door softly behind him. The moment was gone.

I lie in the bed. The clock blinks 4.30 a.m. My head hurts. I stare at the tea-coloured 1970s woodchip on the ceiling, wondering why, if he's lived here for three years, he still hasn't managed to strip the horrible wallpaper?

Do I really know him? We went out with each other for just eleven months. I've always felt like he was special, that we'd had something unique, but maybe I've just been kidding myself. Maybe I look back at that year – 1994 – and merely put my own interpretation on what it meant in the scheme of my life, like some colonial mapmaker travelling over the continent of Australia in a balloon and contriving what lay beneath.

Can you invent the past, just as you can imagine the future?

I turn to face the door, wondering if I'll hear the creak of floorboards and the door handle turning. I imagine Neil standing there in the doorway, naked, his erection already rising triumphantly in silhouetted profile. I imagine him climbing on me, thrusting deep inside me. The thought of him makes me wet, for the first time in months.

I want him to open the door. I want to feel desired, to feel dangerous, to feel electric. To feel alive. I want him to take my body and hurt it.

I listen once more.

Silence.

I don't want him to come. I want him to come. I don't. Do. Not. Do. Not.

I open the door to Neil's bedroom. I'm naked. I feel the frame of the door which is cold and damp. The light in the room is a dull ethereal orange from the streetlamp below his window, and the air is cold on my thighs and belly. He's lying on his side, a massive body covering three-quarters of the bed. My foot remains locked in the angle of streetlight, unable to move forward.

Suddenly, I find myself picturing Raj there, lying next to Neil on the bed, a dwarf against his bulk. I am shocked. In that instance I sense the memory of Raj's body against mine, my curves fitting his angles, female against male, my pelvic bone curved around his small taut backside as if hewn to it.

'Night, night, don't let the bastards bite.'

His refrain always makes me smile.

I wait for a sign. For a sound or a movement.

No cars pass, no gulls call. Neil doesn't move, his breathing deep and regular. When I can't sleep I lie up against Raj, my hand on his side feeling his lungs rise and fall like small tropical waves.

I walk quickly back to the spare room and pull on my knickers and T-shirt, and climb into bed, dragging the sheets over my head.

Staring into the dark cocoon, I recall my doctor's tired eyes as she tells me that I was right to make an appointment. There is a lump in my left breast, but she can't tell if it's malignant. I hear her measured voice inform me that I will require a biopsy.

She shows me examples of mammograms. They seem strangely beautiful. Like a chart of a river system, the fragile white veins snaking outwards from the source. I admire them, trying to feel reassured by the neat map of tissue, the illusion of order and control.

I see my watch on the day of my hospital appointment, showing the time I'm meant to be at the hospital, and I see the hands move on as I sit at my work desk. I hear the secretary leave the first answering machine message, then the following message, urging me to come in for another appointment. A note through the door from the GP Surgery Nurse: please will I come in to talk about the situation urgently.

The situation. Urgently.

A seagull cries out. As the dawn light seeps in slowly from the street, I think that here I am in Brighton and I haven't even seen the sea. It makes no sense. No sense at all.

POSSIBILITY

I've called Molly seven times, leaving four messages. I'm beginning to wonder whether she wants to talk to me.

It's been three days since Brighton. I caught the train back to London with Gemma. I told her about the epi-pen fiasco, and she tried calling Molly, but her phone was switched off. Gemma refused to talk about her night, merely revealing that, 'I slept in the spare room, nothing happened, I had fun, we'll talk on the phone,' in a tone that suggested there was nothing more to say on the matter.

Feigning sleep against the juddering train window, I was surprised to sense a flicker of satisfaction that things seemed not to have worked out so well between Gemma and Neil. I reproached myself for feeling it, finding it strange that Gemma's discomfort brought me a degree of gratification, since it was me that had suggested the whole Neil scenario.

Was I that mixed up? Was the idea to visit Neil in Brighton some sort of subconscious plan to take Gemma to the very depths so that I, Ian Thompson, could be the knight in shining Nikes once more, bringing her to salvation? I'm not that perverse, am I? I'm not that devious?

Then again, Gemma didn't seem too concerned that her sister had walked out on me. Maybe she too was relieved.

Despite Gemma's reiteration that I can stay at Raleigh Street as long as I want, I'm beginning to wonder if she's growing tired of my presence in the half-finished house. I feel bad. I know it's difficult for her to ask me to leave. I should be the one to take the initiative. I just have one problem. I have nowhere else to go.

I lie down on the sofa and turn on the television.

It's depressing, when you think about it. I'm thirty-one, and I've nowhere to sleep, apart from my parents' house in Cambridge (which for obvious reasons would be even more sad than being homeless). In my twenties such an itinerant lifestyle, with its lack of ties, possessions and responsibilities, was exhilarating. But ever since turning thirty, I've been feeling increasingly unsettled by being unsettled.

I could call around my travel-writing colleagues and ask to sleep on someone's floor, but most of them are away writing again, now September has returned the summer tourist hoards to their jobs and schools. There's always Justin Wilson, my old footballing friend from Sheffield, but he and his wife have two small children. I met their girls once at a chaotic lunch party during which the oldest, Amy, screamed incessantly, and the youngest, Mary, smeared excrement on the cat. Even if Justin said yes to my request for a bed, I don't think I could last more than a single night in their hectic, toy-strewn house.

I consider booking into a cheap hotel. I could probably afford a week. But the thought of limping into a Travelodge makes me feel more miserable and alone. It's all my own fault. I have to take responsibility. That's what my father would say.

I turn back to the television. It's the *Antiques Roadshow*. An old lady is quivering gently as a man with a droopy moustache appraises a china chamber pot. Her eyes light up when he informs her it's worth £250. For the first time today, I smile. The old lady seems so happy, as if the notional price of this vintage piss-pot has somehow increased her own worth.

The next hopeful, a slender middle-aged man with thinning hair, is carrying a mid-sized picture frame. The expert appears to stifle a yawn. The middle-aged man hesitates briefly, then turns up the picture as flamboyantly as a clue on a game show. It's a map. The camera zooms in. I sit up on the sofa. It's a map of the Middle East.

'Well, well, well . . .' declares the expert, one hand absentmindedly caressing the left dangle of his moustache.

'It was my great-grandfather's . . .' mutters the middle-aged man hopefully.

I lean closer to the television. The map is almost identical to the one I gave my father for his birthday. The same size, the same red, blue and brown shading.

'May I take it out of the frame?' asks the droopy moustache. The middle-age man frowns, then acquiesces. The expert takes the map very delicately, I think, for a man with sausage fingers. He turns it over. I exhale.

'Remarkable.'

'Yes?'

The camera zooms in. On the back of the map are two signatures in expansive flowery styles.

'Sir Mark Sykes and his French counterpart, Charles Georges Picot,' declares the expert in a resounding tone that suggests these two names should be as well known as Tom Cruise and Madonna.

'In 1916 the Allies drew up a plan to divide the Middle

East between France, the blue area, Britain, the red area and a neutral International zone, the brown area. Sykes and Picot were the two diplomats involved. I believe there were only four copies of this map circulated, to the British, French, Russians and the Americans. This really is quite a find . . .'

I grasp my crutch tightly.

'HOW MUCH!' I feel like shouting, but something in the expert's measured demeanour discourages such greed. I remain quiet, heart beating faster.

'My great-grandfather worked for the Foreign Office . . .' whispers the little balding man. The droopy moustachioed expert nods, squinting closer at the map.

'Fabulous detail . . . this really is very valuable.'

I turn up the volume on the TV set.

'We keep it in the downstairs toilet,' admits the middle-aged man, with a hopeful laugh.

'Ha, ha, ha . . . it might be a good idea to find another location for it. I would say, for insurance purposes, you should consider valuing this map at . . .' the expert pauses, with practised television dramatics, giving his moustache another fondle. The middle-aged man nods eagerly, like a dog waiting to be walked.

'Come on!' I below.

'. . . At least . . .'

Another moustache fondle.

'Get on with it!'

'. . . Thirty thousand pounds.'

The middle-aged man seems to crumple. The expert, evidently used to the powerful reaction his words create, catches the man's arm.

'Well, I never . . .' mutters the middle-aged man, his eyes darting around him, as if thieves and kidnappers are already massing.

Bloody hell! I can't believe it. Thirty grand. At least. Did I imagine it? But the map looks the same. I picture my mother's face, tears of joy streaming. My father will smile gently, that smug look that suggests he was expecting this all along. I'll have to stop them giving it all to charity. I'll have to sit them down, convince them that retirement is expensive, that they could use the cash as part payment on a flat somewhere, a nice modern flat with a small garden for my mother.

I think about getting on a train to Cambridge. Instead I dial their number. My mother answers.

'Hello dear. I'm sorry but we're in the middle of a coffee morning for the Romanian refugees . . .'

'Just a quick question. You know the map I gave Dad? Is it okay? I mean, did he get it framed?'

'I don't think so. Not yet. But it's safe in his drawer. You know how he cares about his maps. Sorry Ian, I really should get back to serving coffee . . .'

She puts down the phone. I breathe out and punch the air like a goal-scorer.

I sit on the unfinished concrete terrace holding a mug of cold tea, staring at the walnut tree. The sun has disappeared into a bank of clouds. It's chillier, a first breath of autumn. As I gaze at the tree, I wonder how far its roots descend. I think of the family tree my father carefully mapped out when I was a child, using a red and black fountain pen.

'It's up to you to grow new branches,' he'd declared, patting my six-year-old head.

When Gemma returns at 6.30 p.m., I'm still sitting on the concrete terrace.

'What are you doing out here?'

I gesture towards the bottom of the garden. 'I like that tree. It's majestic.'

'You and Raj. I wanted to cut it down to let in more light, but Raj said it was protected. Some preservation order or something. Bloody ridiculous if you ask me, preserving a tree, I mean it's not like we have a shortage of them in this country . . .'

'I'd preserve it,' I mutter, more forlornly than I intended. I glance up to see her looking at me. When I meet her gaze, she looks away. Her eyes, I note, are just as beautiful as her sister's – a dark hazelnut that seems old and newborn at the same time.

'What's the matter?' Gemma asks. I look up again, cursing her feminine intuition.

'Molly won't speak to me.'

Gemma looks at me. I continue, stammering.

'And I got my dad a map for his birthday, and on *Antiques Roadshow* they had one just like it that was worth thirty grand.'

Gemma looks puzzled.

'What are you going to do?'

'Sell it. Give my parents the money.'

'About my sister.'

'I don't know.'

Gemma squints against the sun which has just peeked out from behind the clouds. I remain silent. I realize I'm hoping Gemma might provide an answer, like a UN resolution that enables everyone to feel less personally responsible.

Gemma is silent.

I am silent.

'Can I ask you a difficult question, Ian?'

I nod. Her tone is direct, business-like. I am suddenly worried about what might be coming next.

'Are you sure you want to be in a relationship?'

'What? Yes. Of course. Everyone does.'

'No they don't. And maybe you don't.'

Her eyes are narrowed. I get the feeling that she's embarking on a speech which has been formulating in her head, but which is only now finding true voice.

'You've become detached, Ian.'

'Detached?'

'That's why women fall for you, but that's also why they leave you.'

'What do you mean, detached?'

'You come and go, you don't really make an effort to connect with people.'

'Bollocks . . .'

'That's why you're a travel writer, so you can make a living from being distant, you never have to connect with any of the places you visit.'

'I'm a travel writer because I like seeing new places, expanding my horizons. Unlike some I could mention . . .'

I'm annoyed with her facile explanations, her school-teacher tone. I wonder if she's channelling her own confusion about her relationship situation into a desire to categorize and condemn everyone else's.

Gemma seems to ignore my jibe.

'But don't you think there's something deeper going on here?'

'And what would that be?'

'Travelling enables you to run away, to not have to deal with your emotions. You can put on your travel clothes, your black combats, your linen shirt, those horrible old Nikes, it's like a suit of armour that protects you against feeling anything.'

I laugh, sarcastically.

'They're just clothes, Gemma.'

'There's another thing.'

'Great.'

'I think you like to travel because when you're away you know your parents worry about you.'

'What?'

'Yup. You know they're worrying about you, and that gives you the feeling, for once, that they love you. You travel because you feel loved by your parents when you're away.'

I look at her. It's the craziest thing I've ever heard.

'What the fuck are you talking about, Gemma?'

She looks at me.

'Call her.'

'What?'

'Call my sister. Sort it out.'

'Why?'

'Don't run away.'

'I'm not running away!'

We stand there, facing each other, and I feel angry, as if Gemma is an enemy, an adversary. I've never felt alienated from her like this before. As I'm trying to decide whether to return the jibe, Gemma walks up to me and hugs me tightly. In an instant, my annoyance and rancour vanishes.

'Sorry. Maybe I overdid the analysis stuff.'

'No. Maybe you're right. I'll think about it.'

She pulls away, gently.

'All I'm saying is, life is short. To coin a cliché.'

As she says this, tears appear in Gemma's eyes.

'Sorry, sorry . . .' she wipes her eyes. 'I don't know where that came from.'

I put my arms around her. Her body is warm, hot even. I wonder if she's feeling unwell.

'I'm sorry, Ian. It's . . .'

Her cheek is wet against my neck.

'What is it, Gemma?'

She doesn't answer. Instead, she pulls away, strides into the house and returns with the portable telephone.

'Call her.'

I climb the stairs to the spare room, attempting to plot out in my head how I'll embark on a conversation with Molly. I will be friendly, not desperate. I will make it clear that I've thought about everything, and that I over-reacted about her seeing her ex-husband. I will offer a hand of reconciliation, and hope that she reaches out and takes it.

When I'm satisfied with my strategy and the different routes I am prepared to take, I dial her mobile. It's strange linking the numbers. I've dialled it so many times before, without thinking. But now the combination of digits seems alien, a dangerous, forbidden code. It feels illicit. It feels exciting.

I almost hang up, but then she answers and I say hello and I think I hear her breathe in sharply.

'Hello, Ian.'

'Hi,' I mutter, unable to think of anything more cutting to say. 'I'm sorry.'

Silence. Then she replies.

'Me too. I overreacted in Brighton.'

I'm adrift. I've not planned for this outcome. I was prepared to be the one to apologize, to try and win her back. Now she's handing me the power, and I don't know what to do with it.

'Well . . . I overreacted to your meeting with Will.'

'I don't blame you . . .'

I feel fine. This is fine.

'Can I see you?'

Molly appears to think for a moment.

'I'm up to my eyes at work, but my birthday's next Thursday. Maybe we can do something then?'

'I'd love to.'

'Great.'

'Next Thursday.'

'Yeah.'

'See you then.'

'You too.'

She puts down the phone. I breathe out. I'm not sure quite how I got here, but I feel . . . comfortable. Satisfied.

I sit in the bedroom for a while, staring out of the window at the concrete garden. Sometimes, when I'm travel-writing, the places that I think will be spectacular, or fascinating, or simply provide good material for my article, turn out to be just plain dull – the museums shabby and uninformative, the bars tame and predictable, the beaches dirty and overcrowded. Quite often, another place – an unplanned stopover in a strange little fishing village, or a hidden beach resort recommended by a fellow traveller – turns out to be a much better story.

Maybe it's the same with Molly and I. We haven't taken the obvious route, but perhaps we've ended up on the best path. I thought that Molly seeing Will Masterson was the end of our relationship. But maybe, like Molly claimed, it's just the beginning.

I feel strong. I didn't run away. I'm not like Gemma's description of me. I was mature enough to listen to Molly. I feel as if things are somehow clearer now. Imagining life without Molly has made me realize that I need her. I want the security of knowing we are together, that I am part of a couple. Unlike Gemma, who has sought liberation and independence, I am seeking unity and connection. Perhaps, I think, I am finally ready to settle down. It feels liberating. It feels grown-up.

As I open the door to head back downstairs to tell Gemma what has happened, I wonder if this is what love really means.

QUESTIONING

A week after Brighton, I receive another envelope from the Surgery Nurse. The hospital has evidently passed the task of tracking me down to my doctor's office on Lauriston Road. I put the envelope in the bin, tie the plastic yellow strings shut and leave the bag out for the dustmen. I know, in my head, that I'm being foolish (worse than foolish, potentially life-threatening). But I've reached a plateau in my emotions, a 'mid-project' juncture where I feel numb enough to get up each morning and go to work, to get through the day (enjoying moments, I can't deny), returning to the house, where Ian has cooked me something, and going to bed. It's a normal, humdrum existence. It seems miraculous after all that's happened.

I know I should tell Ian to leave, but I can't. I don't want to be alone.

Monday morning, the second week of September. The final sultry days of August have given way to the first gusts of autumn, trees shaking, leaves flickering earthwards. I get dressed, ignoring the small red mark on my left breast where the needle entered, easing on my most expensive La Perla bra, pulling up the Prada skirt I bought the previous Christmas (I have lost weight, haven't I?).

I glance at my body in the mirror, observing the sagging. At any other time, I would be ecstatic, like one of those beaming women in the television commercials for pink dieting drinks who wriggle suggestively into their jeans. At another time, losing ten pounds would have made me whoop and dance through the streets of east London.

Absentmindedly, I glance out of the window at number 22, at the black railings, the black front door. Since Brighton, I've returned to my spying on the house. Yesterday evening, a well-dressed couple called at the black door as I was getting back from work. I waited in the shadows by the motorcycle bay, hoping for a glimpse of the house interior. But the door opened and closed swiftly. The couple did not come out again.

Then, this very morning, two more younger men in suits disappeared quickly into the house at around 8 a.m., only to reappear a matter of minutes later, walking away swiftly, hands deep in their pockets.

I have a sudden urge to call Raj, to tell him about the early morning visitors. Yet what once seemed so normal is now an impossibility. I can't call him, I'm not allowed. I told him that I didn't love him. Relationships are horrible – the connection, then disconnection, a house you love, then leave behind without a word.

Why shouldn't I call him? We haven't taken a vow of silence. My hand trembles as I punch the numbers, hearing the ringing. I'll keep it light, just say hello, chat in a friendly but detached way about our mysterious neighbour and the comings and goings at number 22.

Voicemail. The perfect rounded vowels, the calm, paced delivery.

'This is the voicemail of Raj Singh. Please leave a message after the tone.'

I'm about to hang up when I realize that my number

will have registered on his caller display, so I leave a hurried message asking him to call. He calls back three minutes later.

'Were you screening your calls?' I ask, without thinking.

'So what if I was?' he replies, tersely.

'Okay Raj, I didn't call you to fight.'

'Why did you call?'

'I . . . I just wanted to see how you were.'

'I'm fine. Busy. Is there anything else?'

Suddenly, my stories about the man at 22 seem to belong to another time, another relationship. Another me, another Raj Singh. I have to think of a bigger reason to justify my need to call him.

'I'm sorry Ian came by . . .'

'Did you send him?' His voice is curt, accusatory, the perfect prosecution counsel.

'No, he was just passing, he was just trying to help . . .'

'Yeah, sure.'

His sulky tone annoys me.

'Ian's been really kind . . .'

'Oh, I bet he has . . .'

'Stop it, Raj!'

'Stop what?'

'Oh, just forget it, I don't know why I called . . .'

'I don't bloody know either!'

And we slam down our phones.

I burst into tears. Something about his tone has shattered the last wall preventing the terror from taking my body. I shake, my arms shivering, my heart trembling, teeth grinding down.

The most painful thought is that I might never be a

mother. I might never feel my child against my breast. I have so many plans – drawn up since I was young. The three names – Chloe, Sarah and Daniel; the house where we'd live – four bedrooms, large garden, my studio office under some trees where the children would burst in after school, full of tales of painting and spelling tests and netball matches.

I don't want to die. It's a simple, overwhelming desire that wracks my body.

In the bathroom I try to stop sobbing. I have to focus on what is right in front of me, like when I'm drawing a detail of a building project and I have to concentrate solely on the small and the intricate, trusting that it will eventually fit and work in the whole. Think positive, I hear a voice say. First things, first. The voice sounds like Raj, but I shake my head to rid myself of it, like turning the dial on a radio.

Ian knocks on the door and asks if I'm okay. I tell him I'm fine. I listen to his limp thump slowly down the stairs.

I'm meeting Neil at the bar by Smithfield Market. 7.30 p.m. Neil. My first love. I take down my make-up bag and choose my favourite items – a Lancôme juicy tube, my most sophisticated Christian Dior lipstick and my Mac face powder. Then I do two things I hadn't realized I was going to do. I go to the medicine cabinet and take three condoms from the box of 'Elite Pleasure Ribbed'. I feel a strange mixture of thrill and dread. Next, I pull off my wedding ring. It slips off my finger with surprising ease. I place it on the glass shelf above the sink. Wiping my eyes one last time, I drag on my coat and head for the door.

'Have a good one . . .' chimes Ian, smiling broadly. I pretend to smile back, and close the door gently behind me.

Suggesting the surprise birthday party for my sister was inspired. Ian has been in such a good mood since I gave him the task of planning it. He's treating it like a travel article – researching caterers, compiling the guest list, tasting wine and champagne. I hadn't realized how much he needed a project.

As the bus passes the canal, I marvel at the ease at which men can feel happy. There's something Pavlovian about Ian's puppy demeanour now he has my sister's birthday to occupy him. Then my irritation slips immediately to guilt. Why shouldn't he be happy, just because the thick-thighed, cancerous Gemma Cook is not?

I'm not jealous. It's just . . . I'm not sure about Molly. I think I know why she wants Ian back. Turning thirty-two definitely has something to do with it – impending birthdays have always intensified Molly's need to be loved, to be looked after, to be considered special.

Yet I should reserve judgement, shouldn't I? If Ian is happy, and Molly is happy, that should be enough, shouldn't it? Just because I'm not happy doesn't mean I can interfere. I can't let my own troubles influence my judgment concerning my sister and my best friend.

I haven't told either of them about my imminent date with Neil. My secrecy makes me feel a little smug. I sense Ian was relieved, pleased even, to discover my Brighton night didn't turn out to be the great romantic occasion I'd hoped for. His satisfaction surprised me, since he was the one to suggest tracking down Neil Farrelly in the first place. It annoyed me too – it seemed to confirm my long-term suspicions that Ian likes me best when I'm downtrodden, troubled or in distress.

Molly has called once since Brighton, asking how I was doing before moaning about how much work she had on. We didn't talk about Ian. I listened and wondered for the thousandth time whether I could tell my sister about the lump in my breast and the terror that prevents me sleeping most nights. I almost confessed, on more than one occasion, but something about Molly's habitual dismissiveness prevented me, and prevents me still.

'When did I become a woman of secrets?' I wonder, as the bus careers along Cambridge Heath Road.

Just as the bus pulls up to my stop, I sense panic rising. What if Raj goes back to the house, to pick up fresh clothes? What if he goes into the bathroom and discovers my wedding ring sitting blatantly on the shelf? What if he sees the condom packet on the toilet seat, freshly opened and missing three of its regiment? Did I do these two things, I wonder, because, in some twisted, subconscious way, I want to bring about this final rupture in our relationship?

I step off the number 55 and walk the three hundred yards to the office. The morning light seems more luminous, more full. Today, anything can happen. Please God.

The morning passes quickly. Duncan Archer is nowhere to be seen – Sandra the secretary says he's away on site somewhere. As usually happens when Duncan is away, everyone on my side of the office seems more relaxed. Some appear positively merry. I hear laughter from one desk, then singing as one of the senior architects carries a model out to reception. It feels, in some ways, like a last day at school, or the Friday before a long weekend.

Everything else is so routine, so mundane, that I feel almost heady with normality.

I finish a couple of new drawings for the bar project, changing the length of the counter, adding an extra table to the dining area. I enjoy the neatness of the lines, the tiny exactitude of the writing alongside each measurement. I wonder, not for the first time, whether my interest in architecture has more to do with the presentation of the plans than the actual building being constructed. Unlike most of my colleagues, I never relish a site visit. I hate the dirty, temporary mess that builders seem to thrive in.

After lunch, my breast begins to hurt. I try to ignore it. Over the past few days, I've started a new tactic. I'll convince myself that there's nothing wrong, and in so doing, force my body to believe the same thing. I want to be a concrete tower, impenetrable and indestructible.

I need a couple of Nurofen. I take my bag to the ladies' toilets and stand in front of the mirrors. I look so tired. But I can't give in to pity. I have to fight it. I unzip my bag. Where is the bloody Nurofen packet? I know I put it in here. I open the bag wider, bending over slightly to look into its depths. As I do so, I sense someone behind me.

'Hello, Gemma . . .'

I turn swiftly. My bag swings round, the contents hurling outwards, a shower of pens, hair-pins, make-up, tissues, tampons and a bottle of perfume, clattering onto the cold linoleum floor. Duncan Archer stands there. I step back. I can smell alcohol on his breath.

'This is the ladies, Duncan!' I stammer. On the floor I see my make-up bag, my smashed perfume bottle in a pool of Gucci Envy, my hairbrush, and, by Duncan Archer's dark brown Camper shoes, three green condom packets, shining like precious jewels. Before I can do anything, he's bending down, a chuckle forming in his throat. He picks up one of the condoms. He stands and looks at me with a wide grin.

'"Elite Pleasure Ribbed". Well, Gemma. Saucy. Very saucy.'

'This is the ladies . . .' I stammer again, as if these words are the only spell that might cause the evil troll to disappear. His eyes are bloodshot and as he speaks he fingers the condom packet suggestively.

'Just in case, hey, Gemma, ha, ha, ha . . .'

He rips open the packet, pulling out the condom. It dangles from his thumb and forefinger like a slip of severed skin.

'Duncan . . .'

'When were you going to use this then, you saucy girl . . .'

He steps closer to me, I step back, but my spine hits the frame of the cubicle. I have nowhere to go. He thrusts the condom towards my face. I can smell the bitter latex, mixed with the stench of booze on his breath. As I move instinctively to one side, his left hand appears on my hip, gripping me into him.

'Duncan . . . please . . .' I whimper and in that instant I wonder if telling him about my breast and the lump might somehow dissuade him from his advance. But I know there is no time for logic.

I draw back my right leg, and knee him hard in the balls.

'Urrghhh!'

He staggers backwards.

I push him hard. Duncan Archer collapses against the sink, gasping for breath. His eyes bulge, his tongue loose and lolling. I nod once, with satisfaction. I am still quick, still strong. Perhaps I shouldn't have given up playing netball and tennis after I married Raj.

'Duncan?' a voice squeaks, behind me. I whirl round. At the entrance to the ladies' toilets stands Gwen Jones, the office manager. She looks worried. Very worried.

Duncan Archer gabbles.

'I was just talking to Gemma . . .'

I cut him off.

'Duncan attacked me. He tried to molest me.'

I wonder for a moment if Gwen will believe me, but one glance at the office manager's face confirms that she does. This gives me strength.

'Gwen, please get Duncan out of the building. I'll see you in your office in twenty minutes.'

Nobody looks up as I exit the toilets. I make tea and sit at my desk, flicking through drawings on the screen. At three-thirty I walk over to the office manager's cubicle.

I speak quickly.

'I did not in any way encourage this, Gwen.'

'I believe you. You have every right to sue for sexual harassment. I know your husband is a lawyer . . .'

'That is one option.'

'All I ask is that you consider how completely out of character this was for Duncan. He's going through a very tough time at the moment . . .'

'Oh, well that's fine then. Let's forget the whole fucking thing!'

My voice is strident. It seems like someone else's. I like it.

'No, no, of course not . . . It's just . . .' Gwen lowers her voice. 'He's been drinking. He needs to go away for a while, perhaps to a clinic. We are looking into it . . .'

Gwen tails off, evidently trying to regroup. I remain silent, yet my mind is racing.

What should I do? What can I do?

I could sue. I enjoy, for an instant, a picture of Duncan Archer's terrified face on the front page of a morning newspaper. It could, given the right exposure, destroy him. I imagine the faces of his colleagues as he clears out his desk. I picture his wife. She'd throw him out for good, and he'd undoubtedly hit the bottle even harder. I see his two little daughters, what are their names? Emma and Susan. I see their laughing faces in the office one Friday afternoon a few months back as their father lifted them up to see one of his designs. I recall the impressive drawings he showed me when I first joined, and the passion with which he talked about his earlier work.

If I sued him, I'd have to appear in court, the defence would rake over my own background. They'd find out about the cancer, everyone would know. Maybe they'd even use it against me.

Perhaps I should just pretend nothing has happened.

It's tempting. Why not? Duncan Archer is going away, I could just come to work and tinker with the plans, redraw the renderings, stay focused on the nineteen-inch screen for the rest of my life and never have to deal with anything terrifying or hurtful or difficult, ever again. Would that be so bad?

I want to hide. Like when I was a little girl and I'd race away from my sister to the toilet under the stairs and lock the door and wait for my father to come and talk gently from beyond the darkness, convincing me that all was safe and good and right once more.

Why was I so vehement about telling Ian what I thought of his tendency to run away to foreign countries? Did I get annoyed with him because deep down I'm angry at my own predisposition towards fleeing responsibility?

I feel a little sick. Gwen Jones is still trying to think of something to say. Then an idea hits me, appearing suddenly, like an itch or a nosebleed.

I have the power to save Duncan. I can forgive him.

If I forgive Duncan, I will be better than him. Better than all of them. He could be encouraged to change, to dry out. He could love his two daughters as they deserve to be loved.

The strength of my voice surprises me.

'Okay Gwen. Here's what I propose. I'll take two weeks off. The bar project is almost finished, Stan can take over the final drawings. You'll put me on treble pay. Then I'll come back and we'll talk about the future.'

'Okay.' Gwen looks a little startled, like a child caught stealing.

'Things will have to change.'

'Yes. I . . . Of course . . .'

'And now I need three thousand pounds, up front. I need to pay the builders working on my house.'

The office manager looks at me as if trying to decide whether I'm telling the truth. I feel like laughing. I feel so strong.

'All right. There'll be a cheque on your desk in ten minutes.'

'Good. I'll leave then. You can tell people I'm taking holiday time to get my house in order.'

I'm pleased with the phrase.

'Are you sure?'

'Positive.'

'Thank you, Gemma.'

I catch a cab to Smithfield Market. It's 4.00 p.m. I have three hours to kill before my date with Neil. I am light-headed. It's a feeling that reminds me of the night Raj asked me to marry him. I feel deliriously well.

I pay in the £3,000 cheque at the bank. I wander around a bookshop on Cowcross Street, stop for tea. I feel suddenly hungry and order a large slice of chocolate cake, which I eat, slowly, with small deliberate forkfuls. I don't know why I asked for the money. I know it means I'll never be able to sue for sexual harassment, and I know that this is why Gwen Jones was so quick to give it to me, but I don't care. I want the money to pay the builders in order to get them back in, so that they can tidy up what they've started, and leave the building in a state where Raj and I can sell it.

As the light softens and evening approaches, I feel

butterflies in my stomach. It has been a very strange day. I wonder how it will end. Will I sleep with Neil? Will this day prove to be the turning point in my life? Will he come with me to the hospital and hold my hand as the doctor tells me the terrifying news?

I go into a couple of clothes shops, glancing along the rails. It's been months since I've bought any new clothes – I didn't feel able to once the work on the house began.

The third shop I enter is having a sale. I survey the trousers, the skirts, the shirts. Then at the end of the rail, I see a little black dress. I've been looking for one for a long time, something for Christmas parties or dinners with Raj's work colleagues. I am surprised to see it's my size, a 12. I take it hurriedly to the changing rooms, suddenly filled with teenage excitement.

There are two full-length mirrors in the changing rooms. I undress quickly, not wanting to look at my body. But I can't resist a peek as I stand there in my La Perla underwear. I've lost weight. There's no doubt. Not that the thighs show any sign of thinning. Instead, the pounds have disappeared from my face, my arms, my breasts. I seem older, more pinched. God, I hate my body. More than ever. I touch my left breast, take it in my right hand. I want to tear it off. I want to cut off my skin, my fat, my flesh and step out of my body as if it's a wetsuit. My arms fall flatly to my sides.

When Neil touched me, the first time, I felt invincible. For days afterwards I sensed men looking at me and I revelled in the power. Even with Raj my body caused him to exhale, pausing for that magical moment before entering me.

But now I feel rotten. Like dying fruit.

'I'm so scared,' my reflection says, repeating the words in case the big-thighed woman in the La Perla underwear opposite didn't hear them.

'I'm so scared.'

I order a double vodka and tonic and sit at the table in the window so I'll be able to see Neil arrive. I'm forty-five minutes early. I watch the videos on the TV above the bar. The barman, a cute Australian, smiles at me. I look down at my drink. Time passes. I begin to feel better. I try to empty my head, to leave myself open and optimistic for the night ahead.

7.20 p.m. I know he won't be early. Neil isn't punctual like Ian. I've always liked that about Ian, that you can count on him. Not that Raj is ever late either, but he always gets mad if he has to wait for you longer than ten minutes. Not like Ian. Although he's punctual, Ian doesn't seem to mind others being tardy. One time I was forty-five minutes late for a coffee, and he simply laughed, teasing me for being an airhead.

I wonder if I should call Ben Keane to tell him that I now have the money to finish the first (and now final) stage of the work on 26 Raleigh Street. I rummage around in my bag, trying to avoid contact with the metallic condom packets. I can't find his number. Instead I take out the pocket-sized London *A to Z*. I want to look at the city, to see where I could live when we sell the house. As I turn the front page I notice Raj's name written on the inside cover. I curse quickly. He'll be furious. He hates it when I borrow his *A to Z*, he claims I never give it back (which is true, often I do forget I've borrowed it, but then what are husbands for?).

Oh well. There's no use worrying about it, he will have already bought another one, cursing me as he pays out the £4.99.

As I turn the book over, I notice a scribble on the tattered inside page. I look closer. It's a jaunty inscription, the sort I remember from teenage school books.

Raj ♥ Gemma.

The letters are small, but painstakingly inscribed. He's coloured in the heart, leaving no white behind. I close the book quickly, and slip it back into my bag.

It's 7.35 p.m. The barman smiles at me again. Another video comes on. I have no idea who the band are. They screech and throw themselves around the screen, tossing their hair like women in shampoo commercials.

7.45 p.m.

Neil was always late, when we were going out. Initially I found it charming, he was so boyishly disorganized. But as the year progressed I found myself getting more and more irritated. But I didn't tell him, I blamed myself for being an uptight cow.

At 7.55 p.m. the bar gets suddenly busy. A group of people enter. Neil is nowhere to be seen. At 8.05 p.m., the barman comes over to me.

'Fancy another?'

I look up at him.

'No. Thanks.'

When he turns his back, heading to another table, I stand, take my coat and bag and walk from the bar.

Outside in the street, I call Neil's mobile. He answers, breathlessly.

'Gemma, I'm sorry, the tube was late, I'm almost there . . .'

'Don't come.'

'What?'

'I can't see you.'

'Look, Gem, I'm sorry I'm late, but there was a signal failure at Kennington . . .'

'No, Neil.'

'I'll be five minutes . . .'

'This isn't right, Neil.'

I am surprised at the firmness of my voice. He is silent for a moment. A police car passes, siren wailing in distress.

'How do you know?' he asks, quietly.

'I don't. Maybe I'm wrong.'

Silence. Then he speaks.

'No. Maybe you're right.'

I didn't expect him to be so easily dissuaded. But I've set out on a path. I can't turn back.

'Let's see,' I say, more gently. 'Take a time out. Okay?'

'Okay.'

Silence again. Does he hate me?

'Will you be okay?' I ask, loudly. 'You're staying with friends, right?'

'Yeah. Look, why don't we just meet up, have a quick drink . . .' His voice lacks conviction, as if he thinks these words are expected of him.

I think about it for a moment. You cannot relive the past. It's another country. I read that somewhere, ages ago. I've drawn a map, high up in my balloon, but it bears no resemblance to the reality on the ground.

'No. I can't, Neil. I'm sorry.'

'You're sure?'

Silence. I'm not sure of anything.

'Yes. I'll call you.'

More silence. I want to hear him breathing, but there is static on the line.

'I'm seriously thinking about going to Canada,' he says, resolutely.

'I think you should.'

'Really?'

'Yes.'

'Okay.'

Another silence. I don't know what I'm doing.

'There was a signal failure. At Kennington . . .'

'I believe you.'

'I . . .'

'I'll call you, Neil,' I say, conclusively and put down the phone. Standing there, by Farringdon Station, the Monday night crowd surrounding me, passing this way and that, men and women laughing and shouting, I know I won't call him again. I feel unbelievably sad. I reach into my bag, take out a £20 note and hand it to the man sitting on a dirty sleeping bag by the ATM machine.

'Ta, gorgeous,' he mutters, with a vacant, happy stare.

As I approach the house on Raleigh Street I slow. The light is on at the entrance to number 22. The black door shines brightly. By comparison, three houses away my own front door is dark.

It starts to rain. I walk quickly. I take a breath, and hit the knocker against the door, three times.

Nothing. No sound inside. I withdraw my hand. As the raindrops hit the pool of light from the lamp they seem to glint like diamonds. My heart is beating. I feel like I'm watching a film.

I knock again. Nothing. Films aren't real. This isn't real. I turn to go.

'Yes?'

He stands there in a black suit, with a black polo neck. His hair, I realize, is dyed, pulled back in a small pony tail. He looks like a retired member of a seventies rock band. I want to laugh.

'Can I help you?'

'I'm your neighbour. At number twenty-six. Gemma . . . er . . . Singh.'

I hold out my hand. He takes it. His hand is very warm, his hold soft and gentle, like a girl, I think.

'John Major.'

'No? Really?' I stifle a giggle. He smiles.

'Yes. Unfortunately. Do come in.'

The house is beautiful. Not in my modern style, but in period Edwardian, all dark hues, lush curtains and elegantly upholstered furniture. Green plants stand in porcelain pots. On the walls are several large antique maps, surrounded by gold frames against the dark green painted walls. I try to list the countries as I walk by. Russia. Romania. Albania. I follow him to an antechamber containing a dark brown Chesterfield sofa and two armchairs. He gestures to the sofa. I sit down, smoothing my skirt, my hands clasped in my lap protectively. Suddenly I feel very young, as if I'm back at school.

'And what can I do for you, Gemma?'

'Er . . .'

A clock ticks somewhere. The house smells of incense. The dark blinds allow a soft dusky light to bathe the room. It's a light that reminds me of my room as a child, as I lay awake hearing the evening birdsong, waiting for my sister to come upstairs (our bedtimes were 45 minutes apart until I turned 14). Then I hear a voice. It sounds like mine.

'I might have cancer . . . I'm so scared. I didn't tell my husband. He's seemed so distant, like his work was always more important. So, I told him that I didn't love him. I think I wanted him to fight to keep me, but he just packed his bags. He ran away and left me . . . People always leave me. My father died of a brain aneurysm when I was fourteen. I'm terrified of dying. I don't know what to do.'

Half an hour later, I walk down the steps feeling lighter. At my door I pause. I wonder for a moment if anyone has seen me leaving the man's house. Then as I unlock the door, closing it softly behind me, I realize that I don't care. I feel light, I feel brave. I don't know what I'm going to do next, but I know I feel stronger. I check the small plastic bag in my left pocket, and step into the dark, empty, unfinished house.

Rejoicing

It's going to be Molly's best party ever. I've decided to host it at her flat, with the help of a catering company. There are three reasons for this:

1. It's a fabulous apartment that everyone will get a buzz out of being in.

2. It'll be easier to dupe Molly into turning up at her own home without suspicion.

3. It's free. I can spend my limited budget on top-class booze and catered nibbles.

Gemma thinks it's a great idea. She has spare keys so we can set everything up. She's even offered to be the lure – she's going to call Molly half an hour before our fake dinner reservation at Moro and ask her to pop back to her apartment to bring Molly's favourite cashmere cardigan for Gemma to wear to an important business meeting the following day. It's going to be perfect.

I've tasted the wine and champagne, I've negotiated a good deal with the catering company. I've called all Molly's friends from the list Gemma supplied me with. I've even drawn out the timetable, in five minute intervals, right up to the point at approximately 8 p.m. when Molly enters her apartment and we all shout 'surprise'.

I know I'm being pedantic, but I don't have much else to put my efforts into at the moment. A few further calls to travel editors of publications with even smaller circulations has yielded three 'no's and one 'call back in the spring'. Gemma keeps suggesting that I think up a proposal for a book, but I have no ideas and anyway the publishing industry is in as much trouble as the newspaper business, isn't it?

The truth, I suspect in more desolate moments, is that I have messed it all up. That I've chosen the wrong path. Now I need to get back on track.

My plaster cast is due off in five days' time. I can't wait – I've decided that the removal of the punishing plaster shackle will herald the start of a new era. A new Ian Thompson. I will be free. I will start again, the curse of the Venezuelan Virgin Mary lifted once and for all, to be replaced by the blessing of the Far-From-Virginal Molly.

My new plan will be revolutionary, I tell myself at secret moments during the day. I will stay with Molly, emotionally and physically, I will think of a book idea, and Molly and I will get married.

I can't believe it. I can imagine myself putting the ring on her finger. I can imagine her, in luxuriant white (will she wear white knickers, perhaps a white thong?), at my side. I can imagine our intoxicating honeymoon, perhaps on a beach on Lamu, or perhaps Salvador in Brazil, or maybe that amazing hotel I stayed at once on Haggerstone Island just off the Great Barrier Reef. I will get her to travel, to share the joys I feel every time I walk up to the check-in desk at Heathrow.

I call my parents, but I don't tell them of the potential value of the map. Instead I say I'll come back to Cambridge to pick it up soon, in order to get it framed.

'It's fine Ian. I can get it done here in Cambridge. I know you're a little short of funds at the moment.'

'No, Dad. I'd like to. All right?'

To my surprise, my father says he'll bring the map up to London himself. He's attending a Church of England working group on asylum seekers at Lambeth Palace on the day of Molly's birthday. We arrange to meet for lunch. My father sounds unduly pleased.

'We'll have a bite and a chat,' he says brightly. As I put down the phone, I can't help but feel a little pang of joy.

I meet my father in an old-fashioned coffee shop in Soho, one of those establishments that seem stuck in a smoky, paper-doily age long before the invention of cappuccinos and comfy sofas.

'How's the ankle?' my father asks, as if this is a joke.

'Fine. Just another week to go.'

'Splendid. Any luck with finding a new flat?'

'I've seen a couple of places. I've a few to see this week.'

'Something will turn up.'

'I know.'

My father hands me the map of Palestine. I inspect it, heart racing. It appears identical to the one on the TV programme. I flip it over. I want to sing. The two signatures are there. Sir Mark Sykes. Monsieur Charles Georges Picot. My two new favourite people in the world.

'It's very kind of you to get it framed for me.'

I nod. The money from the map could really help them. Ian, their only son, could really help them. I decide the moment is right to reveal my good news.

'I was watching *Antiques Roadshow* the other day . . .' I begin. My father cuts in.

'Your mother watches it occasionally. Can't say I'm a fan. Dull as dishwater, if you ask me.'

'This map was on it. Or at least one that looked a lot like it.'

'What's that?'

'They said there were only four drawn up, for some agreement to divide the Middle East in 1916.'

'Really?'

'Yeah. Look, here are the signatures of the diplomats involved . . .'

I turn the map over. The Reverend John Thompson reaches out for it. His right hand trembles. I know I have to ask him, I have to confront it, confront him, but I don't know how. I'm too scared of what it means.

'Dad . . .' I stammer. My father interrupts me.

'Well I never. Is it . . . valuable?'

'Thirty thousand pounds, or more.'

'No! My goodness.'

'That's what they said.'

The map quivers in the Reverend John Thompson's right hand. I raise my left hand and grasp the map firmly. The parchment stops trembling.

'I got it from that antiques market behind St Paul's.'

My father looks up, eyes clear and focused.

'You have to take it back.'

'What?'

'The poor man who sold it to you evidently had no idea of its value. You have to take it back.'

'Why? I bought it. It was a fair deal.'

'But he didn't know its true value.'

I feel like screaming. It's as if my father delights in creating hardship for himself. There is something masochistic about him. Or perhaps he just likes putting his only son in his place.

'It's thirty grand, Dad! In case you had forgotten, you and Mum are not exactly rolling in it!'

'He didn't know its true value.'

True value. My father has the infuriating habit of making any sentence containing an abstract word sound as if it belongs in a sermon.

'That's his problem!'

'No, Ian. It's our problem. We have to be honest and return this valuable item to its rightful owner.'

'Rightful? He probably bought it for a fiver off some old lady!'

'We don't know that. He may just have made a terrible mistake. I strongly believe we must return it and tell the vendor its true value. It will be up to him to decide whether he wants to share any ultimate financial gain.'

'Oh don't be so bloody self-righteous!'

The Reverend John Thompson looks at me. He shakes his head slowly.

'Please don't get angry with me, Ian.'

The tone is sad and weary.

'Angry? I'm not angry . . .' I lie, instant and familiar shame spreading from my chest to my face.

We both fall silent. I look down at the white tablecloth with the embroidered flowers at the borders. I wonder if it is handmade, imagining a little old woman sitting in a small low-beamed room darning cloth after cloth. My father coughs. I know this is a ruse, to get my attention, but I continue staring at the yellow daisies.

'I'm sorry, Ian.'

I look up. My father is sitting with his hands in his lap, shoulders hunched. The map lies on the white tablecloth. I wonder if I've heard correctly. I decide to wait and see if the words are repeated.

'I've been somewhat stressed recently.'

Maybe I did imagine it.

'Well, you'll be retired soon. You'll have all the time in the world to relax.' I know that my father will never relax. He'll probably be busy in his grave, directing the worms and lecturing the beetles.

'Not really.'

'Why not?' I ask, the two words seemingly charged suddenly with all the years of rancour and pent-up bitterness.

My father doesn't answer. I wonder if he's trying to contain himself, trying to be the forgiving disciple of the Lord. If only he wasn't so righteous, if only he could lose his temper, curse and stamp his feet. If only he could be human. I watch my father pick up the tea cup, then place it down in front of him. When he looks up to meet my gaze, his eyes are solemn and watery.

'I have Parkinson's.'

'What?'

'That's why I'm in London.'

'Parkinson's?'

Someone has hit me. I can't breathe. I stare at my father in disbelief. He is hiding his right hand beneath the table like a child concealing stolen candy. Immediately my anger vanishes and I'm filled with shame and pity. I feel an urge to lean over and touch him. Hold him.

'I lied about the asylum seekers thing,' continues the Reverend John Thompson, his voice trembling like his hand. 'The truth is, I'm here for tests at Queen's Square.'

'What's Queen's Square?' I ask, wishing this could be a simple enquiry about London geography rather than a fearful question about my father's future.

'The Hospital for Nervous Diseases.'

My father's voice is small and scared. His body seems to have shrunk in the instance of confession, hunching into a shrunken, concave shell. The Reverend John Thompson breathes in deeply, evidently seeking strength from somewhere deep inside.

'Look, I'm sorry, Ian, I didn't do this very well. It's funny, having spent so many years giving other people bad news, you'd have thought I'd be able to give my own with a bit more sensitivity . . .'

'What does it mean, Dad?' I ask, quickly.

'Every case is different.'

'What happens? Normally.'

'Usually there is a gradual deterioration in function of muscles and limbs. The ability to walk, to move the arm, or hand, facial expressiveness. There is this thing called dysarthria . . .'

'What's that?'

'A difficulty in articulation.'

'Articulation?'

'Your speech slows, it becomes slurred. You can't talk properly any more.'

'Is there a cure?'

'No,' my father intones softly. 'I don't think so.'

I want to cry. My father's sermons boomed through my childhood, through my adolescence, through my university years. I heard them from Quito to Papua New Guinea, at the top of Kenyan mountains, at the bottom of Australian coral reefs. The Reverend John Thompson lives for his Sunday address, he comes alive the moment he crosses himself in the pulpit. It's not fair. It's not right. I want to shout.

'How did this happen?' I bark, angrily. 'Why did it happen?'

'There's no reason . . .'

'So much for the Grace of God!'

'Ian . . .'

'You see, it's just proof . . .'

'There's no blame . . .'

'Why not? Why would a benign God do this to you? Why?'

I glare at my father as if glaring at the very Word made incarnate. My father stares back at me, eyes ringed with bruised fatigue.

'I don't know. I don't have any answers.'

'Why not?'

'I just have to accept it.'

I look away. I wish I'd managed to contain myself. My father doesn't need my baiting. In attacking his God I am attacking him. I should be supportive, caring, loving.

'It'll be all right,' my father concludes. He's trying to sound brave. I remember this tone from when I was little. Had my father seemed as unconvincing back then?

'Does Mum know?' I ask, more quietly.

'Yes. She's trying to be strong.'

'I'm sorry Dad. I'm so sorry.'

My father looks down. I see tears in his eyes.

'I don't know what to do, Ian.'

Immediately, without thinking, I step around the table and open my arms and quickly place them around my father's back. I'm surprised at how wide and strong my father's body feels. I can feel the older man stiffen at my touch. I wonder for a moment whether he will push me away. Then I feel his muscles slump. I hear a brief sob. I hold him more tightly.

We remain, son behind father, as I hold him tightly for a moment. I know everyone in the coffee shop is watching us, but I don't care.

'Thank you,' my father whispers.

'I love you, Dad.'

I kiss my father's cheek.

'I don't know what to do,' my father murmurs, gently.

Outside, the sun is shining. It's warm, and most of the passers-by are wearing shorts and light dresses. Everyone seems exuberant, joyful even in the Indian summer heat. We stand for a moment, father and son, blinking in the bright light.

'The appointment's at two.'

'Why don't I come with you?'

'No. Thank you. Somehow I think I'll feel stronger on my own.'

'You're sure?'

'Yes. Thank you.'

We walk through Chinatown to Leicester Square underground station. We stop at the barriers.

'I'll come back to Cambridge in a couple of days,' I say, trying to sound strong.

'That would be nice.'

'I'll think about the map. I'm not sure what I'm going to do.'

My father nods, but says nothing.

'I'm going to help you through this, Dad.'

My father looks at me. I feel tears welling in my eyes. I put my arms around my father once more. Two hugs in . . . what? Twenty years?

'Thank you.'

We look at each other. I hear the words in my head, but I'm unsure if I can say them. My father seems to be searching for his own conclusion.

'Look Dad, I'm hosting a surprise birthday party for Molly at her flat this evening. It's not far from Liverpool Street, you could stop by before you go back to Cambridge.'

'Oh no . . . I wouldn't want to cramp your style.'

'Just come for a quick drink.'

My father's face breaks into a smile.

'Well . . . why not. I'll try. Thank you, Ian.'

My father pats my left shoulder, and turns to place his ticket in the machine. He takes the ticket, the gates open and he passes through. I watch my father walk slowly down the steps until the last bob of his head. Then he is gone.

I sit on a bench in the sunshine and watch the late-summer shoppers stroll through Soho Square. They seem so normal, so carefree. I wonder if they too are carrying secrets,

their everyday bodies harbouring diseases or derange-
ments, microbes or viruses, terrors or confusions. I want
to stop them, to ask. I want to know that my father is not
alone. I want to know that my mother and I are not the
only ones worrying. Not the only ones hurting.

In that moment, I remember the letter in Gemma's bed-
side drawer. The University College Hospital Women's
Health Clinic. I should be brave and ask her if she's okay.
Maybe she's hiding a terrible secret like my father.

I'm scared. My father seemed so helpless. I think ahead
ten years. The Reverend John Thompson will need constant care. My mother will need support, she'll be lost
without her husband to show her the way. It's up to me
to save them. To provide salvation. I am their son, the
only son of the father.

I pay £25 for a safety deposit box at my bank in
Paddington, where I leave the map in a padded envelope.
Then I return east to Gemma's house, shower, dress, and
head out into the early September night.

I arrive at Molly's flat at 5 p.m., just before the caterers
are due. The plan is simple. When she comes through the
door, all her friends, some work colleagues and her mum
and mum's boyfriend will be there. I've bought six crates
of champagne, the nibbles are being catered. It's costing
me £500 but it's worth it. Molly's been stressing about her
birthday. This will help her feel that thirty-two is still
young enough to enjoy yourself.

I've bought a new T-shirt from a shop off Carnaby
Street that reads 'What If I'm Not Paranoid?'. I've also
dug out some old baggy Levi's that fit easily over my

plaster cast. Usually I feel a little embarrassed wearing them, but somehow, on this day, I feel they make me look cool – like Eminem or someone. Almost.

Picturing the diminutive Detroit rapper makes me think of Gemma, who for some reason likes his music. There's so much I want to tell her about Molly, about my father, about my hopes, fears and plans, but I recognize that this is a time when my best friend needs a bit of space. I can be selfless. And tonight I've planned a surprise for her, which I'm hoping will make her happy.

I go through my list, checking that everything is perfect. Molly is going to love this party, I'll make sure of it, and afterwards she will love me, in several passionate and creative ways. For this evening, at least, I need to forget about my father, about the future. This is about here, and now. It's about getting drunk, having fun and sex and not worrying about tomorrow.

It's allowed, isn't it?

I call the DJ's mobile, to verify he's on schedule. I check the cake (large and chocolate-laden, with strawberries – Molly's favourite). I put up the last of the gold streamers, and blow up the remaining twenty balloons. The barman arrives, and I go through the drinks list with him.

'Do this for a living, mate?' the South African grins.

'What?'

'Party planning?'

'No. I'm a travel writer.'

'Wow. Cool.'

I nod, feigning false modesty, and attach the last balloon to the bathroom door.

*

The guests are all here, her old school friends and work colleagues. Her mum is sipping champagne in the corner with her 'friend' Stanley Myers, who's wearing a bow tie and green-checked jacket. I attempt to be charming and deferential, and I'm pleased to see that my confidence seems to make her mother smile and then laugh. Stanley Myers shakes my hand firmly. I think I've made a good impression.

Justin Wilson is one of the first to arrive, carrying a bottle wrapped in shiny blue paper.

'Gift for the birthday girl. I'm dying to meet her.'

I feel a small rush of affection for my friend, whom I haven't seen since the aborted lunch party at his house five months previously. He seemed excited to get the invitation when I called him, although he was worried about what to wear to 'an uptown bash' as he insisted on calling it.

'Casual. Whatever you'd normally wear to a bar.'

'I only go to pubs. Not bars.'

Justin has evidently settled on his own version of *Dawson's Creek* chic – khaki trousers, finely checked shirt, and Timberland shoes; a look that sits uneasily between the smart Italian work suits of the bankers and the shabbily expensive glamour of Molly's friends who work in media and the arts.

'Have a beer – it's all free.'

'Thanks for inviting me, Ian. I haven't been out like this in months.'

I smile, wondering if Molly and I will ever be like Justin and Sarah – staying in every night to read bed-time stories to their children before collapsing into bed at 9 p.m. I can't see it.

I meet a few more of Molly's friends, who all compliment me on what a cool idea this surprise party is. Everyone seems to like the canapés I've chosen after going through seventeen different selections at the caterers. A pretty dark-haired waitress wearing low-slung jeans and a black vest top carries drinks to everyone, her careful, measured stride followed by lustful male gazes.

'This flat's amazing,' Justin declares, watching the waitress's progress. I nod, sipping another beer. The waitress smiles at me as she passes, and I feel a surge of wellbeing, a feeling that tonight, for once in my life, everything is going to be perfect.

Justin and I chat briefly, catching up on his career and the kids, on the Wilson family's plans to move from Balham to Barnes, while I keep my old acquaintance well fed with chicken vol-au-vents and questions. As Justin speaks, I wonder if he feels like I do, that it's nice to see an old familiar face, but not so nice to realize how little you have in common any more.

Justin must realize that he's being overly zealous in talking about his children, because he pauses abruptly, sips his lager, and asks:

'Enough about me. How's life with you, apart from the gorgeous squeeze? How's the travel writing lark?'

Justin, I note, is one of those people who consider any job that doesn't require you to take exams to be inferior, if not downright shady.

'Fine. I was in South America, but I did the ankle . . . once the cast's off next week I should be able to start travelling again . . .'

Then, for some reason, I find myself making up an

intricate and impressive lie about a forthcoming travel writing commission from *The New York Times*. As I'm wondering why I feel the need to invent this story, Gemma appears at my side. I turn quickly, immediately grateful for her presence. She looks great – she's wearing clothes I've not seen her in before – a low-cut black top and faded combat trousers.

'Everything's set, Ian. Molly's on her way.'

'You look great, Gem. Remember Justin?'

She smiles at the balding doctor, who shakes her hand brusquely.

'Hey, read my ass!' Gemma declares, turning to show us her backside. We peer closer. Across the seat of the combat trousers is emblazoned the word 'VELVET'. She laughs, coquettishly, and struts over to get a drink. Beyond, her mother looks on disapprovingly.

'Wow,' exhales Justin. 'She looks great! I haven't seen Gemma in, what, eight years? She's lost weight. She's quite the babe.'

'Gemma?'

'Yeah. Quite the babe.'

Drinks are flowing, voices rising. I look at my watch. 7.35 p.m. Molly should be here in about twenty minutes, if I know her well enough. I'll have to tell everyone to be quiet, to hide for her entry. I look around for Gemma. She's standing chatting to the South African barman. As I start towards them, my father walks up to me.

'Hello, Ian.'

'Dad. How are you doing?'

My father attempts a smile, then looks around the apartment.

'This is quite a pad . . .'

'Yeah. Molly's done very well for herself.'

My father takes a glass of apple juice.

'So . . . how was your afternoon?' I ask, falteringly.

'Fine. It was just an initial consultation . . .'

I nod. We stand, three feet apart, as music pounds around us. I have a sudden urge to hug my father, but I can't, surrounded by all Molly's friends and work colleagues.

'Hello, Reverend Thompson!'

Gemma is at my side, extending her hand for my father to shake. My father looks puzzled, she's holding out her right hand which demands that he holds out his right hand, but it's clasped firmly behind his back. Slowly, he unfolds his arm and his fingers are outstretched, his hand shaking uncontrollably. Gemma shakes it quickly.

'Good to see you, Gemma,' says my father, as if everything is fine. Gemma releases my father's hand, which falls to his side before creeping up to hide behind his back once more.

'I've been at the hospital all day . . .' says my father, as if this is an answer to a question that Gemma has posed him. Gemma, of course, looks confused.

'Dad's having tests, they think it might be Parkinson's,' I stammer, quickly. Gemma looks concerned.

'That's terrible . . .'

'Gemma's no big fan of hospitals either, Dad' I continue, clumsily, 'She never goes to her appointments . . .'

'What?'

Gemma is looking at me, her eyes narrowed.

'I saw that letter from the hospital about that appointment you missed . . .'

'I don't know what you're talking about!'

I look at Gemma, surprised. Her tone is angry, emphatic.

'Oh, sorry. Maybe I got the wrong idea . . .'

Beyond, by the bar area, the pretty waitress is trying to open another bottle of red wine. I turn and walk quickly over to her.

'Do you need a hand?'

She looks up and smiles.

'Obviously I should work out more often.' She hands me the wine bottle and I pull up the cork with relative ease. She smiles. I smile. I look back at my father and Gemma who are now talking animatedly. I wonder about Gemma and the hospital appointment. I must find a way to ask her if it's serious.

As I look at my watch (7.50 p.m.) and then around the room at the thirty-five people I've invited to Molly's surprise birthday party, Raj appears by the vol-au-vent table.

I breathe out. Suddenly my great plan for Gemma seems foolhardy. I realize that I didn't really believe that Raj would show up. I left him a message on his work number, telling him about the party, and asking him to come, just to say hello to Gemma. It made me feel better about the whole Neil scenario, which I was still feeling a little guilty about.

Raj sees Gemma, but Gemma's back is turned so she doesn't see Raj. I watch the lawyer pause. He's evidently trying to decide whether to get a drink first, or to say hello to his estranged wife. I wonder whether I should go up to him, but I don't want to appear until after the husband and wife have spoken.

Raj takes a drink from the pretty waitress, a glass of red wine. I watch as he glances over at his wife. He seems to inhale, as if trying to muster strength. Then he strides purposefully over, until he gets to within a step of her. And then he stops.

Gemma is in full flow, relating some story to Justin Wilson and my father. Raj doesn't want to interrupt her. So he waits, her shadow, shrinking smaller with each second that passes. I want to shout out to Gemma, like a child at a pantomime:

'Behind you!', but I've sworn myself to non-intervention. It's as if they are frozen, once more, in a tableau of separation.

Then Gemma pauses, Raj coughs, Gemma turns, and drops her drink. The glass shoots from her hand, as if sucked, to the floor. The glass shatters, the drink splashing her combat trousers. Gemma doesn't react. She stands, rigid, white-faced. My father steps back. Justin Wilson laughs. Raj falls to his knees, and hurriedly begins picking up pieces of glass. As he does so, Gemma turns and walks away.

I hobble fast to catch up with her.

'Gemma . . .'

Her glare is brimming with passionate fury.

'Why didn't you tell me? You bastard!'

'Slow down, Gemma, please . . .'

I catch hold of her wrist. It's always surprised me how thin and fragile her wrists are. My fingers meet around it. She stops.

'Look, he's just here for one drink. Have a quick chat, then leave it at that . . .'

Gemma looks at me, a hard stare, as if she's attempting to define some darker ulterior motive behind my words.

'Who do you think you are? Jerry bloody Springer?'

'Come on Gemma, what have you got to lose?'

Five minutes later, Gemma and Raj are sitting on the sofa by the window. I remain near the front door, wanting desperately to hear their conversation, but knowing I have to be alert to Molly's arrival. I am nervous. I think I hear the lift mechanism clunk. Footsteps in the hall.

Is Molly the one, I think suddenly? Is this it?

SEPARATION

I should be angry, I know, but I don't have the energy. I dropped the wine glass in surprise rather than fury. Part of me, I have to admit to myself, is intrigued to see Raj. It's a meeting I've imagined countless times, since the moment I heard the front door slam and the Audi charge away down Raleigh Street. I've pictured his face in various moods, from fury to contrition. Yet recently, my firm image of what he looks like has dissolved a little, like a television picture flickering and waning during strong winds.

He's thinner and more diminutive than I remember him. His slender body seems shrunken. His dark brown eyes look tired, ringed by dark shadows. He's nervous, I know by the way he holds his hands together, kneading the fingers as if they are clay. It shocks me a little to recognize his every gesture, his every intonation, his every look. I know him so well, whether I like it or not.

Raj leads me to my sister's hideous white leather sofa. I'm surprised by his forthrightness. Once installed, I swiftly review the numerous scenarios I've imagined for our first meeting since the split. I decide on the one which shows me in the best light – the trusty old 'Polite Grown-up Superficial Conversation Approach'. This will be the best tactic to avoid confrontation, at least to begin with.

'Well, this is a bit of a surprise . . .'

'I wasn't going to come. I didn't sleep at all last night. But I had to come . . .'

'How's the hotel?'

'I'm back at my parents. It was too miserable . . .'

I feel sick. The Singhs know. It's gone further than I expected. In a brief flash of panic, I wonder if Geeta Singh has called my own mother, to remonstrate. But my mother is standing by the window, laughing uproariously at another of Stanley Myers's terrible jokes. If she knew, she would have marched up to me and demanded an explanation the moment she saw me.

'Oh. What do they think about it all?'

'They're sad. And confused . . . They don't really understand . . .'

'Do they hate me?'

Raj looks at me, but not with the irritation I'm expecting following this somewhat self-centred remark.

'No. Of course not,' he says quietly. I realize I'm keeping my left hand hidden, underneath the cushion. I don't want him to see that I'm not wearing my wedding ring. But I shouldn't hide it. I should be strong.

I place my hand in my lap. His eyes flicker. He registers the ringless finger. I wait for him to say something, to protest and remonstrate. But he says nothing.

There's silence between us. I look away, not able to stay within the suffocating gaze of my estranged husband. I see one of Molly's friends, Amy, the really pretty one that all the men fancy. True to form they are all sneaking glances at her. Except Raj. He's still staring at me, I know, without looking back at him.

'Molly and Ian seem to be getting on well . . .'

'I've been thinking, Gemma . . .'

'What? What have you been thinking about, Raj?'

'About everything . . .'

There's something about his tone that scares me a little. He sounds . . . resolved. I turn back. He's looking down at the sofa, jawbones prominent, indicating clenched teeth. I feel my stomach tighten. What if he decides to divorce me? That's what it sounds like. Perhaps seeing me without my wedding ring has been the last straw. I've thought about such a possibility a thousand times in the past few weeks, but here, now, as it's happening in front of me, it seems too big, too horrible, too dreadful. Maybe he'll announce it here, in front of all my sister's friends, in front of my mother. If he divorces me, I will be alone. Completely alone.

'Raj . . .'

'No, Gemma. Let me speak. You owe me that much.'

I close my mouth. It's a childish gesture, I know, but instinctive. I can be respectful.

'I want to say sorry.'

I look at him, eyes narrowing, trying to detect which direction his speech is going in. My heart is beating fast. I wonder if he can hear it.

'I'm sorry I put my red socks with your underwear.'

'What?'

I look at him. What the hell is he talking about? Then I remember. The pink laundry. I'd forgotten about it – I'd simply bleached the vests to something approximating white, and the panties and bra had been consigned to my 'weekend slobbing' drawer.

'It doesn't matter, Raj.'

'It was a mistake.'

'I know.'

'I didn't mean to.'

'I said it doesn't matter!'

He's silent for a moment. I sense anger simmering. Was this all he wanted to say? Does he just want forgiveness for a minor domestic incident, so he can head off into a new life with someone else, happy in the knowledge that he can once again be trusted to do a woman's knicker wash?

When he speaks again, his voice is quieter.

'I know why you said what you did that Saturday.'

I decide to remain silent, suddenly terrified that he's known about the lump in my breast all along.

'I neglected you.'

'Raj . . .'

'Just listen, please!'

I close my mouth again, the human goldfish. He begins to speak, and there is something in his measured tone, in his exact and careful choice of words and stress, that tells me he's written this, probably on the computer, and practised it several times before coming to Molly's flat.

'I felt so rejected and hurt by you, Gemma. By what you said. I didn't know what to do.'

'So you just ran away? Like a bloody child?'

'I didn't know what to do! Yes, it was childish, but I was shocked. You'd rejected me. I had to get out. I went to work and I felt a little better. It was somewhere to hide. But the harder I worked, the less happy I was . . .'

I look at him, noting his wide open eyes, imploring me to believe in him. It's a shame his boss doesn't consider him feisty enough to plead in front of a jury. Any woman seeing those eyes would fall straight into them.

'Then, after Ian came to my office telling me I should talk to you, I wondered, had you sent him?'

'I didn't, I told you . . .'

'I know. But I wanted you to have sent him.'

'Why?'

'Because that would have meant you wanted me back.'

He looks at me, and I recall the same look three-and-a-half years ago, at the bar in Hoxton, a mile away from where we are on this night. It's the same mixture of confidence and extreme vulnerability. Back then I lost a breath on receiving that gaze. Tonight, it seems like a device, a ploy from the prosecuting council.

I say nothing. After a moment, Raj speaks again.

'I need you, Gemma. I haven't slept in weeks. I lie awake in that bed I slept in when I was ten and all I can think of is you.'

He breathes in deeply, and in doing so seems to straighten a little, growing as he talks.

'I love you. I will do whatever it takes. I'll give up work if I have to, find something else, something that allows me to spend more time with you. If you'll only give me a chance. Please?'

He finishes this typical reticent Raj performance with a small smile. It's his greatest weapon, and I'm sure he knows this. I wait, count to five, Gemma, and then nod twice.

'Well, that's just fine then. Thank you, Raj. You've done

your thinking. You've got it all sorted out. You will stop work and everything will be fine. Brilliant! Why didn't I think of that?'

My sarcasm is heavy. It's not a tactic I've used in a long while, and I'm pleased to discover that I'm still good at it. I have my sister to thank – Molly, the queen of the caustic reply.

'Please Gemma. I'm being serious . . .'

'So am I! God, men are so stupid sometimes!'

'Why? Why is this stupid?'

'You're just doing that typical male thing, you think that just because you've made up your mind, everything will be great. What about me? What about where I'm at?'

My sudden vehemence stems from relief, I know. He still wants me. I am still in control.

'I just thought . . . you were right about me not putting enough time into our relationship. I was too caught up in work. I don't care about the stupid bloody partnership . . . if I can't have you. I want a partnership with you!'

It's a good line, I have to give him that. He sounds more sincere, more desperate than I've ever heard him. I sense tears welling. I fight them back, with anger.

'You're overreacting, Raj! What good will that do, you giving up the job you love? You'd just resent me. It would be a nightmare . . .'

'I don't love it.'

'Yes you do!'

'THAT'S WHAT I'VE REALIZED, GEMMY! I HATE MY BLOODY JOB! I HATE THE WANKERS THAT WORK THERE!'

He's shouting now, but no one seems to hear him,

they're too busy in their own London conversations. He continues, his voice deep and surprisingly booming.

'I did law because I wanted to prove something to my parents. To myself. I wanted to fit in, because I've never felt like I've fitted in. But I hate the firm, I hate the people I work for. The only person who accepted me was you. You took me for who I am, not the colour of my skin, not my education, not my background. For me. And then you rejected me . . .'

'Don't turn this round, Raj!' It's my turn to raise my voice. 'I rejected you for a reason. For a good reason. You were taking me for granted. You thought you could just buy that bloody house and everything would be hunky-fucking-dory . . .'

'Gemma . . .'

'Don't you fucking Gemma me! I will fucking swear if I want to . . .'

'FUCK YOU, GEMMA!'

His face is suddenly flushed with rage. It's immensely attractive.

'What?'

'Fuck you!'

'Fuck me?'

'Yeah. Fuck you!'

'Jesus, Raj . . . fuck you too!'

I sit back, firmly, arms crossed. Rage crackles between us. For people who never fight, I think, this is a pretty good skirmish. I'm surprised how grown-up it feels. How good.

I look down at my lap, teeth clenched. I sense Raj is doing the same.

I might have cancer.

The words I should have said that Saturday night so long ago. Just four weeks ago.

But still I cannot say them.

I look up. He's still looking down at his shoes, hand kneading hand.

Can I say it? Can I? Instead, I hear myself say:

'I bought some cocaine.'

He looks up.

'What?'

'The layabout. He's a drug dealer, he sells cocaine, but just to his friends. So I bought some.'

'What the fuck are you talking about, Gemma?'

'Number twenty-two. The black door. I called by, and he sold me some Charlie.' I laugh as I say this, a high-pitched girlish out-of-control giggle. I sound ridiculous, like some sketch on a comedy programme in which a posh woman tries to talk about drugs. Raj knows I've never done drugs, not even marijuana. I've always maintained I don't need narcotics to get a buzz, even when my friends laugh at me.

'It's in my pocket. Come on, let's go and try some. In the toilet.'

Raj stares at me. He shakes his head.

'Don't be silly, Gemma.'

'You think I'm joking?' I plunge my hand into my bag and pull out the small plastic sachet of white powder. 'See?'

'Jesus Christ, Gemma, put that away! Are you crazy?'

I hold the sachet in front of him.

'Come on Raj. Live a little. Come and try some.'

'Please Gemma, can we just talk about things sensibly here . . . ?'

I stand, hurriedly.

'That's just your problem Raj Singh. You're too sensible. You're the most sensible, boring bastard I've ever fucking met!'

I lock the toilet door and sit down on the closed seat. My heart is thumping. When Raj didn't follow me, I cursed him until I got to Molly's large white mosaic bathroom and closed the heavy door behind me, one of Ian's balloons butting the wood happily, as if in celebration.

I know my sister will be arriving any moment. But I don't care. I want to be locked away in her toilet, taking drugs for the first time in my life.

I survey the small plastic bag of white powder. It looks so innocent. I open the bag, dip my finger in. The powder is soft, like baby talcum. I wonder, in this instant, whether anyone has ever rubbed cocaine into a baby's back by mistake.

Suddenly, I wish that Ian were here with me. I feel that in his presence, standing guard at the door, I would be able to do it. He would look after me. Unlike Raj, who cares only for himself, who was motivated to come to see me by loneliness and childish despair rather than wholehearted deep-seated love.

I feel sorry for my husband. He doesn't know how to live. I am only just beginning to know how.

I extract my finger. It's coated with white powder, like frosting. I've seen movies, I've read novels in which people stick their powdered fingers against their gums to ingest the last grains from the mirrored table top.

My finger trembles. It is, I realize suddenly, my ring finger. I look at the white line where my wedding ring used to be. An inch from the tip of white powder.

I rub the powder onto my right upper gum. Immediately the gum goes numb, as if from a dentist's needle. I taste chemicals and bitterness. I remember putting Ajax cleaning powder on my tongue as a little girl. This is similar. I spit hard into the toilet bowl once, then twice.

I empty the cocaine into the toilet, pull the flush, and place the plastic bag in Molly's bin. I exit quickly, heading for the front door. I open it, and step into the hallway. The lift is coming. I can see the number ascending, so I head for the stairs.

'Gemma?'

It's Ian's voice, but I cannot look back. I have to leave on my own. I have to be strong. I have to survive.

TREACHERY

'Gemma!'

I call after her a second time, but she doesn't look back. I think about heading after her, but then I see the lift dial flashing. It's Molly. I duck back into the flat, closing the door.

'She's coming!' I exclaim.

The music dips, everyone turns to look at the front door. My father smiles at me, I slap the light switch, the room darkens.

My heart is thumping. Faces turned in smiling expectation. Something thuds against the door, a key scratches in the lock. I can sense the rows of faces behind me, each holding their breath, the six syllables forming in their lungs, and the door swings open.

'Happy Birthday, Molly!' I shout, as Molly falls through the open door, her skirt around her waist, her knickers around her ankles, her blouse wide open revealing a naked breast popping out of a black lacy bra. With her falls a large man, his trousers around his knees, and as he tumbles I see a swift flash of erect penis.

Molly and her ex-husband Will Masterson are having sex.

They land on the floor at my feet.

Gasps ring around the room like air bubbles. Faces staring.

'What the fuck?' Molly's face is a snarl. Will Masterson is scrabbling at his trousers, desperately trying to stuff his genitals into his boxer shorts.

'Molly . . .' I stammer, my voice squeaking. I stare down at them, seeing Molly's beautiful white thighs, the dark triangle between her legs, the cream of her breast. I want to take her right there and then, but Will Masterson has got there first. Long before me.

'Molly . . .' The voice sounds like mine. Frantically, Molly pulls her skirt down, pushes herself to her knees.

I feel my anger fold like a blanket, smothering me. The sickening pain of betrayal.

'What are you doing?' My voice is cracking, I know tears are not far off. I struggle to breathe, to prevent myself crying. Molly is kneeling, holding her blouse shut.

'Shit, Ian, I don't know . . .'

I don't understand. She seems a different person. Or am I the different person?

'How long have you been fucking him?'

'Oh Ian . . .'

'Leave her alone!'

I turn. Will Masterson has jumped to his feet, trousers zipped, standing at Molly's side.

'Fuck off,' I say.

'Leave her alone, mate.'

'Fuck you!'

I step forward, Will Masterson reaches out and pushes me firmly. I stagger backwards, then rage roars through me and before I know what I'm doing, I swing my right fist at him. He steps nimbly to one side, my punch misses by twelve inches, and I continue forwards, ploughing straight into the pretty dark-haired waitress who is standing admiring the scene, holding a tray laden with champagne.

I fall hard. My knee clunks against the floor. My nose strikes something sharp and solid.

'Ow!'

I turn my head. I am lying on someone. I look up to see a pair of breasts. The pretty waitress struggles under me. I'm lying in her lap, pinning her to the floor. My nose throbs. I wonder which part of her body I've struck against.

'Help . . .'

A tray lies at her side like a fallen shield. I try to ease myself up. As I shift, the waitress manages to roll out from under me, springing athletically to her feet. She looks down at me.

'"Excuse me" would have sufficed,' she says softly. To my surprise, she doesn't seem angry.

The barman appears, pushing people aside. The waitress turns quickly to him.

'It's fine Zack, I slipped, that's all.'

I try to stand, but I feel too tired. Will Masterson offers his hand.

'Piss off,' I say, firmly.

'Go, Will!' Molly barks. Will Masterson steps swiftly away, exiting through the open front door.

I hold up my hand to my nose. There's a spot of blood, although it doesn't seem broken. Behind Molly, I see faces – her friends, her mother, Stanley Myers. And there, amongst the faces, my father stands, his face white and confused. He meets my gaze for a second, then jerks his head away.

'Sorry,' I repeat to the waitress. I reach clumsily into my pocket, pull out a twenty-pound note and thrust it up at her.

'It's okay. It was an accident.'

'Please.'

'If it makes you feel better.'

I push the note into her hand.

'Sorry,' I say once more. She smiles again. It is, I think for an instant, a very kind smile.

'Anything else broken?' She gestures at my plaster cast.

Everything's broken, I think. I shake my head. She nods quickly, and starts to pick up the broken pieces of glass.

The tears well in my eyes. In that instant, I wish Gemma were still here. I know she'd take over, she'd say the right damning, enraged words to Molly's face, before escorting me swiftly but proudly from the flat. I have to think like Gemma.

'Molly. Please tell me. What . . . what's going on?'

For a moment, Molly's face is impassive. I try to think of other words, to force some change in her facial expression. Then she nods once, biting her bottom lip. I love it when she bites her bottom lip. She looks so vulnerable. But it's just a trick. She's playing me, like a professional.

'Why, Molly?'

She speaks, finally.

'I don't know. I couldn't help myself. I'm sorry.'

Her voice is small. I am going to be sick. Another voice rings out.

'Ian!'

I look up. Raj is pushing through the faces, thrusting out my crutch towards me. I take the metal neck and push myself up.

'Thanks,' I mutter. Raj nods, then shrinks back into the onlookers.

I have to move.

'Ian . . .' Molly whispers. I hobble past her to the front door. I walk out in to the hallway and close the apartment door behind me.

I wait for the lift. I wonder why I don't feel more angry. I just feel exhausted. I want to leave, to disappear. I want to get on a plane and go to somewhere hot and difficult, where I can be worthy and interesting and detached.

The door to Molly's apartment opens. Justin Wilson appears. He's wearing a Barbour jacket over his checked shirt.

Justin holds out his hand. I shake it.

'Tough luck, mate.'

I can't look at him, shame burning my neck and cheeks.

'It's . . . I don't know . . .'

Justin nods, once.

'Thanks for the party.' He pats me on the shoulder and pushes open the door to the stairs. I look down. Justin turns round once more.

'You really are a stupid fuck, aren't you Thompson?'

'Pardon?'

'Either that or you're just stubborn.'

'Stubborn?'

'Don't you see it? Molly isn't worth it. She's a looker, but she's not a stayer. She doesn't deserve you.'

'Why not?' I want Molly to deserve me. I want us to be together. I want my plan to work.

Suddenly, Justin's hands are on my shoulders, grasping me tightly.

'You're only going out with her because she's a replacement for her sister!'

'What?'

'Gemma is the one, you crazy bastard! You two have been nuts about each other since the first time you met!'

'Nuts?'

'Yes. Fucking nuts! You fucking nutter! For fuck's sakes, go and do something about it!'

Just as suddenly, Justin releases me.

'What are you talking about?'

'As plain as raisins. You love Gemma, and she loves you! It's so bloody obvious! It always has been. Nobody can believe you two never got it together.'

I stare at him. Justin smiles broadly, then pushes the door, and disappears down the stairs.

I am a nutter. I am nuts about her.

Suddenly, it's clear. I know what I have to do.

I open the door to Molly's apartment. Fortunately, the South African barman is in the hallway.

'Pass us that knife would you?'

'What?'

'The knife you were using to cut up the lemons.'

'Sorry mate, . . . I can't do that . . .'

'Come on, just for a moment. I'm not going to do any damage . . .'

'What do you need it for?'

'I'll show you. Look, here's ten quid.'

The barman looks at me. He takes the ten-pound note and hands me the substantial serrated black-handled knife.

I lean down, slip the blade into the small gap between my shin bone and plaster cast, and pull the knife upwards. The plaster parts a little. I start to saw, back and forth, down the length of the cast. The dull top edge of the blade digs into my flesh, but I don't care.

'Hey . . .' the barman is leaning around the door, watching me. I look up.

'It's fine.'

The plaster splits easily. I pull the sides away with my left hand, ripping, tearing, enjoying the energy, my anger wrenching the innocent white plaster apart.

'No, you'll break the knife . . .'

'It's fine. I'm fine,' I look up at him with a wide, maniacal grin. I split the last of the cast, drop the knife to the floor, and rip the plaster shoe in two. My ankle and foot seem so thin, fragile and white, like something dug up after two thousand years in a bog. I wriggle my toes. They feel okay. I am free.

I hand the barman the knife.

'I'll have to wash it now,' the barman moans. I pick up the pieces of plaster cast, cradling them in the crook of my arm like precious relics.

'Do you have a bin?'

'Jesus Christ mate, anything else you want?'

I nod.

'How much for your shoes?'

I head due east, along Old Street. The barman's Puma trainers are just a little too small, which, considering they

273

cost me £120 in cash, is far short of a bargain, but they are better than the alternative of walking two miles wearing a single boot.

I push my right foot down gingerly on to the pavement. It hurts, I can't put too much pressure on it, but the ankle seems to hold. I wriggle my toes once more as I push off, curling them round as my foot steps down again.

I stare ahead, the shimmering tail-lights of the cars clear and brilliant in front of me.

Justin is right. How can I have been so stupid? All those years of friendship, of banter, of help and solace, of comfort and joy. Of course it was desire. Of course it was love.

Champagne courses through my veins, electricity sparking, my heart hammering my ribcage. I gulp in air, which on this London September night tastes sweeter than any I can remember. I see Gemma's face, her gentle smile; she has the prettiest smile, the loveliest laugh. Her beautiful breasts, I can't believe I've never imagined them before, her legs, a little chunky but powerful, they could wrap round you, and the dark place of pubic hair that I saw that night on her roof terrace, the centre of her.

The older you get, the fewer people you meet whom you really connect with. Gemma is great. Gemma is precious. Gemma is unique.

I want her. I want to kiss her, to feel her lips, her skin, her hair. I want to be inside her. I want her to be mine. This is my plan. The greatest plan of all.

I reach Hoxton and hobble across the road just as the lights change, the cars screeching their horns at me as I reach the other side, victorious, righteous, a man changed for ever.

Understanding

The house is dark. The builders have finished the plastering, added the rail to the top floor balcony, repaired the stairways and banisters. The concrete garden has been cleaned up, the watery holes filled in. £3,000 has cleaned up the mess. In the house at least.

It's a long way from the finished vision I planned so meticulously all those months, all those years ago. It's unrecognizable from the dream I luxuriated in, too excited to sleep, lying on the double inflatable mattress on our first night in the house of my dreams.

But it is presentable. We will be able to sell it. Raj will be able to move out and move on.

I cried, in the taxi on the way back east through Shoreditch, turning my face to the window so the driver couldn't see me. I hadn't meant to be so nasty towards Raj. It wasn't my plan. I reacted well to his appearance at the party, I tried to be light and superficial, and then I lost it.

Oh well.

Fuck it.

He seemed so physical when he swore at me. So unlike my husband. Remembering his snarling mouth, his glaring frown, his gruff deep voice, his clenched fist, I sense a pang of something strange that confuses me further. It feels like desire.

I smile, unexpectedly, despite myself.

God, I am a mess.

I climb up the ladder into the attic and crawl out to stand on the top floor balcony. The moon is full above the orange glow of London. I breathe in the night air. It's cooler now, a mid-September chill. I place my hand on the metal rail. It's pleasantly cold against my palm. Suddenly, I want to feel my cheek against the cold smooth metal. I kneel down and lean my head against the railing.

Tomorrow. I have to call the hospital tomorrow.

The hum of the nocturnal traffic. The beat of my heart. 'Help me, Dad.'

The doorbell rings somewhere deep below in the bowels of the house. I don't move. I can't move. It rings again. Suddenly, I'm scared. It's nearly midnight. Who could it be? Raj? I haven't the energy to have another slanging match. The police? Perhaps they've been carrying out surveillance on John Major, the drug-dealing ex-Prime Minister? But they have no proof I bought cocaine from him. Unless he told them. Perhaps it's John Major himself, wanting to sell me more drugs? I'll tell him, politely, to go away. I'll be firm, but friendly.

I decide not to answer.

The bell rings again, louder and longer.

I climb down the ladder, slowly. Hopefully by the time I get to the stairs, whoever it is will have gone away. I pause on the landing.

Silence. A creak from somewhere that makes me jump. Then the bell rings again, shrilly. The neighbours will be woken. I could shout at the person to go away. I could threaten to call the police.

I step down the stairs noiselessly and hurry into the kitchen. The bell rings once more. I open the drawer and take out a large kitchen knife. Again the bell rings, a long hard insolent buzz. I pause for a moment, in front of the front door, wondering what the hell I am doing with the knife.

'Go away!'

A muffled voice, possibly male. I can't make out the words.

'I'll call the police.'

Silence.

The bell rings again.

'Piss off!'

The bell rings once more.

'Go away!'

The bell rings three times, short bursts.

Holding the knife firmly, I open the door to the length of the short chain. I smell aftershave and sweat and wine. Somehow I recognize the smell.

'Ian?'

'Please, Gemma, I need to talk to you.'

I cannot deny that I am pleased to see him. Pleased, and worried, and angry and unsure. And, above all these other emotions, there flutters a strange excitement that I cannot categorize. It feels like a dream.

'What happened, Ian?'

'Molly. She's a fucking bitch.'

He's furious, that is obvious, his face red, the vein descending the left-hand side of his neck pulsating like an angry insect. But the interesting thing is, he doesn't seem sad, he doesn't seem hurt. He seems angry – an energetic, muscular, confident male anger. What is the word for it?

Righteous. His anger seems righteous. It is, I have to admit, very attractive.

'Molly was fucking Will Masterson. They were screwing in the doorway. Everyone saw them, my dad even saw them . . . I tried to punch him, but I missed, I knocked down this waitress . . .'

'You punched a waitress?'

'No, I sort of broke my fall . . .'

I notice his feet.

'Jesus, Ian. Where's your cast?'

'I cut it off. With a knife.' He looks up at me. 'Like that one. What the hell are you doing, Gemma?'

I look down at my hand. The fingers and the kitchen knife they clasp do not seem to belong to me.

'Protection.'

'Fuck me. Samurai Gem.'

I place the knife carefully on the countertop.

'Oh Ian . . .' I say, and it strikes me that I sound just like my mother, admonishing my father all those years ago.

'So that's it. Fuck Molly.'

He seems resolute. But it could be a front, hiding the real fear and panic. I decide to probe gently.

'You seem . . . I don't know . . . relieved?' I say, softly.

He looks at me, eyes narrowing, a small frown lining his forehead.

'Relieved? Yeah. I don't know. I feel fucking stupid.'

I nod. I have to admit that discovering I've been right

all along about Molly makes me feel awkward. I am glad in a selfish evil way, but sorry for Ian.

He shakes his head.

'I'm sorry to pitch up like this. I didn't really have anyone else to turn to . . .'

'Don't worry. What are friends for?'

Could it be like the old days? The two of us telling each other our problems, our fears, our hopes? Our plans? Our future? Can we be open and honest, about everything?

As I think this, the words form in my head, clear and bold, and I can hear them approaching my lips. I can tell him, can't I, about my lump, about the thing that is lodged within me, the terrible parasite. I can tell my best friend, my oldest friend. Ian will know what to do. Ian will sort it all out.

Even the worst case scenario, the scenario I am dreading with stark terror, will be better if Ian is here.

'Ian . . . I might . . .'

'Molly is such a bitch.'

I can't tell him. He's too caught up himself, in my sister, he's still under her evil spell. I glare at him.

'How does this work, Ian?'

'What . . . what do you mean? With Molly? We're finished . . .'

'Not with Molly! With me! With Gemma!'

It feels good to shout. It feels vital to shout. He looks at me blankly.

'What do you mean?'

'How are we, Ian? To each other?'

'We're friends, Gem . . .'

My heart is racing, my hands hot and damp.

'I mean . . . that thing we always talked about, what are we to each other? What do you want from me, what do you get from me, how does the whole fucking thing work?'

'Work?'

'"When Harry met fucking Sally!" Can a man and woman ever just be friends?'

'Gem . . .'

'Can they help each other, hang out with each other, hug each other, confide the truth to each other, and not slip into that horrible shitty trap of having to fancy each other, having to fuck it all up by wanting to go further?'

'It's okay, Gemma . . .'

'WHY DID YOU NEVER WANT TO SLEEP WITH ME?'

At architecture school, we went to Doncaster to watch the demolition of a 1960s housing block. When the building was dynamited, there was a moment after the explosives had detonated when nothing happened. Time was frozen. Perhaps, I thought, watching with my hands over my ears, it had all been a sham. Perhaps nothing would happen. Nothing would change.

Ian's mouth opens but no sound comes out. I cannot breathe. My muscles have locked. The words remain in the air, like the imprint of lightning on the eye.

This is it. The moment before the building falls.

Then, all at once, there is a rushing in my ears, and I take a snatched breath, and when I speak my voice is small and meek and dazed.

'I'm sorry . . . I don't know what I'm saying . . .'

He takes my face in his hands, and kisses me.

His fingers are cold. His nose is wet. He stinks of booze. His lips are flesh, not fire.

The kiss stops.

His hands drop to his side. I step back. I flick a strand of hair from my face.

'Wow.'

His word, but it's not joyful, not thrilled.

'No,' I whisper.

We stand, unable to move. At that moment, I remember my grandmother's funeral, my sickening sense of grief that something would be no more.

'Shit.'

His word again.

'Ian . . .'

'I should go.'

'No . . .' My voice possesses no conviction. 'Yes . . .'

'I'm sorry.'

'Don't be.'

'I'm really sorry, Gemma.'

'Me too.'

'I should really go.'

'Okay.'

I take his bag of clothes from the second bedroom and hand it to him. It feels like helping a stranger on to a bus. He says thank you, puts the bag over his shoulder and opens the front door.

'Bye.'

'Bye.'

I close the door slowly behind me. My hands are shaking. The building has fallen, and there is nothing left but dust.

VULNERABILITY

I do not know where I am going, but this in itself is my plan. I don't want to know where I'm going. The city is mine – all I have to do is to possess it, to walk down its streets and claim them for myself. I am a travel writer. I am an explorer. Anything might happen.

'Don't look back,' the voice in my head tells me. 'Keep going.'

I keep going westwards. I get to St John Street, where I try to remember who St John was, whether he was John the Baptist, or John the disciple. I sense I am trying to think of anything but the evening I've just been through. Perhaps it's the way the human brain copes with trauma, by stuffing the synapses full of irrelevant, unrelated thoughts.

St John was a disciple of Jesus. He wrote the last of the gospels, the only one to wholeheartedly push the idea that Jesus was the Son of God, that God dwelled in man and man in God. His was the last epistle, written many years after Jesus' death, when John could sit back and look at everything that had happened, and piece it together, point by point, place by place, to draw up the first map for the Christian church.

My father's name is John.

A sob swells in my throat, but I fight it back, speeding up my pace. The strap of the bag cuts into my shoulder, but I don't care. It feels like a fitting punishment.

Now I am into Clerkenwell, and the streets are full of Thursday-night drinkers who have been forced to vacate their pleasure-holes, but who seem reluctant to head home, aware perhaps that this is one of the last warm nights of the year.

I look at my watch. 1.30 a.m. I am three streets away from Molly's apartment, the scene of my first humiliation. The apartment I'd spent so long decorating, where I'd spent so much money to hire caterers, a DJ, a barman and a pretty waitress. I wonder if I have the strength to go back there and confront the birthday girl, to demand the money, in cash. But I can't. The shame would be too great.

I carry on, head down, walking faster and faster, to try and beat out the pain with each painful step.

I reach the looming arches of Smithfield Meat Market, which is alive with the barking cheerful voices of the butchers, small burly men in white coats stained with blood. The huge refrigeration trucks hum along the flanks, back doors open to reveal ethereal mists, lit by yellow lamps, in which large pale carcasses hang like fatty ghosts. I shudder. The air is thick with the curling stench of dead flesh, decay held at bay by ice and frozen air.

I wonder if I can climb into one of the trucks without being seen. They say freezing to death is the easiest way to end your life. After the first creeping pain, you feel nothing at all.

But I'm not brave enough. I realize now, I'm a coward. In so many ways.

I start to walk even faster, the bag thumping against my side, out of the market, along the side of St Bart's Hospital, down Little Britain. Suddenly, above me soars the huge white dome of St Paul's Cathedral, as spectral as the moon. I stop, breathing heavily.

Looking up at the great bone-white cathedral, I remember my first trip to London. I couldn't have been more than eight or nine, and we'd taken the train from Cambridge to the capital.

St Paul's Cathedral had been at the top of my father's list. I was secretly disappointed, having had my heart set on Madame Tussaud's or the London Dungeon, which my classmates had all been to, but I'd kept quiet because there was a childish excitement in my father's voice that I'd never heard before.

We climbed the rickety wooden steps, up and up and up. Near the top, I suddenly became very afraid, snatching terrified glances two hundred dizzying feet down to the marble floor below. But I was too afraid to show it, being at that age when boys want to prove that they are tough and independent and able to climb towering staircases without terror, without needing to hold their father's hand.

But I couldn't go on. My knees were jelly, my heart thudding like a small bass drum. Then, at the very moment I thought I might collapse, my father reached down and took hold of my hand, saying:

'It gets a bit steep for the next bit, perhaps we should help each other . . .'

And the hand was so large and strong and warm that the terror vanished in an instant.

We walked out from the musty bell tower on to the

narrow curved balcony with its gilt gold railings and I wanted to shout for joy at the panorama of London stretching for ever below us. My father stepped up beside me and lifting me up he pointed out all the famous landmarks of the city – Big Ben, Tower Bridge, the memorial column to the Great Fire of London, and in the far distance, the communications mast at Crystal Palace.

As my father talked, other people around us stopped to listen. Perhaps realizing he had a crowd, my father continued his verbal tour of the city, the city where he'd studied theology, where his first parish had been, telling tales of history, architecture and social intrigue. He took out a pen, and on the small cathedral brochure he drew a quick map, naming all the bridges – east to west – Tower, London, Southwark, Blackfriars, Waterloo, Westminster, Lambeth, Vauxhall, Chelsea, Albert, Battersea, Wands-worth, Putney, Hammersmith, Chiswick and Kew. He recounted how London Bridge was demolished and moved to Arizona, he talked of the Blitz and how each morning Londoners would gaze towards St Paul's to see if it was still standing, how its daily survival gave them hope and belief that the war would eventually end, and that God in His mercy was looking out for them.

The people around us applauded, and I felt my heart swell with pride. My father, suddenly embarrassed, took me by the hand once more and we descended quickly to meet my mother in the shop at ground level. I kept the map of the river for many years, in the bottom drawer of the night-stand by my bed.

Now I look up at the white columns, the silent stoic statues, and above the great dome, the gold cross. As I stand, the bells chime. It's 2 a.m. A massive, absolute peal that seems to shake the very building, the soaring columns, the vast wooden doors, the steps, and the city of London, which trembles at the voice of the Lord.

I shiver. The bells stop.

For a brief moment, London, England, the United Kingdom, the World is silent. Then, from the silence, come six words.

'Please God, let my father be okay.'

I don't think the voice is mine. But no one else has spoken.

I stand in the middle of Blackfriars Bridge and take out my *A to Z*. I have to decide where to go, I have to find refuge for the night. I recall seeing a hotel on a previous visit across the bridge, but I can't remember which street it was on.

I survey the *A to Z*, the two pages of streets and parks and stations and river, trying to figure out where I've been and where I'm going to go. I need landmarks, I have to figure out a route. As I stare at the map I see Gemma's face, after I kissed her. Her eyebrows raised, eyes wide with a bemusement that was gentle, not angry, her lips parted slightly, as if she'd just spat out a cherry stone.

'No!'

I have destroyed my one solid landmark in this city, the one edifice I need to orientate myself in the chaos of my life.

Gemma.

My best friend. My relationship with her is the only thing that has made me feel grown-up. The only thing that has made me feel real, feel attached to something beyond my own thoughts, my own interior, imaginary world. She has been the one constant in my life for the last twelve years.

I look out at the shimmering lights of London, a city of eight million people, covering 610 square miles. I stand, feeling miserable and utterly alone, on the cold old bridge.

In this moment, I remember sitting on a dusty step at Volubilis, a ruined Roman city in Morocco. A tour guide approached with a party of Australian tourists.

'Over there, is a wonderful example of early Etruscan frieze work . . . above the right shoulder of the man sitting on the step.'

I turned to look at where the guide was pointing, only to hear a commotion from the tourists.

'He's moved.'

'Which shoulder?'

I realized the man sitting on the step was me. The tour guide smiled my way, apologizing for using me as a reference point, a Meridian line, a 'You Are Here'. I smiled back. For a moment, then, I felt vitally important. I was the centre of everything.

'Fuck!' I shout, and throw the *A to Z* hard into the river. It falls through the orange light from the street lamps, pirouetting once, then hitting the water with a small splash. A wave gulps, swallowing the book of maps beneath the Thames.

For an instant, I think about throwing myself after the book. I imagine the cold ancient water hauling me down, into the swirling darkness. No one would know. Until it was over. I smile, bitterly. I will never jump into the river. I am not strong enough.

Beyond, the dome of St Paul's shines more brightly than the moon. To my left, a train eases itself out of Blackfriars station, seemingly reluctant to begin its journey at this early hour, yawning with fatigue at having to trundle forth into the weary depths of the night. I see the figure of the driver, hunched in his cab, and wonder whether he too, on this September night, is feeling the extreme cutting loneliness of the big city. Above the cab, I read the illuminated destination, which makes me laugh out loud, a self-pitying exhale.

Brighton via Gatwick Airport.

Brighton. I never want to go back there, to the place and time before I managed to fuck it all up. Brighton is now on my hit list, my own personal axis of evil (which includes very few places, to be fair – just Norfolk Virginia, Casablanca, Canberra, Belgrade and Switzer-land).

The train rattles slowly by, most of the brightly lit carriages empty except for a few seats occupied by people guarding large suitcases and roller luggage.

Gatwick. It's impressive that trains run at this hour to the UK's second biggest airport.

Gatwick.

I pick up the holdall and run for the first time in four months, towards Blackfriars Station.

*

The 3.06 Thameslink service from Blackfriars arrives ten minutes late at Gatwick Airport, stopping at 4.02 a.m. I am surprised to find the south terminal inhabited by several groups of holidaymakers – flights seem to be leaving all through the night.

I check my bank account at the ATM machine. I have £77 in my current account, and £2,025 in my savings account. I sit down on the row of seats opposite the Quickflight Shop. The board on the wall announces numerous potential aeronautical bargains. San Francisco £199, Cyprus £89, Kuala Lumpur £319. The shop will open, according to the sign, at 5.30 a.m.

I do not sleep. I do not reminisce. I stare at the list of flights to the world's favourite holiday destinations, and I picture myself in every one. Then I panic. Where is my passport? I open the bag, and rummage quickly. To my relief I locate the brown envelope containing my life's documents. I empty the envelope onto my lap.

My passport lies, smugly, with its reassuring burgundy cover. I flick through the other papers – my driving licence, the now-defunct rental agreement for the flat on Norfolk Place. And a letter with the *Daily Times* letterhead. I look at it. It's my commissioning letter for Venezuela.

To whom it may concern,
Ian Thompson has been commissioned by the travel editor to write an article about Venezuela for the Daily Times, *which has a circulation of over 1 million. Any assistance you can provide him will be credited in the newspaper.*

I go to the toilets and open the bag once more. In the musty, overheated cubicle I pull out my black combat trousers, my linen shirt and my worn pair of Nike walking boots and put on my armour once more.

WONDERMENT

I sleep for the first hour, missing pre-breakfast drinks, much to my annoyance. What is the point in flying Business Class (the letter from the *Daily Times* procured me the usual upgrade) if you don't avail yourself of all the luxuries on offer? The stewardess smiles sweetly and informs me that she will be more than happy to bring me a cocktail of my choosing if I can wait for a minute or two. I wonder for an instant if I should ask how I might feel 'more than happy', when most people can't admit to being 'happy', but already the hot croissants are being handed round, along with more champagne, so I shake my head and ask for two glasses of bubbly.

'To catch up.'

The stewardess's smile becomes less sugary. She hands me two glasses of Lanson, and turns on her attractive heels.

This isn't like me. Usually, on a travel writing assignment, I am reserved, careful not to make a fuss or abuse the abundant hospitality on offer. But on this Friday morning, I don't care. I have nothing to lose.

While I pick at the omelette, which is gratifyingly fluffy and light, I wonder, not for the first time in my travelling career, what would happen if the passengers seated in the higher numbers ever found out about the disparity between the food offered on either side of the cotton drape that divides Business from Economy like West from East Berlin. There would be a 1989-style Gorbachev revolution. Flat-bed seats would be ripped up and the individual DVD players hurled on to the airport runway.

I ask for another glass of champagne.

From across the aisle, a young father glances over at me, eyes narrowed. He is evidently concerned that I am a problem drinker, on course to alcoholic obliteration, and as such present a clear and present danger to the peace and tranquillity of his travelling family – a little girl and a baby, who at this moment is nuzzling covertly at its mother's breast. It is, I can't help but notice, a very pretty breast. Like Molly's. My girlfriend. My ex-girlfriend. The woman who has ruined my life.

You think you know everything, and then you realize you know nothing.

I have to focus, I have to avoid thinking. I stare at my omelette and decide to cut it into the smallest pieces I can, tiny forkfuls, which I stab, minutely, one by one. I put on my headphones and glance at the film, which seems to be something starring Al Pacino and a gun. But I feel so weary. I down the last of the champagne and close my eyes.

The exuberance I'd felt at the gate when they'd told me I would be upgraded has vanished. I feel queasy. I wonder whether eggs and champagne are the best combination at 35,000 feet. I try to focus forward, to imagine what will happen on landing, to possess and control the future, as an antidote to the confusion and chaos of the past. Usually, I am good at this forward strategizing, it helps me complete my assignments on time, it's vital to plan every hour of every day in the destinations I visit.

San Francisco. I know the city relatively well, having been there three times before. I can find a cheap hotel in the Castro. I can eat for next to nothing in the Mission. I can spend my days walking, maybe catch the ferry over to Sausalito, or rent a bicycle and cycle over the Golden Gate Bridge into Marin County.

My return ticket is for three weeks' time. It's a perfect plan, to head to the city of Kerouac and Armistead Maupin, to gather myself, breathe in the big Pacific air, and map out what I will do next. And there is, I tell myself, always the chance of meeting a beautiful Californian girl, and an immediate fast-forward to a wedding on the Bay within a year. Perhaps this is what is meant to happen all along. Perhaps this is the first step on the final, glorious route to Ian Thompson's Perfect Future.

The plane hits turbulence, the seat belt sign flashing. My stomach leaps into my mouth. I grip the armrests. Usually I don't mind shaky plane rides, I can think my way out of the airplane to my destination, or to some pleasant memory that usually involves a naked woman. But at this moment, I feel terrified.

The plane lurches again, dropping through an air pocket. I feel immensely sick, a dizziness that is familiar – I am back at St Paul's, twenty-three years previously, with the earth rushing towards me. The plane dips, somebody screams. I grip the armrests tighter.

No one knows I am on this plane. No one knows I'm going to America. And no one cares. Molly doesn't want me. Justin Wilson thinks I'm a fool. And I've destroyed everything with Gemma.

My parents will care, I know that. But my father has

Parkinson's. Before long he will be incapacitated. My mother has more to worry about than her moneyless, friendless loser of a son. I am on my own.

My fingers dig into the metal armrest. The plane plunges again.

Why am I running away? Why is this always my first instinct, to get on a plane and flee? To seek out the anonymity of foreign places, to crave the irresponsibility of being a stranger in a strange land? Why do I always do it? Why can't I face myself?

The engines roar as the 747 climbs steeply, the sound almost deafening. The young girl opposite is cowering in her father's arms. The pretty wife is white with fear as she cradles the screaming baby. I turn to them and say:

'It's okay. I'm a travel writer, I fly all the time. These 747s have amazing computers, they can fly through anything. It'll pass.'

I sound calm. The woman nods.

'It's perfectly normal.'

The plane levels. The turbulence stops. Two hundred and thirty-six people let out a sigh of relief, as one.

I turn to the window so no one will see the tears which fill my eyes and begin to run down my cheeks.

A while later, the Captain informs everyone it's safe to leave our seats. I stand and head to the toilet. The man and his wife smile briefly at me as I pass.

I wipe my swollen, puffed eyes and look into the small over-lit mirror. The reflection that stares back at me looks older than I'd expected. In the slightly receding line of its hair, in the more sunken setting of its eyes, in the gentle encroaching looseness of the skin under the chin, I recognize someone else. For the first time in my life I see how the son will become the father. It makes me sad. But it is also a relief.

I want to speak to my dad. I want to tell him that I miss him, that I am still a son who needs kind words and advice. I want to prove to him that I am worthy of the Vicar's love and time and affection, as much as his congregation, as much as the poor, deranged and infirm who flock to the Vicarage, the lost sheep.

Back in my seat, I try watching the film once more, but I can't make out the plot and my headphones aren't working properly. I think about complaining but then I drift into sleep. I wake some time later. The sun is cutting in from the opposite window. I wonder if I can ask the young husband to close it, but he is asleep with his wife's head on his shoulder, the little girl curled in his lap, the baby asleep in a travel cot on the floor. They look so peaceful.

I open the blind by my window. Below, I can see white land, probably Greenland. In the bright sun the ice shines blue and silver, extending to the horizon. Small flecks of icebergs dot the dark sea. I imagine myself, Ian Thompson, alone on the ice, an explorer in furs with yapping dogs at my heels, striding forth to map out new lands. It's an image I created many years before, as a child, reading *Adventure Stories for Boys* by torchlight, beneath my sheets.

Yet at this moment the image of the solitary heroic Ian Thompson fills me with dread. I don't want to be out there, in the wilderness, on my own. I want to be back in London. I want to see Gemma, and apologize. I want to see my parents, to ease their stress and their fear. I want to sell the map of Palestine and give them the money. For the first time in my life, I want things to go backwards, to return to the time before.

The stewardess asks me if I'd like a pre-lunch drink. I order a coke, which seems to please her. She pours it, smiles sweetly once again, and places the drink and a small bowl of cocktail snacks by my left arm.

'Good sleep?' she asks, softly.

'Yes, thanks. Really good.'

I know what I have to do. I take a sip of the coke, reach out and take the Airphone from the back of the seat in front of me. I've never used one before, but it seems straightforward enough. I swipe my credit card in the slot, and dial Gemma's mobile number. To hell with the cost.

I feel a flash of excitement as the crackling silence becomes a dull ringing. I will say I'm sorry, say I want things to be like they've always been, that I am her best friend and I want nothing more from her than her trust and laughter and ability to listen to me in a way no one else can.

As I wait for her to pick up, I take a snack from the bowl. It's salty. I bite quickly and swallow.

I know immediately.

'Shit!'

I look at the bowl. It's full of walnuts. As the two nutty pieces disappear down my throat I feel the tingling. I cough, trying to regurgitate, but it's too late. Just a speck of walnut affects me. I've never eaten a whole one before. I gag, spit rising. Where is my adrenalin shot? Where is it? WHERE?

Then, in a moment of absolute terror, I remember. My

epi-pen stabbed Molly's thigh. I threw it away. I've been meaning to get another one, but with everything that has happened . . .

I drop the phone. The receiver hangs forlornly, swinging back and forth. I punch the SERVICE buzzer in the armrest. I rip open my seatbelt. I can feel my hands itch, my back, the swelling of my skin, my throat beginning to close, I can't breathe properly, I fight for breath.

'Please . . .'

I stumble into the aisle, the young husband looks up, dazed and concerned.

'I . . . ate . . . a . . . nut . . .'

I clutch my throat. The stewardess steps out from behind the curtains, and hurries towards me.

'Are you all right?'

I'm clutching my throat like a character in a bad horror movie, I rasp for air, but I know what is happening, my throat is swelling, closing the air passage, my heart rate dropping, I feel dizzy, faint, my back and armpits and groin swelling in a mass of hives. I can't breathe. Anaphylactic shock. It happens so quickly . . .

I lurch forward, arms outstretched.

'Nuts . . . aller . . . gic . . .'

'Oh my God! Do you have medication?'

But I can't suck in enough air. I stumble and kneel and then collapse on to the floor of the aisle. I can't see clearly, my vision blurring. I can feel the hard sticky carpet beneath my head, and I turn, looking back upwards and faces are staring down at me in concern and fear.

Fight it, Ian, fight it.

I have to breathe, but each breath is becoming more

difficult, my lungs seem to be shrinking, smaller and smaller, my mouth is full of spit and the horrible, alien toxic taste of walnut and I want to be sick, but I have to keep breathing.

I sense movement above me, and voices, but I am feeling lighter, as if the blurriness of my vision is seeping into my blood. Then, at once, I sense myself lifting, and I am looking down at my body lying prone in the aisle of the Business Class section of the British Airways 747, unknown people crowding around me. It is both strange and strangely familiar.

Keep breathing. Don't give in . . .

Yes. Yes. Yes. I have to breathe. But I can't.

I see faces, but they aren't the people from the plane, they are familiar faces – Justin, Raj, Molly, Gemma, my mother and my father. Suddenly I am filled with a surge of love for each of them, a feeling that makes me tingle and swell. As I choke, I see again moments in my life when I've felt overwhelmingly happy – the view from St Paul's as my father describes the history of London, my first kiss with Sarah Lawrence, meeting Gemma at the pizza-eating contest at Sheffield, my thirty-yard goal for the first team against Manchester University, my first travel writing article, a sunset in the Maldives, Molly's small nose against my neck, my father's smile at the café in Soho.

I breathe out. Maybe my father has been right to believe all along. Maybe everything is connected by an invisible thread that is only detectable at the end. Maybe the head does not rule, maybe it is the heart that has to be followed, because the heart knows what the head and eyes can never know, that love does indeed make the world go round, and all we need is love.

The plane banks. Sunlight strokes my hair. It's the most beautiful light I've ever seen.

'See Dad? That's Him, isn't it? That's Him.'

'Yes Ian. That's Him.'

I am happy. I am more than happy. I part my swollen lips and try to smile. Then, swiftly, before I can say another word, the plane banks again, and everything fades into darkness.

XENOPHOBIA

My mobile rings but when I answer all I can hear is loud
static. I wait for a moment, but no voice emerges from
the crackling din, so I turn off my phone. I have drawings
to annotate, I have materials to select, I have costings and
invoices from the bar to go through.

I sit at my desk, enjoying how comforting it feels to be
back in my space, with my large white monitor, my wall
calendar, my selection of coloured felt-tip pens and my
big black stapler that is so solid and dependable, unlike
the men in my life.

I walked into the office like Clint Eastwood, I think
(with the steadfast stride, but without the poncho and
cheroot). Gwen Jones looked up, nervously.

'I want to get back to work,' I declared. 'There's no
hard feelings. It's all forgotten.'

'Er . . . all right. Fine . . .' Gwen stammered. 'Welcome
back, Gemma. And, er . . . thanks.'

Clicking through the client drawings I am relieved to
find that everything seems on track. It is good to see all
the layouts in order, everything organized and correct and
on course to meet the October deadline. It's all so neat,
so sensible. I feel my stomach relax, my lungs open. I find
myself humming a song, something that seems familiar, a
Top-40 hit I heard blasting from a kid's headphones on
the bus.

'Love me, hold me, I'm yours eternally . . .'

I try not to think about Ian. He will be all right. He is resourceful. I suspect that he'll get on a plane and travel somewhere for a while. I don't blame him. After all, I am escaping myself, returning to work. Flight from trouble is a natural instinct, I think, much more so than staying put to face the onslaught. It's only human.

Yet, I don't feel like I am escaping. For some reason, on this sundrenched Friday morning, I feel stronger. Something is different, as if elements have shifted and are now in a better, more cohesive alignment. I can't define it. I can't map it, or plan it out, hard as I try. I just feel better.

'Gemma?'

I jump, swivelling round on my chair. Duncan Archer steps back. He looks exhausted, but well groomed, his skin taught and freshly shaved, his eyes sunken and sad. He is wearing a sombre grey suit and a light blue T-shirt.

He holds his hands together, as if embarking on a prayer.

'I am so very sorry. I will never forgive myself. I was completely out of order. It will never, ever happen again. With anyone.'

I have always found the expression 'to wring one's hands' comic, but here, now, in front of me, Duncan Archer seems to be doing exactly that – his two hands clasped together, swinging up and down like a small bell. He seems smaller. I feel sorry for him. But I'm not going to let him know that.

'I should have sued you, you bastard.'

He nods, like a small boy.

'Yes. It was unforgivable.'

There is silence between us. He wants forgiveness, I decided from the outset to grant him forgiveness, but at this moment, I'm not sure I want to give it to him. I glance left and right, to see if others in the office are watching, but everyone is working at their desks, heads down. Evidently, no one else knows what has happened between us.

'Why did you do it, Duncan?'

'I was drunk, but that's no excuse. I'm sorry, Gemma. I'm so . . . so disorientated. I love my wife . . . now, of course, I want her so much. And I can't have her. And it's my fault I can't have her.'

He seems defeated, but anxious to talk about his defeat.

'I've ruined everything, and I've only realized the damage I've caused now that it's too late. I couldn't see what was in front of my own eyes, it was there, in front of me, but somehow I couldn't see it. I feel like some bloody old-fashioned explorer who thought he'd found El Dorado, only to find he's completely in the wrong place and about to be eaten by cannibals!'

I imagine Duncan Archer in safari suit and pith helmet being stewed in a cannibals' cauldron. It's not an unpleasant picture.

I nod, once. This is as supportive as I want to be. I say nothing. Duncan Archer coughs, then continues:

'Anyway . . . I am taking some time away from the department. Nigel and Gwen will run things. If you feel it's appropriate, I'd like you to be Project Manager on two new commissions, a restaurant conversion in Borough and a retail space in Brixton. We'll double your salary, you'll have a team of five people working under you, you can select whomever you want.'

He coughs again, his eyes narrowing to a beseeching frown.

'Please Gemma. Stay. I trust you. You are honest, unselfish and you care about the people you work with. I want you to help build the future of this department, whether I'm involved or not.'

I look at him. Two years ago I would have dreamed of hearing these words. But now I feel overwhelmingly sad. It's likely that I will not have a future, at this company or anywhere else. Can I tell him that?

'I'll think about it.'

'I'm in therapy, Gemma.'

I nod.

'The Borough restaurant is a great project, I've drawn a sketch, it's on Snowfields, do you know the area?'

'I don't think so . . .'

'It would be fabulous if you could start Monday . . .'

I nod, reaching in my bag. As I take out Raj's *A to Z*, I remember the front cover. I open it.

Raj ♥ Gemma.

I hold out the page to Duncan.

'Look.'

He smiles.

'Very romantic.'

My finger lingers over the worn black ink.

'Yes,' I say, firmly. 'It is.'

After Duncan departs, I sit at my desk, unable to take my eyes from the black heart on the white cover. Why did

Raj draw it? Why did he spend so long neatly colouring it in? It's a perfect heart.

On our first date, we went to dinner at a small French restaurant in Soho, where the candles stood in wax-caked bottles, the wine was cheap and the tablecloths red-checked. Raj's knife was dirty, and he asked for another one. The peppery onion soup made me cough, and I asked for a glass of water. We've been back several times – on each occasion ordering the same meal – onion soup, steak with Roquefort sauce, crème caramel, coffee and armagnac. Each time he has asked for the knife to be changed, and I've coughed after a mouthful of soup, in remembrance of our First Dinner.

Ritual, I realize, makes a relationship. We are encouraged to believe it's the one-off occasions, the incredible once-in-a-lifetime moments that cement two people together, but it's not. It's the repetition, the small, inconsequential things that become vital and huge. The mortar between the stone.

His signature, so small and restricted.

His toothbrush, always blue, always medium bristles.

His 'Ummm' while he thinks of the next thing he wants to say.

The way I always forget to check there's a towel in the bathroom, and the way he always admonishes me, but always brings me one.

The personal history of a couple that is like and unlike any other couple.

In that moment, sitting at my desk on a sundrenched Friday afternoon, I realize for the first time why I told my husband that I didn't love him. When I said 'I don't love you' I was saying it to myself. My self-loathing.

I blamed myself for the lump in my breast. I felt it was my punishment for not being satisfied with my easy, luxurious life, when my sister and my mother had suffered so much. I hadn't been content with my handsome, successful husband, my fabulous four-storey house, and my job at one of the five best architecture firms in the country. So I had to be punished.

Molly was the one who was meant to succeed. She was the eldest, the good girl. Not me. I had upset the plan, I was wrong. And the tumour had appeared to tell me that.

'You must be destroyed,' it had said, 'because you are not worthy. Not only have you been granted these things in error, but you do not even appreciate them.'

And so I pushed Raj away. Because I was not worthy.

'I don't love you any more.'

I realize more, as if understanding a language for the first time. I said those words in the hope that he would protest, that he would not leave, that he would stand up for his love, and force me to reveal why I'd said them. It was a test that I'd set for him, just as I'd tested Neil, so disastrously, all those years ago.

Is it because of my father's death? Do I have a deep-seated fear of being abandoned? Does this result in my subconscious need to test people, to ensure that they will not leave me?

Whatever the reasons, everything seems clearer now. Now I know.

I know for certain that a career is important and promotions are important, and that money is necessary and a nice house that will impress your friends and your relatives and your milkman is of value, and that holidays to new and interesting and sunny places are indispensable, but that when it comes down to it, all these things don't mean very much, unless you have someone in your life whom you trust, whose flaws and talents are known to you more than anyone else's flaws and talents, and whose back fits into your chest when you curl into them in the darkest hour of the night.

I catch a cab to Moorgate. The receptionist recognizes me from an office drinks party and tells me to go through. I walk up to Raj's desk. I will not tremble, I will not flinch.

'Hi.'

He looks up, and his mouth opens but no sound comes out. I look at him, and I picture him as an old man.

Perhaps this is the challenge in life. To make a decision to love someone and stick to it.

'I have something to ask you.'

'What, Gemma?'

He seems scared, as if this might be the end.

'Will you come to the hospital with me?'

'Why? What's the matter? Are you okay?' There's panic in his voice.

'Will you come with me right now and be there whatever happens?'

He pauses before answering, seemingly aware that what I am asking is serious and big. I wait, knowing that the tone of his reply will tell me if I've been right to take this gamble.

'Yes.'

He picks up his jacket and turns to a tall man I recognize as his boss, Peter Saville.

'I have to go. I'll call in later.'

'But the Samuelson report is due at the New York office by close of play their time, Singh . . .'

'I'm sorry Peter. I have to go.'

'Singh . . .'

But Raj is already walking away. I can't help a quick high laugh as we stride from the office.

'Wow.'

Raj turns and smiles.

'Maybe the leopard can change his spots,' he murmurs softly.

We walk out into the bright light, and I stumble slightly. His fingers brush against mine. He steps to the curb and shouts for a taxi, and as we wait for the black cab to pull up, I reach out and take his hand. I squeeze gently. His hand is warm. It feels like home.

Yin-yang

Three weeks later.

I find the place. Page 30 of the London *A to Z*. Burleigh Street, Covent Garden. The coffee shop, Pietros, is halfway down, next to a Burger King and a branch of Pret a Manger. I wonder why he chose this place. Probably because of its old-fashioned Italian espresso machine and the wizened old man sitting in the corner. Authentic. That's what he'd call it.

I order a cappuccino and look at my watch. He's five minutes late. But I can forgive him that, after all that has happened.

Suddenly, I feel nervous, an anxiety fizzing through me. I sip the coffee which is thick and creamy. No more nerves, please, I think. No more terror.

But it's unavoidable. I am fretful, yes, I am full of fret, because I have no idea how this meeting will work out.

He called me. I listened to him, feeling a rush of conflicting feelings as he explained what had happened. We arranged to meet.

'Hi, Gemma.'

I look up. He is standing there, by my table. He must have walked in as I was fretting. He looks well, better than I'd imagined. I beckon for him to sit down opposite me.

'Do you fancy a coffee?'

'Please. Espresso. They're really good here.'

I look at him, trying to divine what has changed in him. He has a vague tan, his hair is shorter, eyes are bright. He looks as if he's had a lot of rest. But I know any real changes will not be visible. They will have to be deduced.

'Well . . .'

He looks worried.

'Well . . .'

'It's good to see you, Ian.'

He smiles.

'It's good to see you too, Gemma.'

We order more coffee and I listen to his story, as I've listened to countless stories he's told in the past, and as I listen, my head nodding occasionally, my mouth interjecting 'ummm' and 'no way' at intervals, it is pleasantly familiar.

Ian tells me about eating the walnut, and losing consciousness, and the passenger who raced up the aisle with his own epi-pen of adrenalin, ripping down Ian's trousers and plunging the needle into his trembling thigh before anyone could stop him.

'He saved my life. This undertaker from Oregon, in his forties, a little normal-looking bloke, you wouldn't look at him twice, and he saved my life. An undertaker. Isn't that funny?'

I nod.

'Wait. It gets stranger. It turns out that he'd only been diagnosed with a bee-sting allergy three days before he was due to travel; it was his first ever trip outside the States, for this undertakers' conference in Slough, so he'd bought the epi-pen because someone told him there were lots of bees in England. He'd never even used it before, but he said he was pretty used to sticking things in corpses. Morten Chambers. From Eugene, Oregon. I sent him a case of champagne. He's invited me to go and stay with him and his wife next time I'm anywhere near the west coast. They've got two small kids. I might go. It's strange. I feel this weird bond to him.'

'Well he did save your life.'

'Yeah. An undertaker saved my life. How strange is that?'

Ian explains how the plane was diverted to a Canadian airfield called Goose Bay, where he was taken to hospital for observation. Apparently the airline were great about it, as were the passengers. They clapped and cheered him off the plane.

'It was like I was a hero. I'd cheated death.'

I nod and smile once more. Perhaps everyone glimpses their own mortality as their twenties end. Or perhaps Ian and I have been in some way privileged.

It's clear that now Ian has finished the story he's been so excited to tell, he is feeling uneasy. It's as if he's been racing up a mountain, and has stopped to see how far he's come, only to realize how far he has still to go. I sense my own discomfort returning, the gap between us expanding once more, like a pool of icy water freezing as it spreads.

I sip my coffee which is now cold and bitter. Ian picks up his espresso cup, then realizes it's empty and places it down. A car passes. There's laughter from someone on the street.

'I was calling you . . . when I ate the nut.'

I look up at him.

'What? From the plane?'

'Yeah. I just wanted to say . . .'

His voice trails off. Suddenly I am terrified that he is going to tell me that he loves me and he wants me and that he'll do anything to have me. It would be too horrible. I don't want him like that. I was just lonely and jealous and confused, that's why I said those things about sleeping with each other. I don't want his passion. I don't want his love. I want him as my support, my diversion, my confidant, my friend. I want the old Ian, and the old Gemma. Too much in life is new and difficult. I want continuity, I want connections to everything that has gone before. Is that too much to ask?

He speaks again.

'I guess I wanted to tell you that there were definitely a few times, at the beginning, when I wanted to sleep with you.'

'It doesn't matter, Ian . . .' I interrupt him, quickly.

'I mean who wouldn't? You're attractive, you're wonderful, of course I'd want to have sex with you . . .'

The old man in the corner peers over the top of his paper. The café seems deafeningly quiet as Ian continues:

'. . . in some ways I've always been jealous of your boyfriends . . .'

'Of Raj?'

'Yeah. I guess so.'

I want to leave, things can never be the same again, I've been so stupid, so naive to think they can be.

'. . . That's the curse of being male, I guess, sometimes you think with your dick.'

I glance up at the waitress, who seems to be smirking behind the cappuccino machine. My face burns scarlet. I cough.

'Look Ian, maybe we should talk about this some other time . . .'

'What I'm trying to say is that, you know . . . you're my best friend.'

He looks at me.

'I love you more than I've ever loved anyone . . .'

'Ian, please . . .'

'Not romantically . . . not anything like that, but more as . . . I don't know . . . a sister. That's it. I feel like you're my sister, even though I've never had a sister, but I can't think of any other way to describe it, it's like you and I, we learn so much from each other, don't we? I mean we can . . . Look, Gemma, can we forget everything? Can we start again?'

I look at him. I want to laugh. He gazes back at me, blushing.

'How about it? Would you be my sister?'

He is the old Ian, both frustratingly and inspiringly childish. I smile, a comforting yet reproachful smile that I know I've copied from my mother, but for once I don't care.

'We can't choose our family, Ian.'

This seems to stop him in his tracks. He looks down at the table for a moment, as if trying to translate my words into a language he can understand. Then he looks up and smiles.

'Yes we can. We have to. Because there aren't any rules any more. How many people turn their backs on their parents, their brothers and sisters, their children? How many families end up divided, never talking to each other? The old ideas of family don't exist any more, Gemma. So we have to make new ones. We have to make a really big effort to choose, even our own parents, we have to look at them and say, yes, I choose you and I'm going to stick with you through everything, because I've made that choice . . .'

It makes sense, in a strange way, I suppose. I've rejected my own mother, my own sister. Perhaps Ian is right. Perhaps I have to choose them again. Perhaps I have to make a firm and happy decision to accept Susan and Molly Cook, and not constantly complain to myself that neither of them is right for me. They are who they are.

'What do you think?' His voice is wavering, uncertain.

'Maybe you're right.'

'So . . . how about it? Will you be my sister? We could sign the deal here and now, on this napkin?'

He spreads out the napkin, and takes out his pen. I smile.

'If I was your sister, that would make Molly your sister, which means if you tried to screw her again it'd be incest.'

'Er . . .'

'I'm joking, Ian.'

'It was a mistake with Molly.' He sounds grave. I nod.

'I know. I realized it wasn't personal. After all, you're just a guy.'

I push back my chair, standing to pick up my bag.

'And she is a bit of a babe. It runs in the family.'

We walk on to Waterloo Bridge. It's almost lunchtime and office workers are hurrying towards the South Bank and its sunny benches by the river. We do not speak, but I feel lighter, a weight lifted.

I think about the countless times people have told me that Ian and I should be more than friends. I have spent twelve years denying it, yet secretly wondering, the sexual tension flickering inside me like malevolent mercury.

But we have overcome it. Yes, I think, with a rush of excitement. We have been lucky. The kiss was an instant antidote, as powerful as the undertaker's adrenalin that saved Ian's life on the plane. Lips on lips for less than ten seconds and we knew. Sex was not going to happen, ever. That moment released everything. It was like some strange fairy tale, where the Prince and Princess kiss only to find they were never meant to be together.

We stop in the middle of the bridge. The river is gold, shimmering. I look back towards the Strand, as I always do on Waterloo Bridge, picking out the window that used to be my father's office where he greeted his two little girls with hugs, forehead kisses and presents of coloured paper clips that we put in our hair.

I wish Bill Cook were alive, I wish I could take the rickety elevator to the sixth floor and walk into his tobacco-musty office and sit in the green leather armchair and tell him about everything that has happened, about the hospital, about my job, about the house, about Ian. About Raj.

But I can't. He's gone. And Ian is here.

'So, Thompson, what are you going to do next?'

Ian smiles at this time-honoured question, gazing out over the river. I sense at this moment that we might be back on track. I breathe out, enjoying the sun on my face.

'Well, I'm completely fucked with the *Daily Times*. The BA press woman called the travel editor, they were worried about me and wanted to notify the paper. Old Martin Foster threw an absolute fit, he didn't care about me almost dying, he was just furious that I'd forged the letter. Not that I give a monkey's . . .'

'You can still write for other papers . . .'

'You know, I think I've had enough of the travel writing thing for a while. It's not like there's anywhere left to explore. I told you I was born in the wrong century. I should have been born in the 1870s, not the 1970s.'

I nod. I've heard it all before. Secretly, I've always thought that Ian would have made a pretty useless explorer. He isn't ruthless enough. But I've never told him this, and I'm not about to start being brutally honest now. As I imagine Ian as an intrepid traveller, crossing ice floes and sand dunes in a variety of nineteenth-century costumes, I recall Duncan Archer's words about trying to find El Dorado.

'Maybe we are explorers Ian,' I murmur, softly. 'We are exploring new territory, new lands . . .'

'How's that?'

'Love, emotions, relationships.' My voice is stronger now. 'It's like you said about family, everything's changed. There are no maps, no charts. We're like those people who went out to Australia in the 1800s; they had nothing to tell them what was there, they had to draw their own maps, build new roads, new towns, new railways . . . We're the same . . . with relationships. Everything's new, the old maps don't work any more. Don't you think?'

He looks at me, eyes narrowed in quizzical questioning.

'You know what I think?'

I shake my head.

'I think it's great to be back together, Gemma.'

He steps up to me and puts his arms around me. His grip is loose, as if he's waiting for me to move closer to him, to grant him approbation. I lean in. His torso is more slender than I remember, more fragile. I feel as if I could pick him up. I move my arms around his back and give him a quick squeeze.

'Yeah,' I say softly. 'Me too.'

ZENITH

After Gemma goes to meet Raj for lunch, I stand for a while in the middle of Waterloo bridge, enjoying the warm early autumn sunshine on my face and hands. I watch the lunchtime crowds – tourists, office workers, businessmen and women, bike couriers, accountants. Everyone seems in good spirits, appreciating the last vestiges of summer, the last few hours that their British forearms will be exposed to the sun for another six months.

It's funny. Nothing much has happened, but everything seems to have changed. All right, I almost died in Business Class on a 747 to San Francisco. I have been dumped by my best friend's sister. I almost drove away my best friend, who almost divorced her husband. And I'm not sure if I want to continue the career I've been pursuing for just under ten years of my adult life.

Yet none of these things feel momentous. They are just things that have happened, points on a map, junctions on a road. The change that I feel most is impossible to draw. It's in my head. It's difficult to explain. It's just that . . . what? I see things differently. Like finally getting glasses after years of complaining that everything was a little bit blurred.

The strange thing is that I can't quite categorize what has changed in my head. I feel better. That's all. That's everything. It seems amazing that something invisible, undefined and nebulous can feel so real. So solid.

A middle-aged couple stops on the bridge to my right. They are nondescript, just another slightly overweight man and woman dressed in the same clothes as millions of other British men and women in their forties – he in khaki trousers and a blue shirt, she in jeans and a blouse. Usually, I wouldn't give them a second glance, they don't stand out. They would never warrant a mention in a travel article, unless perhaps one of them had fallen into the river, or taken off all their clothes.

Yet I can't take my eyes off them. As I watch, the woman leans into the man and kisses him, missing his lips and clumsily pecking the side of his mouth. The man laughs, his double chin jiggling with his chuckles, and the woman smiles, placing her hand against the small of the man's chubby back. Two children slouch up to them, evidently embarrassed by their parents' show of affection in the heart of London, the coolest city in England, if not the world. The boy, who looks about twelve, takes out a camera and snaps a shot of a boat going under the bridge. The girl, who is probably a couple of years older, wearing baggy jeans that flare hugely at the ankles and a pink raincoat and a T-shirt that reads 'Wicked', stands in front of her parents with a sulking expression that expresses all her disgust for her brother's nerdiness, for her parents' Marks and Spencer's clothes, for the fact she is being taken to museums and the London Eye when all she wants to do is head to the shops in Oxford Street and Covent Garden.

As the girl stands and pouts, her mother says something to her, with a frown, which seems to harden the girl's sulk, until the father shifts his feet, steps alongside her and ruffles the girl's hair. She leaps back, her hand flicking to her head in outrage, but she is smiling. Then the father says something and his daughter grins, and the mother laughs, and soon all three of them are laughing in the middle of the bridge in the heart of London. The son looks round to see what all the fuss is about, and raises his camera hurriedly, snapping a picture of his laughing family, and I feel a surge of affection for them and the photo that I know the parents and daughter and son will look at independently in years to come and cherish as an image of this unplanned instant when they were all momentarily but completely happy.

And a thought strikes me that has been ebbing through my head since the plane, but which chooses this moment to surge forward, fully formed, coherent and simple. My thought is this:

That I have spent almost all my life mapping out, strategizing and planning ahead, in a bid to distance myself from my parents and my childhood, and yet the times that have been most precious to me are the moments that have surprised me, that I didn't plan, that revealed in some way the truth that I've been trying to flee from for so long – that everything is connected but unmappable and that even in times of grim uncertainty there is a benign force that acts on our lives, and that this is the force that many people call love and my father has chosen to call God.

The family walks away, mother and father hand in hand, daughter slouching behind, son striding in front. I watch them until they reach the end of the bridge and disappear down some steps.

I think about Gemma and Raj and hope that they can figure out their differences, and love each other again. I think about Molly and how she was very different from the woman I'd imagined her to be in my head. I hope she will find happiness with Will Masterson, or whoever she ends up with, and that she will continue to love her work and taxis and takeaways.

And I think about my visit to the Old Seamen's Hall on Gutter Lane. The antique market was open, but the old man with the maps was nowhere to be found. A neighbouring stallholder said he'd heard that the old man had passed away. I asked several other stallholders, but no one could confirm whether this was true or not. The following day, I took the map to a friend of a friend at Sotheby's. The auction house's cartography expert valued it at £35,000. The auction takes place at the end of the month. I called my parents and my mother sounded relieved and a little excited.

'Thank you, Ian,' she said, quietly.

I will see them at the weekend. I hope that even if my father's condition deteriorates, the extra money, and whatever I can help out with, will make things a little easier. I hope my parents can learn to let other people look after them for a change. And I hope that I have the strength to be there for them, to love them whatever happens, for the rest of their lives.

Are such hopes the same as prayers? I don't know. All I know is that they are new and clear and they make me feel better about myself and the world I am in.

I look north and west, I look south and I look east across the city I have somehow become part of, and as the sun comes out from behind the clouds once more, I realize that for the first time in my life, I know exactly where I am.

THE END

I only learned about Gemma's breast cancer scare a couple of years after it had happened. Raj told me one night when I was round at their house watching cricket. I was shocked, then a bit miffed that she hadn't told me about it, and then relieved, of course, that the lump had been benign and she'd been fine after the biopsy. As Raj and I agreed, it helped explain some of what happened during those few weeks at the end of the summer of 2004.

That was four years ago. It might seem a little unbelievable, a little Mills and Boon, but everyone is pretty happy at the moment.

Gemma is pregnant again, the baby due in September. Archi Cook-Singh is two in June, and I've bought him an enormous plastic dumper truck that he can sit on and be pushed around in (I always wanted one when I was little, but such large plastic vehicles were considered excessively lavish by my parents). I'm his sort of godfather, but there wasn't any religious service or anything. Apparently the Punjabi term for it is *papa-ji*, which I like. That's what Archi calls me. Uncle-brother.

Molly is the other quasi-godparent, so we see each other occasionally. It was a bit weird at first, but just recently, we've been able to joke about things. She doesn't get to see Archi as much as I do, since she's now living in New York, working for the Bank of America. Will Masterson is there too, at one of the big Wall Street broking houses. Gemma thinks they'll have children soon.

And me?

I'm happy. Maybe even more than happy.

I've got a regular travel writing gig for the *Daily Times* – Thompson's Trails, my column is called, in which I write about a different walk each week, in the UK and abroad. I got the commission on the back of a couple of articles I wrote about walks around London – one of them following the nocturnal route I took from Gemma's house to Blackfriars Bridge on the night before my nut attack on the plane. They were published in the *Camden Chronicle* (it was edited by a friend of my wife's at the time, who took pity on me), and subsequently read by Simon Rogers, the new travel editor at the *Daily Times*, who called me in. Simon seemed happy to forgive and forget, and employ an erstwhile enemy of his predecessor. It was he who came up with the idea for the regular walking feature. It pays fairly well, and sometimes my wife comes along too.

Kate is amazing. I know we've only been married a year and a half, but I still think she's the most beautiful, intelligent, talented woman I've ever met.

It's strange the way it happened. I ended up renting a new apartment near Paddington Station. One evening a few weeks later, I found myself in Clerkenwell passing a bar where I used to go with Molly when we were dating. I was going to hurry on by, to consign that painful time to my own personal memory bin, but something made me stop, turn back and go in.

I ordered a beer. The waitress looked at me. She was pretty, brunette. I fancied her immediately. Then I realized

I recognized her. And she seemed to recognize me. It was the waitress from Molly's party. We both laughed, both blushing. She offered me a free cocktail of my choosing. She recommended a mojito, which despite my many travels, I'd never tried before. We chatted, she made me laugh, I talked about myself more than I'm used to. She told me about her freelance book-illustrating and her penchant for Spanish cinema.

I stayed until the bar closed and walked Kate back to her flat near Angel. To my surprise, I found the courage to ask her out to lunch. She said yes. Two weeks later she invited me to Barcelona for a weekend and we kissed for the first time. It was a good kiss.

We were married in a church. A beautiful little chapel in a village outside Chester with green and red stained glass windows and a loud ancient organ. Kate's family come from there. Everyone agreed it was a very picturesque wedding, including my bride, which was a relief to all concerned. The best thing was, my father was still well enough to officiate, although his hands shook badly. He gave a great sermon, the gist of which was that the Lord works in mysterious ways.

Which I suppose, if you believe in that sort of thing, He does.

EPILOGUE

Choroni, Venezuela, by Ian Thompson

In the spring of 2005, following a military coup and the election of a new president, the statue of the Virgin Mary was moved from Caracas back to its original home in Choroni. Once more, pilgrims flocked from all over South America to the small fishing village. They came, two to a seat in packed buses, lying on top of each other in beat-up cars, hoping, praying, and believing.

To this day the Virgin has not cried again, but still the pilgrims keep on coming . . .

CIRCULATING STOCK WEXFORD PUBLIC LIBRARIES

BLOCK LOAN
BUNCLODY
ENNISCORTHY
GOREY
MOBILE NORTH
MOBILE SOUTH
NEW ROSS
WEXFORD

GET IN THE MOOD FOR LOVE

WIN

A fantastic meal for two at a restaurant of *your choice* up to the value of £150!

Simply consult your local A–Z, tell us the address and contact details of your favourite restaurant and let Penguin do the rest.

To enter this free draw, just cut out the entry form and send to:

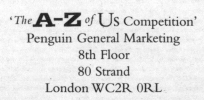

'The **A–Z** *of* Us Competition'
Penguin General Marketing
8th Floor
80 Strand
London WC2R 0RL

ENTRY FORM

Name: ....

Address: ....

Telephone Number: ....

Email Address: ....

Restaurant name: ....

Restaurant Address: ....

....

Restaurant Telephone Number: ....